MARKETING TO HOME-BASED BUSINESSES

MARKETING TO HOME-BASED BUSINESSES

Jeffrey P. Davidson, MBA, CMC

BUSINESS ONE IRWIN
Homewood, Illinois 60430

© Richard D. Irwin, Inc. 1991

This publication is designed to provide accurate and
authoritative information in regard to the subject matter
covered. It is sold with the understanding that neither the
author nor the publisher is engaged in rendering legal, accounting,
or other professional service. If legal advice or other expert
assistance is required, the services of a competent
professional person should be sought.

*From a Declaration of Principles jointly adopted by a Committee
of the American Bar Association and a Committee of Publishers.*

Sponsoring editor:	Cynthia A. Zigmund
Project editor:	Jean Roberts
Production manager:	Ann Cassady
Cover designer:	Michael Finkelman
Compositor:	Carlisle Communications, Ltd.
Typeface:	11/13 Century Schoolbook
Printer:	The Book Press, Inc.

Library of Congress Cataloging-in-Publication Data

Davidson, Jeffrey P.
  Marketing to home-based businesses / Jeffrey P. Davidson.
    p.   cm.
  Includes bibliographical references and index.
  ISBN 1-55623-475-9
  1. Home-based businesses—United States. 2. Home-based
businesses—Canada. 3. Purchasing. 4. Marketing. I. Title.
  HD2336.U5D38   1991
  658.8'04—dc20   91–7978

Printed in the United States of America
1 2 3 4 5 6 7 8 9 0 BP 8 7 6 5 4 3 2 1

DEDICATION

To Bill Adler, Jr., Maggie Bedrosian, Elizabeth Beier, Jonathan Blum, Marjorie Brody, Bill Brooks, Isolde Chapin, Art Close, Daryl Conner, David Conti, Holland Cooke, Jack Covert, John Jay Daly, Nancy Davidson, Ph.D., Shirley Davidson, Susan Davidson, Valerie Davidson, John Domenick, Michael Dolan, Sheri Douglas, Jennifer Enderlin, George Anne Fay, Cynthia Folino, Leslie Gelbman, Donna Gould, Victor Gullotta, Ernest Hecht, Barbara Hemphill, Marty Horn, Elizabeth Jeffries, Deborah Jolley, Peter Johnson, Ph.D., Shawn Kent, Jeff Krames, Deb Leopold, John Mahaney, Ray Marseli, Margret McBride, Peter Niedbala, Arnold Sanow, Robert Shook, Auda Stranere, Richard Staron, Susan Stautberg, Juanell Teague, Bill Thompson, Brandon Toporov, Barbara Vogel, Ron Wagner, Karl Weber, and Cindy Zigmund, among so many others, for their lasting support and outrageous acts of kindness.

ACKNOWLEDGMENTS

Among the many people who contributed to this effort, I would like to thank Susan Kuhn for meritorious writing, researching, and editing assistance; Thomas Miller for superior survey and analysis capabilities; Jo Ann Austin and Douglas Gray for their in-depth knowledge of the Canadian home-business market; Andy Marken for his superior knowledge of marketing research; Alvin Toffler for seeing what others can't see; Judy Dubler for word processing; Carla Mullen for proofreading; and Willis Shen for research and Diane Beausoleil and Patricia Schissel at Carlisle Communications for masterful copyediting and production.

Thanks also to Heidi Toffler, Ph.D., Raymond L. Boggs, Claudia Kohl, Paul Reiss, Eric Adams, Ron Wagner, Thomas Miller, Robert L. Gray, Laurel Cutler, Marcia Kelly, Jan DeYoung, Andrea Davis, Karen Kane, Peter Miller, Eric Adams, Lura Romei, Stewart Wolpin, Georganna Fiumara, Dianne Walbrecker, Dick Connor, Colleen Armstrong, Linda Russell, Joe Jeff Goldblatt, Jack Miller, Lawrence La Porta, Jeff West, John Shea, Cynthia Bronte, Dick Staron and Mark Eppley, among many others.

Finally, I would like to acknowledge all the fine folks at Business One Irwin, a Cadillac of a publishing house, including Jeffrey A. Krames for acquiring and spear-heading the project, Cindy Zigmund for editing, Kate Wickham, Carol DeSelm, Rick Riddering, Sharon Miller, Barbara Novosel, Ruth Bachtell, Louis DeWinter, a one-man foreign rights superstar, and Richard J. Borto.

Jeffrey P. Davidson

FOREWORD

In 1981 it seemed inconceivable that video stores would soon be found in every retail mall and shopping center. In 1986 the impending worldwide break-up of communism was unimaginable. In 1991 the emergence of staggering numbers of home-based businesses across the globe doesn't seem probable. Yet, as Jeff Davidson illuminates for us in *Marketing to Home-Based Businesses,* the spectacular rise of home-based businesses is already in motion. Five years hence, it will be difficult to recall when America, indeed the world, wasn't dotted with teeming numbers of home-based entrepreneurs in every community.

Too often we hear or read accounts of emerging trends in business opportunities. Unfortunately, after investigating the evidence, we discover that these trends are at best yesterday's news in designer clothing, and at worst, in the emperor's clothing. However, the stunning growth in home-based business and the opportunities it presents to business-to-business marketers is irrefutable.

Marketing to Home-Based Businesses is more than just a book about trends. It's an information-packed "how-to" for direct marketers who want to take immediate advantage of opportunities that exist today for reaching this fastest-growing segment of our economy.

A Different Kind of Customer
As Davidson clearly points out in his book, home-based entreprenuers tend to be an upscale, often affluent lot. They

are better educated, earn more money annually, and are more likely to own their own home than most of their colleagues in the office world.

When it comes to stocking their home offices with equipment and supplies that will make them productive and profitable, without question, *they buy*! And something that every business-to-business marketer would appreciate hearing, there are no layers to penetrate to reach the home-based buyer. Most HBEs are one-person operations. The person who answers the phone and opens the mail is also the person who makes all the business decisions. Little, if anything, is done by committee. That's a far cry from the corporate world!

An Insider's View

To get an insider's view of this dynamic market and social phenomenon, Davidson pulled out the stops for this book to capture the essence of who the home-based entrepreneur is, what she buys, what he reflects on, what she's up against, who influences him, what she reads, what he joins, and what she attends. He researched the subject for months on end. He visited more than four dozen home-based offices in 14 different states. He visited the superstores.

He met famed authors Alvin and Heidi Toffler who first predicted the rise of the "Cottage Industry" in 1969 in *Future Shock*. He met with some of the top survey research firms on the topic of working at home. He attended PC user group meetings, and tapped into HBE networks. He uncovered dozens of specialty newsletters and publications, many of which sell their potent lists of HBE subscribers.

The net result of his findings and experience—whether you work in the marketing department of a multinational corporation or in your own home-based office—is that the home-based business market is becoming increasingly easier to target.

If you aren't selling to the home-based market, or are, but without the gusto needed to achieve substantial penetration, perhaps it is time to re-evaluate your business strategy. With nearly 35 million people working at home in 1991 in the United States, and with an explosive growth pattern through the dawn of the 21st century, marketing to home-based businesses is an idea whose time has come.

I hope you enjoy reading this book as much as I did. I always feel a sense of excitement when learning about emerging markets while it's still early enough in the game to become a player. This book spells *marketing opportunity* from cover to cover.

Martin Horn
Vice President
Marketing Decision Systems
DDB Needham Worldwide, Inc.

CONTENTS

LIST OF FIGURES
AND TABLES

INTRODUCTION

THE QUIET REVOLUTION

Nothing worthwhile has ever
been accomplished without
someone's enthusiasm.
Henry Ford

The statistics are irrefutable—growth in the number of home-based businesses is a global phenomenon. Surveys indicate that 34.4 million Americans now perform some or all of their work in their homes, as shown in Figure I–1. This figure could rise by another 10 million by 1995. In many ways, we're about to witness the most profound changes in marketing since the post World War II period. *Marketing to Home-Based Businesses* focuses on who the home-based entrepreneur (HBE) is, and how to tap into this lucrative, ever-growing market.

WHY A BOOK ON MARKETING TO A PARTICULAR NICHE?

Isn't marketing, *marketing?* And aren't customers, *customers?* Yes, but the winners of the world have learned to focus, specialize, and become insiders to the targets they serve. As we're about to explore in detail, the home-based business market is so large, is growing so fast, and presents so much potential to vendors, that if you're interested at all in penetrating this market, you won't want to miss key opportunities.

FIGURE I–1
Home Office Heartland Work-at-Home Trendline

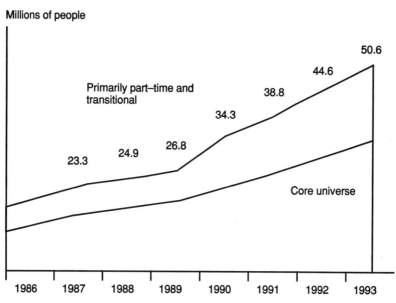

Millions of people

Source: LINK Resources, 1990. Reprinted with permission.

The notion of producing a marketing text for the penetration of a particular market is growing in popularity. *Marketing to the Affluent,* by Dr. Thomas J. Stanley (Business One Irwin, 1989), has drawn considerable interest. Rena Bartos' *Marketing to Women Around the World* (Harvard Business School Press, 1988) is also a solid text, though perhaps not as widely known. Other books have recently emerged on marketing to Eastern Europe, marketing to the Japanese, and so forth. This *is* the era of niche-focused books.

This book will help you grasp the scope and significance of the widespread shift to the home as a work site, and discuss opportunities and strategies for marketing your products and services to this new, exciting, affluent, and spending-oriented market.

A SOLID GROWTH INDUSTRY

Although he coined the term *cottage industry* in 1969 to describe the rise of entrepreneurs working out of their homes, Alvin Toffler recently remarked that the home-based business movement in still *in its infancy.* Its massive growth and broad, sweeping changes on society, however, are inevitable. Toffler observes that even the thinking and planning about home-based business marketing today is simplistic.

Imagine, if you will, an America with no video stores. Can't do it? In 1978 there weren't any; by 1988 they populated virtually every community in America and, in some cases, every neighborhood shopping center. Toffler sees "fantastic" niches opening up for both HBEs and people selling to them. "The demarcation line between the home and offices is blurring," he says.

One signal that home-based businesses are a viable, permanent phenomenon is that none other than 80-year-old Peter Drucker (guru to global organizations, mega-author, and business and social philosopher), operates alone, out of his home.

What of the HBEs elsewhere? Toffler himself received a letter from a gentleman in India who described the home-office movement in that country as magnificent and wide reaching. The letter writer went on to say that the technology to work at home "is a gift to India of the West."

Similarly, large movement is underway in Western Europe, particularly Germany. According to a report in the publication *The Week in Germany,* during the first six months of 1990 more than 100,000 applications for business start-ups were registered in Germany (prior to unification). While nearly half were for retail businesses and restaurants, at least 18,000 were for businesses in other small private trades—HBEs.

Home-office entrepreneurs are springing up within the Soviet Union, the Far East, and Latin America. More

Americans, as well as entrepreneurs worldwide, devote a section of the home, be it a table, corner of a room, entire room, or wing, to a business enterprise. (Chapter 7 is devoted entirely to the burgeoning HBE market in Canada.) The home-based business boom is no passing fancy, here or abroad. It is a way of working and a way of life that will profoundly and irrevocably change society.

Effectively marketing to home-based entrepreneurs *requires new insights and approaches* not covered by other marketing texts. *Marketing to Home-Based Businesses* will help you better understand the needs of the home-based entrepreneurs (HBEs) and identify areas of marketing opportunity, as well as spell out strategies for effectively identifying and selling to targets. This book will help you if you are:

- Eager to start marketing to home-based businesses.
- Considering marketing to home-based businesses.
- Not sure whether to market to home-based businesses, but are interested in effective marketing strategies.
- Currently are marketing to home-based businesses and would like to be more effective.

This book illuminates:

- Who the home-based entrepreneur is.
- What his needs are.
- Who influences him.
- How to get the most mileage out of your efforts.

Fueling the Growth

As I explained in my earlier book, *Marketing for the Home-Based Business,* beyond affordable, reliable office technology, other phenomena have fueled the domestic growth of home-based businesses. As the baby boom generation ages, more people are being squeezed from the corporate ranks—

not everyone can become a middle manager, let alone a top manager.

A Conference Board study in the mid-1980s found that each year 12 million mid-level managers systematically are departing the ranks of the corporate world either through layoffs, dead-end careers, or other pressures. They are opting for careers within existing small businesses or starting their own venture.

An increasing number of working women, as well as the desire among minorities, the handicapped, and immigrants to achieve business success outside of the limited corporate structure, has fueled the hopes and aspirations of millions of individuals. The high divorce rate in our society also has prompted many working parents, who need to care for or wish to stay in greater contact with their children, to seek home-based business alternatives.

As society ages—the median age is 32 and rising—more elderly citizens are discovering the joys of starting their own home-based venture. The American Home-Based Business Association, based in Greenwich, Connecticut, reports that 15 percent of home-based businesses are run by retirees. As the average life span increases to 85 years, we'll witness a dramatic rise in the number of senior home-based entrepreneurs.

Word Usage

The growing use of the word *fax* as both an adjective (fax machine) and verb (fax it to us) has prompted its free use herein, although most dictionaries will not begin to include the term for a few years.

Regrettably, the pronoun *he* and its possessive case, *his,* are used generically to refer to a man or a woman. Women now own one-third of all businesses in the United States, with impressive growth in ownership rates in Europe, East Asia, and South America. By the year 2000, half of all businesses in the United States will be female-owned. The term *entrepreneur,* or *home-based entrepreneur* as used within, unmistakably refers to a man or a woman.

CHAPTER 1

THE ERA OF
HOME-BASED BUSINESS

> Commuting to office work is obsolete. It is now infi-
> nitely easier, cheaper, and faster . . . to move infor-
> mation . . . to where people are."
>
> *Peter R. Drucker*

After decades of predictions by futurists and over-eager
forecasts by industry analysts, the "electronic cottage" has
finally arrived. Home-based businesses are one of the fastest growing social and economic developments in the
United States, and one of today's hottest marketing opportunities.

THE BIG PICTURE

In his book *The Third Wave,* world-renowned author and social observer Alvin Toffler is unequivocal about the tremendous impact of home-based business on America's future:

> The most striking change in Third Wave civilization will
> probably be the shift of work from both office and factory
> back into the home. If as few as 10 to 20 percent of the work
> force as presently defined were to make this historic transfer
> over the next 20 to 30 years, our entire economy, our cities,
> our ecology, our family structure, our values, and even our
> politics would be altered almost beyond recognition.

Marketing strategies will also change.

Until recently, home-based businesses grew at a slower
pace than Toffler and other futurists had predicted. In 1987

2.1 million Americans set up offices at home, according to LINK Resources, a market research firm based in New York, and one of the premier research organizations in the home-based business field. In 1988 1.6 million individuals were added to the home-office universe. In 1989 the number of new home-office workers was 1.9 million. But in 1990, 7.5 million Americans joined the ranks of home-based workers. Toffler's critical mass of "10 to 20 percent" of our society working from home has already been surpassed (Figure 1–1).

The 1990 National Work-At-Home Survey from LINK Resources Corporation, directed by Thomas Miller, found

FIGURE 1–1
A Growing Share of the Work Force Works at Home

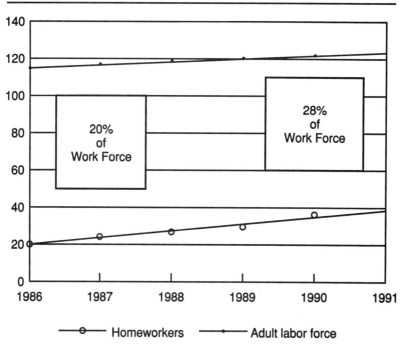

Source: LINK Resources, 1990.

more than 28 percent of the work force (34.3 million Americans) now work out of their homes on a full- or part-time basis (Figure 1–2). This number has been increasing steadily. As more Americans set up office space at home, market researchers are learning how to better identify them, which aids in marketing to them.

Major Subgroups

A market of 34.4 million people undoubtedly has several submarkets, and the home-office market is no exception. About half of the market is **home offices which serve other small businesses.** (The Small Business Administration defines a small business as one that operates on separate premises and employs fewer than 100 people.)

FIGURE 1–2
Number of Home-Based Workers Growing Rapidly

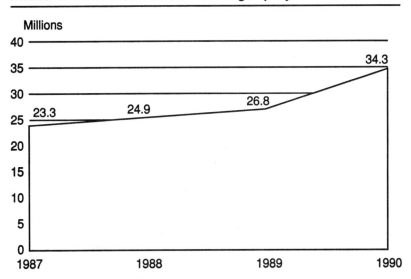

Source: LINK Resources, 1990.

Homeworking Subgroups

- Home offices that serve off-site small businesses
- Home-based entrepreneurs
- Corporate telecommuters
- Corporate employees who work at home
- Homemakers
- Hobbyists

Another group, the heart of this market, are **home-based entrepreneurs** (HBEs). These are revenue-generating businesses in which the work is done in the home. They generally have few, if any, employees although they may use consultants or part-time workers to assist them. Many HBEs look to other home-based business owners to perform tasks such as word processing and marketing rather than hire staff.

Third are **corporate telecommuters** who work at home most of the time and communicate with their offices electronically.

Fourth, there are **corporate employees who work at home,** often or occasionally.

Depending on the type of product or service you wish to market, the distinction between these four types of home offices may or may not matter. There are also two additional subgroups to consider.

Homemakers increasingly set up offices that are used to keep track of family items such as budgets, doctor's appointments, shopping, and so forth. An estimated 4.6 million households have dedicated office space for household management.

There are also **hobbyists** who can be counted on to buy the latest in electronic gadgetry: speedier computers, new software, and fancy phones. Their numbers are best known to the purveyors of these products. They also buy desks, file cabinets, lamps, and many other items that HBEs purchase.

STARTING WITH THE
ENTREPRENEURIAL BOOM OF
THE 1980s

The small business boom of the 1980s helped put the home-office movement into high gear. In the 1970s, there were about 375,000 new business incorporations annually, more activity than in the 1950s and 1960s, but nothing like what was to come. By the early 1980s, new-business incorporations jumped to an average of about 600,000 per year. In both 1986 and 1987, they hit about 700,000 per year.

The small business boom did two things to spur the rapid growth in home-based business. First, it produced a change in attitudes about business and being in business. The entrepreneur became a cultural folk hero. Second, it changed the image of working at home. Whereas before 1980 working out of the home may have been seen as amateurish or even slightly disreputable, by the end of the 1980s running a home-based business was increasingly regarded as the sign of an enterprising, successful professional.

Marketers turned their attention to small businesses during the 80s when their Fortune 500 and large corporation market began to shrink. While small businesses were booming, adding over 14 million jobs between 1981 and 1985, the largest companies were shrinking in work force. The Fortune 500 work force diminished by 2.8 million jobs between 1980 and 1987 alone.

Home offices were responsible for a large share of small business growth. IRS data reveals that in 1987 and 1988, one out of every three new businesses registered with the IRS was a home-based business. Marketers, however, are only beginning to segment the home-based business market from the general small business market. This will irrevocably change in the 1990s. The home-based business is large enough and growing fast enough to be treated as a market in its own right.

THE DISAPPEARANCE OF THE MASS MARKET

Marketers today face the growing challenge of selling their products to fragmented, segmented marketplaces. The mass market is gone. It vanished during the last decade for many reasons. (1) The marketplace actually became overcrowded with good products. As such, marketers narrowed their marketing strategies, preferring to target smaller niches rather than become the second or third choice of a larger niche. (2) The population, at least within the United States but certainly elsewhere, increasingly became fragmented along racial, class, and lifestyle lines, each seeking somewhat different products to meet their needs. (3) Technology facilitates making small batches of specialized products, what marketers call "mass customization."

There is little room for products that people like "a little," or that serve their needs "so-so." To stand out today products need clear identities and must reflect the wants and aspirations of the target market.

Marketers on all levels face this form of market fragmentation. Many companies are organized to sell to America's largest companies. Their products, sales techniques, and advertising appeals to corporate America. After all, corporate America remains the largest and richest market in the world. Selling in that market, however, is extremely competitive, and its growth is slowing.

TARGETING SMALLER . . . SMALLER BUSINESSES

Many marketers took aim at small businesses in the 1980s. The national accounting firms, PC vendors, and long distance phone companies, to cite but a few, recognized that marketing to small business had quickly become a key component for long-term viability. They found the small business market to be different from the corporate market in a number of ways: (1) It is vastly larger, by number of establishments, (2) the average purchase is smaller, and (3) relationships may be more personal.

Now, farsighted marketers are targeting a third major business segment, the home-office market. This market is a cross between a consumer and business market. It buys at retail, but wants business quality. It is motivated by advertising, yet responds to consumer-oriented advertisements in the local newspaper. The HBE market comes complete with its own set of wants and needs, peculiarities, and operating characteristics.

The Opportunity of the Decade

The 1980s boom may be offset by the American economy, but home-based businesses will continue to grow exponentially. In fact, home-based business is one of the few segments of the economy that will grow rapidly in the 1990s. The economy as a whole has been forecasted by many sources to grow by an average of just 2 percent per year in this decade.

In contrast to this is the growth in a particular segment of the economy. Home-based businesses will grow by 53 percent during the same period, according to LINK Resources, Inc.

> With all objectivity, marketing to home-based business offers one of the few bona fide opportunities to grow faster than the economy as a whole in the 1990s.

GROWING FOR GOOD REASON

A broad range of forecasters are predicting that the 1990s is the decade for home-based business:

- By the year 2000, a third of the American work force will work either full- or part-time out of the home, according to research done by an American manufacturer.

- By the year 2000, 22 percent of all employees will be telecommuters, according to business forecaster Marvin Cetron.
- The number of home workers, including both HBEs and telecommuters, will pass 40 million before the year 2000, according to the American Home Business Association.
- "By the year 2000, we'll no longer build large office buildings. People will work from home and telecommute, or just come in for meetings. Buildings are large overhead for a company," says an IBM researcher.

Home-based businesses are booming domestically because conditions in America increasingly favor the small enterprise. The reasons are diverse and run as deep as today's changes in our technology, economy, and society as a whole. As we'll explore in subsequent chapters, these changes are also telltales to the kinds of products and services that the HBE will be seeking.

What are the conditions fueling the growth of home-based business? There are at least four, including information technology, economic turbulence, demographic changes, and family needs.

Information Technology

Since the mass introduction of the personal computer starting around 1980, Toffler notes that some 30 to 40 million people in the United States have learned to use it. This learning came about without a formal plan and without formal education. Many users did not attend classes of any kind. They learned from mentors and friends whenever and wherever they could.

Before it became comfortable and familiar to them, many home-based PC users spent long hours learning word processing, spreadsheet, and database programs. Clearly, something happened on an individual by individual basis resulting in mass change, Toffler observes.

The "electronic cottage" is reverting late 20th century America back to an employment pattern that was common in the 19th century. Then, most Americans worked for themselves; they were family farmers, shopkeepers, and small manufacturers.

During most of this century, those home-based jobs disappeared when new technologies spurred the creation of new industries, large corporations, and big government. Americans became a nation of factory workers, office clerks, and civil servants.

As is increasingly evident, information technology including personal computers (PCs), facsimile machines, copiers, modems, and telephones is sending work back home again. Unlike manufacturing technology, information technology makes it possible to take work anywhere. By linking organizations around the world, information technology is making work "location-independent." Being in the same office as coworkers, or in the same city as clients, is less and less important.

Still, most home businesses *are not* technology-related, although most do use a personal computer. The PC is the single biggest factor behind the home-business explosion. With an investment of as little as $1,500 and a few hundred dollars of off-the-shelf software, a home-business owner can single-handedly manage such tasks as keeping books, preparing mass mailings, and developing business plans. Ten years ago, additional staff would have been required.

In addition to the computer, other low-cost devices have brought big-company sophistication to the home office:

- Fax: Fax machines developed by companies such as Epson and Sharp specifically for small businesses now retail for under $500, and boards which allow computers to send and receive fax transmissions cost less than $200.

- Copiers: Light-duty copiers from major manufacturers such as Canon now retail for around $500.
- Printers: Canon's LPB-4, a personal laser printer that provides top-of-the-line output quality, is now available *with fonts* for under $1,100. Inkjet and bubble jet printers producing nearly comparable output are available for under $500. Both handle different typefaces, allowing the home-business owner to produce sophisticated newsletters, brochures, and proposals. Even inexpensive dot-matrix printers are acquiring this capability.
- Telephone: Answering services, pagers, and cellular telephones allow an HBE to keep in touch with clients from any location, with no need for additional staff.

Economic Turbulence

Economic insecurity is a second driving force behind the growth of home businesses. Global competition, mergers, downsizing, and bankruptcies are eroding the security that employment with a good company once offered. Concurrently, these economic developments are creating many new opportunities for HBEs.

Many workers either leave or are laid off from large companies and start home businesses to gain control over their work life. Fewer jobs or careers are secure today because few companies can forecast their business situation beyond about two years.

Susan Kuhn, a strategic planning consultant and HBE herself, explains that HBEs are able to spread their risk by working with different clients; losing a client who is experiencing a business downturn is easier to absorb than losing a job.

Others start businesses simply to cash in on new opportunities. One woman left a government editing job to start her own desktop publishing and computer training firm. Both her specialties are in such demand that she has been booked solid since starting her business.

Demographic Change

The baby boomers are reaching the peak of their careers at the same time that corporate management jobs are being eliminated. By the year 2000, the Bureau of the Census indicates, the number of Americans between 35 and 54 will increase by 28 percent, from 64 million to 81 million. By 2010, however, the typical large business will have cut its management ranks by two-thirds or more.

Facing limited opportunities for promotion, more employees in this age range will start their own businesses. One-third or more of those will start from home.

Retired Americans are also starting home-based businesses in record numbers. The American Home-Based Business Association reports that 15 percent of home-based businesses are run by retirees. As the average life span increases to 85 to 90 years, more seniors will work from home to supplement pensions and Social Security.

In addition, women and minorities, many of whom have been excluded from corporate opportunities, are increasingly turning to entrepreneurism to fulfill their desire to succeed. Women and minorities have more trouble raising capital to start businesses, and starting from home is the least capital-intensive path.

More than 3.5 million women operate their own businesses, up from only 700,000 a decade ago. Female-owned businesses are growing faster in number than male-owned ventures. The U.S. Small Business Administration predicts that by the year 2000, women will own half of all businesses in America.

The volume of business done by minority-owned businesses grew by 64 percent between 1975 and 1985. Black-owned businesses are increasingly diversifying beyond community boundaries to serve a cross section of customers.

Family Needs

Changes in American family life are also spurring the growth of home-based business. Both married and single parents are setting up home offices to help juggle work and child care. Many have a pioneering attitude, inventing new rules for living and working as they go along.

Some work at home one or two days a week. A magazine editor works out of a converted sunroom on the second floor of his home two days a week. Working at home lets him be around his two young children during the workday; it also allows him to finish more "solo work" (such as writing and editing) than he could in the office.

Some HBEs work at home full-time primarily for the sake of their children. Shirley Bentham, a public relations executive, became Bentham and Associates at age 35 when she had her first child. She now has a second child, and both her home-based firm and her family are thriving. She particularly enjoys being there when her children come home from school.

ALL MANNER OF ACTIVITY

What kinds of businesses are being started out of the home? Consulting accounts for more than one out of five home-based businesses. Other popular businesses include word processing, mail order, accounting, real estate, and graphic arts.

In addition, interior decorating, insurance, advertising, communications and public relations, home remodeling, day care centers, bed and breakfast inns, weight and fitness counseling, tax and financial counseling, software development, professional recording, investment banking, executive recruiting, and product sales are popular. All types of selling can be conducted or managed out of the home.

IRS composite tax records reveal that light manufacturing and equipment repair, as well as ventures such as tailoring, tutoring, and musical instruction, are all flourishing as home-based businesses. Also growing are computer programming, desktop publishing, telemarketing, and telephone answering services. The stigma of professionals working out of the home is quickly dropping away as lawyers, accountants, architects, and psychologists open their doors to greet clients.

The list of businesses that can be proficiently operated or managed from the home is growing:

Actuary
Aerial photographer
Antique dealer
Appraiser

Architectural designer
Architectural historian
Association founder
Audio engineer

Auctioneer
Broadcast engineer
Career counselor
Carpet specialist

Catalog publisher
Chiropractor
Cleaning service
Clown service

Comedian
Computer animator
Computer missionary
Conference planner

Corporate communications
Courseware developer
Court reporting
Design consultant

Dietician
Directory publisher
Disc-jockey service
Draftsperson

Electronic-mail software developer
Electronic marketer
Employment agency
Engraver

Errand service
Event clearinghouse
Event planner
Excavating service

Exercise instructor
Executive recruiter
Expert-search firm
Feed exporter

Fund raiser
Geologist
Glass blower
Gourmet caterer

Graphic designer
Hairstylist
Hot-air balloon school
Housing consultant

Household-cleanser manufacturer
House-repair service
Hydroplane manufacturer
Indexer

Information broker
Insurance broker
Interior designer
Investment manager

Inventor
Jeweler
Landscaper
Laser-cartridge manufacturer

Legal software developer
Library management
Limousine service
Locksmith

Lyricist
Mailing-list service
Manufacturer's rep
Market research

Marketing agency
Massage therapist
Mechanic
Messenger service

Mobile-phone leasing
Mobile notary
Model-kit maker
Music engineer

Musician's network
Networking firm
Newsletter publisher
Nursing service

Office-automation consultant
Organic farmer
Organizer
Parking-lot maintenance

Party planner
Pest control
Pet care
Photo-newsletter publisher

Photography studio
Psychological service
Private investigator
Professional service

Publisher
Radio-TV voice-over
Real estate appraiser
Relocation consultant

Researcher
Reunion planner
Remodeler
Roof inspectors

Sales trainer
Scriptwriter
Security consultant
Sign maker

Silk flower arranger
Shopping service
Songwriter
Speaker

Speechwriter
Stockbroker
Strategist
Surveyor

Teaching nurse
Technical writer
Telecommunications analyst
Title abstracter

Tour operator
Transcriptionist
Translator
Travel agency

Urban planner
Vending machine operator
Wardrobe designer
Washing service

Waste consultant
Water purifier
Wholesaler
Woodworker

SURVEYING THE SCENE

To gain further insight into who's doing what, supported by a home office, let's examine the results of three different surveys.

1. According to a recent study by the American Home Business Institute (AHBI), the top home-based occupation, by far, is "consultant." Many of these consultants are corporate middle-managers whose jobs were eliminated. They either continue to do work for their former employer, practice their profession solo, or compete with their former employers for business. The ABHI consultant category includes: management consulting, high tech consulting, financial consulting, marketing consulting, and public relations.

Following consultants in the ABHI survey comes a wide variety of professionals and marketers, including: accountants, veterinarians, manufacturers' representatives, publishers, writers, editors, systems analysts, psychologists, doctors, dentists, designers, commercial artists, market researchers, income tax preparers, and mail order specialists. These are, for the most part, occupations that have existed for some time.

2. The Association of Electronic Cottages (AEC) conducted a survey to determine the 10 most plentiful computer-related businesses. The AEC survey also revealed the start-up costs and expected annual income range from the businesses shown in Table 1–1.

Home-based word processing services are flourishing. They have seen and experienced a favorable, sharp drop in the cost of equipment needed to set up shop themselves and hence can begin a business with low overall start-up costs.

TABLE 1–1

Business	Start-Up Costs (basic)	Annual Income (full-time)
Computer consulting	$ 3,000+	$30,000 –$100,000
Typesetting service	3,000+	30,000 – 100,000
Bookkeeping service	3,000–5,000	25,000 – 40,000
Writing	1,000	30,000 – 45,000
Data processing	100–1,000	15,000 – 20,000
Information brokering	10,000	40,000 – 65,000
Word processing	1,000–3,000	25,000 – 40,000
Custom programming	3,000+	30,000 – 100,000
Desktop publishing	10,000+	40,000 – 600,000
Mailing list services	1,000	20,000 – 25,000

3. Electronic Services Unlimited, a subsidiary of LINK Resources, Inc., compiled data on the most frequently occurring telecommuting careers, listed below. The common denominator linking these occupations is that results can largely be quantified and easily transmitted.[1]

Accountants

Accounting clerks

Bookkeepers

Clerical support

Computer operators

Computer programmers

Computer systems analysts

Data entry clerks

Engineers

Insurance agents

Lawyers

Marketing managers

Other managers

Personnel/labor relations (job analysts, application processors)

Purchasing agents

Real estate agents

Salespersons (including catalog order-takers and reservation clerks)

Secretaries

Securities brokers, agents, or salespersons

Travel agents

Vocation and educational counselors

Word processors

Writers

---

[1]Marcia M. Kelley, "The Work-at-Home Revolution," *The Futurist,* November–December 1988, pp. 28–32.

Companies with outside sales forces have been managing off-site workers for some time without calling it telecommuting. Sales tends to work well as an off-site occupation because it is results-oriented. Sales managers look at the numbers of calls made, new markets developed, and amount of products sold.

What products could be marketed to home businesses on the basis of occupation? Here are a few ideas:

- Accounting software with custom templates that accommodate the record-keeping needs of a veterinarian, writer, or word processor.
- "Quick-start" guides that provide short tutorials on starting a home-based business, covering business planning, selecting equipment, and so forth, which focus on a particular type of business.
- "Business to business" coupon mailers to help home-based entrepreneurs market to each other.
- A membership association of home-based manufacturer's reps, commercial artists, or financial planners.

BECOMING MAINSTREAM

The sheer number of Americans working from home, 34.4 million, is transforming this arrangement into a mainstream economic choice. The volume of business done from the home is a sizable portion of the nation's gross national product. By some estimates, it is more than 25 percent, although further data is needed to reach an exact figure.

Home-based businesses are also becoming more acceptable legally. Assemblyman Walter M. D. Kern of Bergen County, New Jersey, recently introduced a bill aiming to ensure that telecommuters have all the rights of on-site corporate employees. Some jurisdictions, particularly in the fast-growing Sunbelt, are rewriting their zoning laws to make it legal for home-based businesses to have employees and store inventory.

Part of the reason for this rapid growth is that working at home makes good sense for all involved. The home worker (HBE or telecommuter), the companies that do business with home-based workers, the corporations whose workers telecommute, and communities benefit from home-based businesses.

HBEs and home-based workers in general enjoy the following advantages:

- Greater job satisfaction. Home-based workers are very happy with their lot. *Home Office Computing's* 1990 reader survey found that an overwhelming 98 percent of those responding are happier working from home, and 97 percent would recommend it to others.
- Being one's own boss. This contributes strongly to the high level of job satisfaction.
- Earning more money than one could in a traditional office job, hence having greater purchasing power. A successful HBE, like anyone else in business, is limited only by his or her ability to recognize and capitalize on opportunities.
- No commuting hassles and expenses. One of the biggest advantages of living and working under one roof is eliminating commuting time, which may be as much as four hours per day in congested suburban areas. Expenses associated with commuting, such as bus or subway fare, gasoline, auto maintenance, highway tolls, and car insurance, are reduced as well.
- Lower expenses for clothing. Typically, home workers dress casually when they are not seeing clients, and save their power suits and dresses for meetings.

The advantages to the home worker are more than matched by the benefits to their clients.

- More personalized service. HBEs can provide their clients with more personalized service than a larger company can. In many instances, home-based business owners are more motivated to provide excellent service than, for example, an employee in a large corporation.
- Cost advantages. Working from home lowers overhead, so HBEs can often offer their clients a cost advantage over larger firms.

Corporations, too, enjoy significant benefits when their employees work at home. According to home-business expert Marcia M. Kelly, these are the main advantages:

- Improved productivity. Increases in productivity of as much as 100 percent have been noted, with most gains in the 20 percent range. Let's be frank—many corporate working environments are not conducive to high productivity, but rather represent interruption-oriented work environments. Home workers are subject to interruptions as well, but have much more control over their immediate environment.
- Recruiting advantages. Telecommuting is a highly attractive lifestyle for job candidates in many professional, technical, and clerical areas, and a significant employment incentive in today's skill-short labor market.
- Improved employee retention. Telecommuting helps companies hold onto employees whose services may otherwise have been lost. Both short-term and permanent arrangements are used by flexible companies.
- Greater staffing flexibility and cost control. Telecommuting increases a company's options in staffing. A key employee who is injured can work from home, additional employees can be brought on temporarily without the concern of where to put them, and the talents of highly qualified people who live too far away to commute can be employed via phone lines.

- Office space control. Telecommuters may need some office space in the headquarters, but far less than on-site workers, and that space can be shared. In large telecommuting programs, the cost savings is substantial.

Communities benefit as well. A rise in the number of HBEs means less congested rush hours; less gasoline and motor oil used; schools with fewer tardy, absent, and truant children; and potentially more patronage of local rather than downtown businesses.

The HBE movement may yet spur a macro increase in productivity, though it remains to be calculated. How many managers can come up with a better way to increase their staff's productivity by 20 percent or more?

IN THEIR OWN WORDS

The home-based business movement may be a product of large forces reshaping our society, but it is also a product of very personal needs, experiences, and ambitions. The decision to run a business from home is usually made by one person—one at a time. To better understand the underlying motivations of HBEs, let's explore a few of those individual decisions that are fairly representative of large numbers of HBEs.

Escaping a Grinding Commute

Dan Gorra and Debra Hilson were on the management fast track at Citicorp, but the commute was killing them. Debra had to get up at a painful 4:25 A.M. for her 88-minute train ride to Manhattan. Both felt they would enjoy working for themselves so the ambitious 28-year-olds founded Party Time, a company that handles all the details of staging birthday parties, bar mitzvahs, and graduation parties.

Now they have a 10-second commute from bedroom to living room. Dan can be comfortably at work at 6:30 A.M. He notes that the pair works all the time, but enjoys it so much that it doesn't seem like they're working.

Planning for Retirement

Jack Hersch is 59. He has three years to go before he retires as a mechanical engineer with the local power company. Jack began to plan for his retirement about a year ago. He knew he wanted to work; he did not want to spend his retirement watching television and playing golf.

Jack began investigating opportunities for starting his own business. After a career of working for someone else, he thought he'd give entrepreneurial life a try. His daughter, who works as a marketing manager, suggested that he get into the mail order business. Jack is surveying the products that would be suitable for both his interests and the marketplace, and plans to have his first catalog in the mail within two years.

Earning Money at a Hobby

Barbara Loita has a green thumb. Most Northerners who move south to Florida's sunny climate are surprised to learn how hard it is to grow plants there. Barbara solved the mystery of Florida's unusual growing conditions, then published a book about them. The book has led to speaking engagements and requests for other articles, as well as several television appearances.

In addition to the previously cited reasons for working at home, other reasons given by self-employed home-based workers include the ability to: achieve a more flexible schedule, increase revenue, be more productive, and care for their own children.

SERVING UNMET NEEDS

The rise in the number of HBEs is unmistakably the product
of a host of trends—economic, demographic, technological,
and market-related. As with any rapidly growing segment
of the economy, a host of issues relating to home-based workers remain to be resolved. Among those issues are:

- How can home-based telecommuters be assured of
  the same level of benefits and salary as on-site workers? There have been unfortunate instances of exploi-
  tation and discrimination involving clerical workers.
- How will zoning laws be modified to allow working at
  home? In one case, a zoning official used a law that
  prohibits home businesses to prevent a person from
  working on his computer at home. While a measure
  this extreme is rare, it indicates how current zoning
  laws are out of step with the changes in computer
  technology.
- How will managers supervise cadres of workers they
  see infrequently? Will the home-based worker be
  viewed as a valued specialist, or treated as a second-
  tier worker?
- Will home-based clerical work, a rapidly growing
  area, be a golden opportunity for women's entrepreneurship, or serve to further isolate female clerical
  workers from higher pay and greater challenges?

Society will sort out these issues during the 1990s. As a
marketer to HBEs, your ability to effectively meet these and
other needs to be introduced will spell success in the 1990s.

Let's turn to Chapter 2 for HBE demographics and to
learn what kinds of businesses are being launched.

Insights and Hot Tips from Chapter 1
- Home-based businesses are one of the fastest growing social and economic developments in the United States, and
  one of today's hottest marketing opportunities.

- In 1990, 7.5 million Americans joined the ranks of home-based workers. More than 28 percent of the work force, 34.3 million Americans, now work out of their homes on a full- or part-time basis.
- The mass market, for many reasons, vanished during the last decade.
- The national accounting firms, PC vendors, and long distance phone companies, to cite a few, recognize that marketing to small business is a key component for long-term viability.
- The home-based business market is one of the few segments of the economy that will grow rapidly in the 1990s, at a rate 53 times faster than the economy in general.
- Home-based businesses are booming domestically because conditions in America increasingly favor small enterprise. Changes in at least four areas are fueling the growth of home-based business including information technology, the economy, demographics, and family needs.
- All kinds of businesses are being started out of the home. Consulting accounts for more than one out of five home-based businesses. Other popular businesses include word processing, mail order, accounting, real estate, graphic arts businesses, interior decorating, insurance, advertising, communications and public relations, home remodeling, day care centers, bed and breakfast inns, weight and fitness counseling, tax and financial counseling, software development, professional recording, investment banking, executive recruiting, and all types of selling.

CHAPTER 2

WHO IS WORKING AT HOME?

There is no security on
this earth, there is only
opportunity.
Douglas MacArthur

Who are the entrepreneurs who are turning the home into one of America's major workplaces? This market of 34.3 million Americans is diverse and engaging. It is comprised of individuals who have long been self-employed, as well as individuals starting their home-based business this very instant (see Table 2–1).

The market is made up of some traditional figures such as insurance agents, sales professionals, farmers, and home day-care operators, as well as newer ones—desktop publishers, software authors, geologists, and career counselors. It probably includes at least a handful of your personal and professional acquaintances. Research on the

TABLE 2–1
Basic Facts about the Home-Based Business Market

80.1 percent are married
51.9 percent have children under 18
24.4 percent have children under 6
55.4 percent have a college degree
$49,000 is the average income
38.5 is the average age

Source: LINK Resources, 1990.

home-office market is still in its infancy, so we'll survey the results of several studies to get the full flavor of this group as a market.

BY THE NUMBERS

These home-based workers form an affluent market. They are young (two-thirds are between the ages of 25 and 44), successful, and committed to being even more successful. Three major surveys conducted in 1989 of home-based workers agree in their profile of the home-based business market. As shown in Table 2–2, it is made up of well-educated men and women, mostly married and with children, who earn above-average incomes. Males slightly outnumber females, but both men and women are well-represented.

The 1990 LINK survey found this basic pattern continuing to hold true. The market average income increased significantly since the last LINK survey:

- The proportion of men increased slightly, from 52 percent to 55 percent.
- Based on the 1990 survey, more home workers are married— 80 percent versus 74 percent.

TABLE 2–2
Major Home-Worker Profiles Compared

	LINK	American Home Business Association	Sharp
Age	38–40	38.8	36–54
Male	52%	65%	60%
Female	48%	35%	40%
Married	74%	Yes	85.3%
Children	52%	2	—
Average income	$46,000	$56,000	$42,800
College graduate	51%	Yes	39%

Source: Stuart Wolpin, "In Search of the Home Office Market," *Marketing Communications*, January 1989, p. 49.

- Slightly more have college degrees, 55.4 percent in 1990 versus 51 percent in the earlier survey.
- A higher average income—$49,000 versus $46,000.

The LINK 1990 survey also found a surge in the number of individuals who began to work at home, as shown in Figure 2–1.

Bureau of Labor Statistics figures show that the vast majority, 87 percent, of home-based workers are between the ages of 25 and 54.

The distribution of home-based workers by age is about the same for men and women. Figure 2–2 illustrates that a slightly greater percentage of men above age 55 work at home than do women, reflecting the tendency of men to start postretirement work activities. A somewhat greater

FIGURE 2–1
Number of New Home-Based Workers Escalated Sharply in 1990

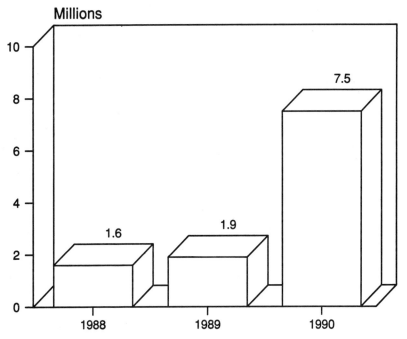

Source: LINK Resources, Inc., 1990.

FIGURE 2–2
Home-Based Workers by Age

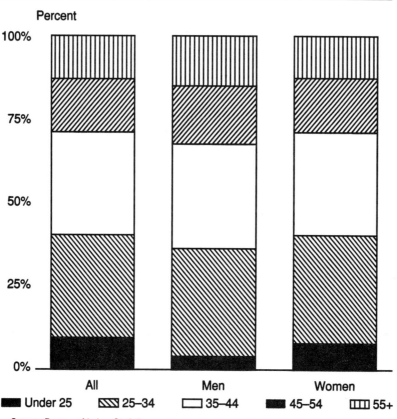

Source: Bureau of Labor Statistics.

share of women between the ages of 25 and 34 work at home, reflecting the interest of women this age in balancing work with care for their young children.

WORK STYLES

When LINK Resources examined the 1990 work-at-home universe, as shown in Figure 2–3, they discovered a wide range of activities in which work was being done at home.

FIGURE 2-3

U.S. Home Work Styles (Many differences, often in the same household)

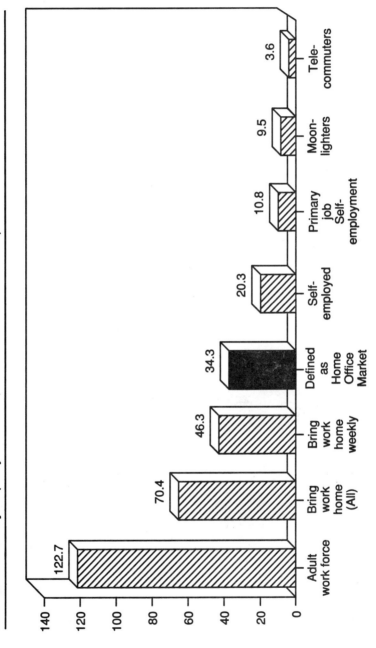

Of 34.3 million home-based workers as determined in the LINK survey, Figure 2–4 illustrates the four different work styles that emerge (which do not necessarily correspond with the four categories of home-based workers presented in Chapter 1):

Home-Office Worker of Small Business

Discussion on this segment is combined within "Corporate Employees Who Take Work Home" starting on page 45.

The Self-Employed

Self-employed home workers, the HBEs, are the heart of the market. Not everyone can start as fast as the 25-year-old millionaire Michael Dell, who launched the fast-growing Dell Computer from his college dorm room. But the

FIGURE 2–4
Key Home Worker Market Segments

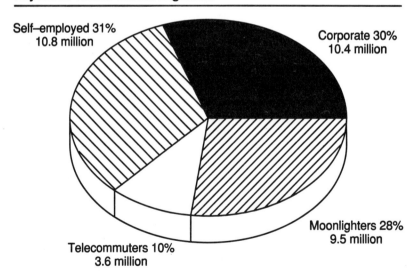

Self–employed 31%
10.8 million

Corporate 30%
10.4 million

Moonlighters 28%
9.5 million

Telecommuters 10%
3.6 million

Source: LINK Resources, 1990.

entrepreneurial drive is alive and well for thousands of Americans starting out at home.

There are two basic varieties of HBEs—those who started at home and those who moved existing ventures to their homes. In either case, most are now committed to staying right where they are. If they need help, they may turn to other home-based entrepreneurs for marketing advice, word processing services, help with research, or other services.

Following are some brief profiles of HBEs in different fields who started at home and have no intention of working anywhere else.

Book Publishing

Neighbors Janet Simmons and Pat Drummond each quit their jobs after having their first child. Soon, both missed the challenge and fulfillment of working, as well as the income. Both had a wide variety of work experience and decided to start a home-based word processing business.

The women purchased a personal computer, a laser printer, and software. They also invested in a fax machine so their clients could speed material to them.

Initially they offered only word processing services, then added list management and repetitive letters, and a resume service. The pair has also become a book publisher. Taking fuller advantage of their PCs, they wrote and self-published a book on starting a home business. They sell the book through direct mail and by advertising in home-business newsletters.

Their next project is publishing a children's newsletter with games, songs, and stories that will be marketed through children's book stores.

Custom-Home Builder

Tom Jellek is following the family tradition by working in the construction business. But while his father is a commercial real estate developer, Tom took the route of custom-home building.

Tom typically works on one job at a time. He hires new workers for every job. He has been using the same architecture firm for the past three years, but has run through an assortment of carpenters, bricklayers, plumbers, roofers, electricians, and painters.

He works out of a converted carriage house and maintains his office upstairs. He uses project management software to plan jobs and schedule workers, enabling him to see immediately what adjustments he has to make when he runs into difficulties.

Tom also uses the computer to market his services. He keeps a referral list on disk and mails a newsletter twice a year to prospects who have inquired about his company. Tom has no plans to move out of his home office. He has acquired off-site, locked storage space to keep blueprints and details of finished projects. Having a home office also helps Tom weather the cyclical fortunes of the custom-home market.

Strategic Planning Consultant

Lisa Bennett knew she wanted to work on her own as a consultant to help companies chart their course. To prepare herself, she held a variety of positions, including researcher at a consulting firm, corporate strategic planner, and director of the planning office for a state government. With that under her belt and a reputation in her field, Lisa hung out her shingle as *Bennett and Associates*.

Lisa works with a variety of clients in the United States and is expanding her business overseas. Her business could not work without her computer and modem. Lisa "teaches" a course electronically at a university in California, even though she is based in Philadelphia, Pennsylvania. She uploads her lecture weekly, and her students download it. They post messages on the course bulletin board, which Lisa and the other students respond to—an electronic version of the classroom discussion.

Lisa's current clients include a school system in the Southwest that is trying to get social services in the schools to better serve its poverty-stricken students, a telecommunications association seeking to market advanced phone features to minority customers, and a medium-sized paper company seeking to set up a system to better monitor changes in its business environment (which could have an effect on the firm's existing products).

Lisa finds working at home more relaxing than in a traditional office. Since most of her work is either writing (easily done at home) or consulting with clients out of the office, she feels she has no need for an elaborate home office.

Software for Schools

Miriam Grabel had a 13-year career as an educator. She taught political science at a midwestern university. Later as an administrator she served as Director of Admissions, and then as Development Officer. Miriam was also a computer buff who has kept a PC at home since 1981.

Miriam could see that there was plenty of room for improvement in the system for tracking student applicants and admissions, as well as for tracking and thanking major donors. She gradually formed the idea of developing an integrated software package for small colleges and private secondary schools.

The package offered development officers on-the-spot performance analyses. It identified lapsed donors and generated thank-you notes to current ones. It tracked the many types of fund-raising events colleges put on, from phone-a-thons to capital campaigns. And it was so simple that a computer novice could use it right out of the box.

Miriam raised capital for her business, then quit her job to start developing and marketing the program. She hired two staff members: a programmer and a marketing associate. From home, they and Miriam developed the core fund-raising program and installed it at 25 schools. After 18 months, due to her huge success, she had no choice but to expand into a commercial office.

Starting the business at home meant that Miriam could put more of her resources into her business. She bought five personal computers, three desks, file cabinets, and other office supplies while the business was still in her home. These supplies formed the core of the company's office furnishings. Her program is now installed in 175 schools and universities.

Telecommuters

The number of corporate employees who rarely set foot in corporate headquarters is rising steadily. Telecommuters now number 3.6 million, comprising just over 10 percent of the 34.4 million people LINK designates as the home-office market. Telecommuters are a creation of the electronic age. They maintain contact with their corporate offices by modem, facsimile, and telephone.

The kinds of jobs that are done by telecommuting tend to be those that don't require extensive personal interaction with the headquarters staff. Presently, telecommuting is growing less quickly than other forms of working at home. Several explanations are plausible:

- Telecommuting requires a major change in the way corporations manage their staff.
- Corporate managers like to see the workers they supervise; employees put in "face time" to impress their bosses.
- It would take a major shift in U.S. culture for managers to focus on measurable output rather than time put in at the desk.

Nevertheless, many companies have found ways to make telecommuting work. The types of tasks that lend themselves to telecommuting include:

- Routine information handling.
- High daily or weekly use of the telephone.

- Relatively little face-to-face personal contact (or personal contact that can be scheduled at the main office and tasks that require concentration can be handled at the home).
- Work that can be done on computer terminals on personal computers.
- Projects with defined boundaries, a structured flow of information, and a predetermined time frame.
- Work that can be performed independently.
- Work with minimal need for support from other people or from complex equipment.
- Work that can be done in a minimal amount of space.

One large consumer products company has a large, supportive telecommuting policy. Following are profiles of three employees participating in the program. Some are permanent telecommuters, while others chose to telecommute for a short period of time.

Exercising the Telecommuting Option

- Retaining the services of mothers on maternity leave
- Accommodating a relocating spouse
- Expanding staff without expanding office space

Maternity Leave

Melissa Renwick and her husband Frank had their first child last spring. Melissa is a marketing vice president. From the time she became pregnant, Melissa planned a six-month hiatus from the office after her child was born, during which she would telecommute.

She read extensively about telecommuting, and gradually shifted some of her responsibilities to subordinates. She and her husband bought a personal computer and modem for the home and had a second phone line installed.

Her six-month telecommuting stint allowed her to continue to lead her division while giving her time at home to adjust to her new family. Moreover, it gave her staff a chance to develop more self-reliance in her absence. Melissa is back in the office now, but she still uses her home office on days when she has quiet work to get done.

Keeping Talent in the Company

Larry had agreed to move to Washington, D.C., from New York to take a new position, but his wife stayed behind to keep her job. Three years of a commuter marriage were taking their toll, so Larry negotiated a deal whereby he would go to Washington one day a week, but telecommute from New York the other four.

Larry would have resigned from his company and looked for another job in New York if his negotiations had not been successful. Telecommuting allowed the firm to keep the talents of a successful, respected executive.

Staff Expansion

A company's educational software subsidiary was developing a new computer game and needed to produce user manuals, a separate guidebook, and a monthly newsletter. They also were setting up a technical support department.

Telecommuters ultimately were hired for all of those roles. After a three-week orientation which was held in the company's auditorium, all 26 staff members went to work in their homes. The writers communicated with the software company's technical experts by modem and phone.

After the software was released, its toll-free 800 number was routed to the technical support staff, who used the company's automated technical support program on their home computers to assist users. Both groups went to the office for meetings with their group leaders. Eight of the telecommuters lived near each other and began to socialize, increasing their camaraderie.

By using telecommuters, the company was able to add staff for a new project without incurring the expense of adding office space. Its new equipment costs were substantially lower, too.

Corporate Employees Who Take Work Home

Senior executives, mid-level managers, and professionals have always taken work home. Some 70.4 million take work home occasionally, and 46.3 million do so weekly. Most of them take work home to catch up on reading, or to keep up with an unusually busy period.

Some 10.4 million of them, however, are serious home workers and are counted among the 34.4 million comprising the home-based market. The time they spend working at home is as critical to their jobs as the time they put in at the office. They make up 30 percent of the home-business market.

Often, their companies encourage working at home by purchasing the necessary equipment for their workers or sharing the cost with them. A readership survey of the corporate employees who subscribe to *Modern Office Technology* revealed how common this arrangement is becoming (see Table 2–3).

TABLE 2–3
Share of Equipment for Working at Home Paid for by the Corporation

Employee's Title	All	Some	None
Corporate management	22.3%	60.7%	17.0%
Financial management	10.3	69.0	20.7
Administrative/operating management	13.7	63.4	22.9
Systems and information management	20.7	53.4	25.9
Support department management	15.7	51.0	33.3
Purchasing	17.9	53.6	28.6
Other	10.4	64.2	25.4
All respondents	17.0	59.2	23.8

Source: Modern Office Technology, August 1989.

The major reasons cited for taking work home are:

- To avoid interruptions.
- To meet deadlines.
- To make up for insufficient office time.

The survey also revealed the types of work that managers found to be best suited to being done at home:

- Reading.
- Strategizing and planning.
- Correspondence, dictation, and research.
- Preparing speeches and presentations.

Many of the managers who responded to the survey said that if their companies would allow it, they could get their jobs done effectively by working at home most of the time.

A Place to Work

When they do work at home, corporate employees make different arrangements for where in the home their work will be accomplished (see Table 2–4).

Over one-third, 37.1 percent, of survey respondents have a separate home office set up to which they take work home. The next largest group, 32.2 percent, has no specific area set aside for work. Another 31 percent sets aside a

TABLE 2–4
Where Employees Work within Their Homes

Location	Percentage of Respondents
Home office	37.1%
Varies	32.2
Designated area	31.0
Other specific locations	5.6

Source: *Modern Office Technology,* August 1989 © Penton Publishing, a subsidiary of Pitman Corporation.

special area of the home other than an office to do work. A small percentage listed other areas such as a kitchen table, a den, a spare bedroom, a part of the basement, or a TV room as the place they did their work.

For many respondents, working at home was a casual affair and did not involve purchasing equipment. This is the case with those who simply read at home and those who take home their dictation equipment to catch up on correspondence.

For those who take other types of work home, particularly work done on the computer, working at home involves major purchases—specialized office furniture, electronic equipment, supplies, and business services.

As more managers use computers for their work, the number who will have home offices is likely to grow to become a majority of this market. Some will use portable computers at home, and could continue to use them at the kitchen table, in the den, and so forth. For managers who work at home a great deal of the time, desktop computers continue to offer a more comfortable, powerful choice.

The Corporate After-Hours Segment
Of the 70.4 million corporate workers who take work home, some 60 million only occasionally take work home. They represent fertile ground, however, and may well start doing more work at home. Two reasons why this could happen are as competition for management spots heats up, workers seeking promotions may work at home to improve their chances. Meanwhile, executives who want to spend more time with their families are leaving their offices at 5:00, but taking a few hours worth of work home with them.

Moonlighters

Moonlighters, 9.5 million strong, are an important segment of the home-office market. Salaries often are not enough to allow families to meet current obligations, own a home, and

save for college tuition for the children and retirement income for the parents. More Americans, in uncertain economic times, turn to moonlighting for additional income.
The number of women who are moonlighting is growing
faster than the number of men.

Moonlighting for Fun

Wilbur Comen has been moonlighting for eight years. By
day, Wilbur is a systems analyst for the federal government. By night (and on weekends) he wears one or more
hats: manager of mailing lists, adult education teacher,
lecturer, columnist, newsletter publisher, and computer
consultant.

Comen does all of this for fun; he says he spends almost
all his extra earnings on trips (a New Yorker, he is fond of
lecturing on the West Coast), new computer equipment,
subscriptions, and other items. He will stay in his government job until retirement, but he admits that he has more
fun with his moonlighting jobs.

Moonlighting Becomes a Second Career

Sometimes, moonlighting can lead to a full-time business,
as it did with Mark Brown. Mark and his wife Cathy are
well-educated professionals in their early 30s. Both had
very good jobs until Cathy's department was downsized in
1987. After some soul searching, Cathy decided she didn't
want to go back to her former field, legal research.

With Mark's support, Cathy explored the job market.
Mark took on some computer moonlighting work to tide
them over. Cathy and Mark gradually decided that they
wanted to move out of their city neighborhood to a small
town. Cathy chose to open a bakery.

They found their dream house, and Cathy opened the
first bakery in their little town. Shortly thereafter, they had
their first child. Mike, now 40, decided to leave his job and
make his moonlighting work his full-time profession. He
wanted to work at home to be with his son as he grew up. By
the time his son was two, he had made the change.

Mike and Cathy's story illustrates dynamism among the work-at-home set. Originally planning only to moonlight, Mike ended up starting a business and working full-time from home. In a sense, Mike moved along the learning curve of working at home.

EVERYONE IS ON THE LEARNING CURVE

The work-at-home movement en masse is progressing along a learning curve. More people choose to work at home because they find it the best way to balance their home and family lives. Companies employing a few telecommuters are learning how to manage them; in three years, they may have an entire telecommuting program.

Workers who are taking their reading home may want to take their budget preparation or sales forecasts home, and buy a computer to make this possible. Individuals who work at home to tide themselves over during a layoff may learn enough to start their own home-based businesses.

ANY REGRETS?

Home-based business owners tend to be a contented lot, but they do miss some things about corporate life.

Home-Office Computing's reader survey found that corporate perks and sociability were missed the most. Some respondents, however, did not miss anything about corporate life.

Q: What do you miss about the corporate world?
A: 1. Company-paid benefits.
    2. Interacting with others daily.
    3. Support services.
    4. Don't miss anything.
    5. After-work socializing.

The survey asked readers what motivated them to work at home. Most people had a combination of reasons, but when all the responses were tallied, the pattern shown in Table 2–5 emerged.

The strongest motivation indicated by HBEs is the desire to run their own show, be their own boss, and increase their earning power. These are the driving forces behind any entrepreneurial venture.

It's notable that these are more powerful motivations than disliking a commute or simply wanting to be more productive. This confirms that the entrepreneurial spirit is at the heart of the home-based business movement. These are a motivated group of businesspeople who want to achieve, and to achieve from home.

PROFILES IN SUCCESS

Jan DeYoung, the training manager at the Small Business Development Center in Ames, Iowa, has worked with hundreds of small businesses and home-based entrepreneurs. Jan notices a pattern that highlights the successful home-based entrepreneur. These success stories:

- Persist.
- Base decisions on factual information.
- Minimize risk.

TABLE 2–5

Motivation for Working at Home	Percent
I wanted to be my own boss.	51
I wanted to make more money.	42
I wanted to change my life.	31
I wanted to spend more time with my family.	30
I'm more productive at home.	27
I'd gone as far as I could in the corporation.	21
I hated the commute.	19

- Learn by doing and getting involved in all aspects of the business.
- Make a conscious, total commitment to the needs of the business.
- Make service their primary goal.
- Start their business with a bare minimum of capital, which forces them to solve problems innovatively.
- Become very aware of their immediate environment—suppliers, customers, employers, friends, and relatives.
- Recognize the opportunity for having fun in their business.

These motivated, professional, home-based business workers are going into business to stay, and are motivated to acquire the best tools to make their businesses work well.

Hot Tips and Insights from Chapter 2

- The home-worker market of 34.3 million Americans is diverse and engaging. It is made up of individuals who have been self-employed for a long time, as well as individuals starting their home-based business this very instant.
- Home-based workers form an affluent market. They are young, with two-thirds between the ages of 25 and 44, successful, and committed to being even more successful.
- There are several sub-groups among home office workers, among them the self-employed, those working for small business, corporate executives who always take work home, executives who occasionally take work home, and moonlighters.
- HBEs miss corporate perks and social interaction the most. They do not miss anything about corporate life.
- The strongest motivation among HBEs is the desire to run their own show, be their own boss, and to increase their earning power—the driving forces behind any entrepreneurial venture.

CHAPTER 3

WHAT THEY BUY AND WHY

... these millions of small private businesses represent one of the world's greatest markets."
The Wall Street Journal, 6/88

The purchasing power of home workers in general and home-based entrepreneurs (HBEs) in particular has risen dramatically in the last four years. In 1986, new home and existing office related purchases totaled $15 billion. Four years later, it had more than doubled.

BIS CAP, a market research firm based in Boston, estimates a $35 billion market, but presumed a base of only 26.6 million individuals, substantially less than LINK's 34.3 million. BIS CAP projected that it would take until 1993 for the home-office market to reach 34.8 million; it reached nearly that size, 34.3 million, in 1990. Hence, the size of the market by 1990 was, *at the least,* $35 billion.

As the number of individuals who establish working space continues to rise annually, home-office purchases will continue to increase markedly for at least the early part of the decade. Any leveling off of total purchases is not likely to occur until the mid to late 1990s, if at all.

Figures 3–1 and 3–2 indicate the percentage of home offices that currently own the products listed:

AT&T sells 66 percent of its two-line telephone to home-office purchasers. Epson, Sharp, Murata, and other manufacturers of fax machines are experiencing a booming business thanks to the home-office customer.

Home offices also contribute significantly to PC sales. Figure 3–3 shows actual figures for 1989 and 1990 and projected figures for 1991, 92 and 93.

FIGURE 3–1
Critical Home Office Products

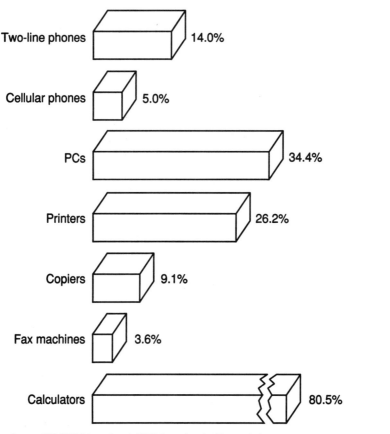

Two-line phones	14.0%
Cellular phones	5.0%
PCs	34.4%
Printers	26.2%
Copiers	9.1%
Fax machines	3.6%
Calculators	80.5%

Source: BIS CAP International, 1990 © reprinted with permission.

NEARLY RECESSION-PROOF

Purchase plans for home offices for many products and services remain on course even in the face of an economic slowdown. HBEs seek advanced products to help them become more personally productive (the primary avenue available for HBEs to expand their businesses).

FIGURE 3–2
Home Office Use of Information Products Increasing Dramatically

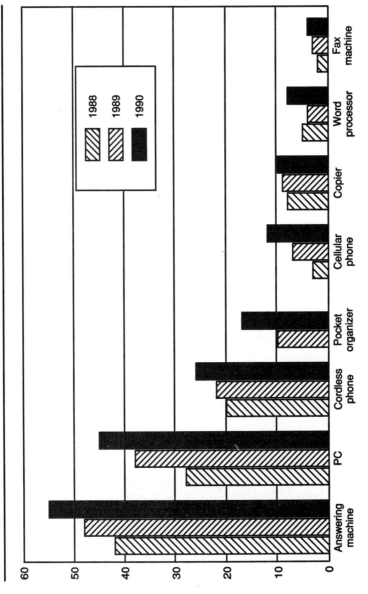

Source: LINK Resources, 1990.

FIGURE 3–3
Personal Computer Market: Fastest Growth in Home Office Segment

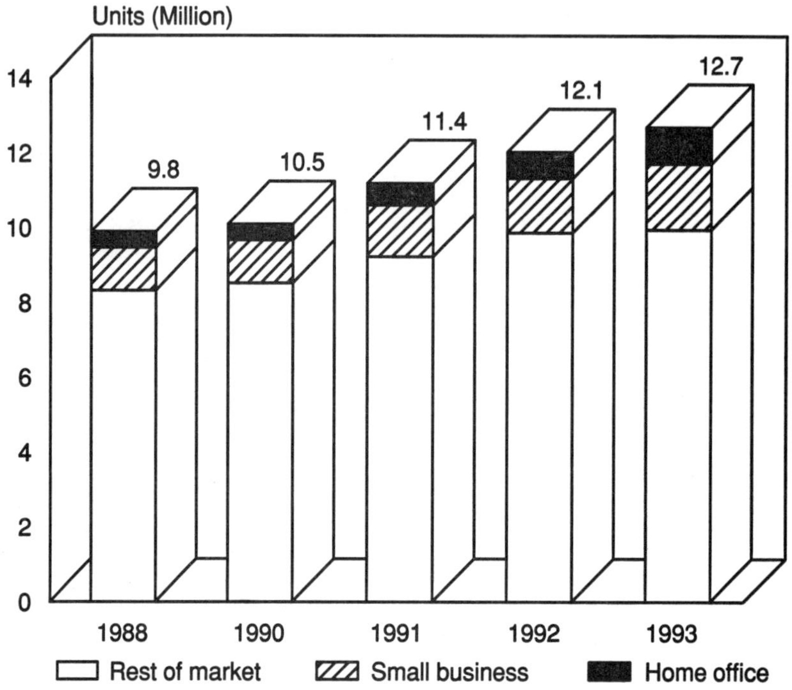

Units (Million)

	1988	1990	1991	1992	1993
	9.8	10.5	11.4	12.1	12.7

☐ Rest of market   ▨ Small business   ■ Home office

Source: BIS CAP International, 1990.

In many ways, home offices often represent a response to economic trouble. Laid-off employees are a significant source of home-based business start-ups. They invest in their home offices to help them earn an income when finding another job may be arduous, and many keep their businesses as permanent arrangements even after the economy recovers.

Typically, HBEs can be counted on to make a sizable minimum number of purchases annually, almost despite their financial footing. Estimates from a variety of sources indicate the extent of their purchasing power. A study conducted by Sharp reveals that the home workers it surveyed (not necessarily HBEs) had planned to spend an average of $2,203 on office equipment in 1989.

The American Home Business Association estimates spending at $9,000 per year for the average home office. This figure reflects a richer concentration of HBEs. Also, the U.S. Internal Revenue Service reports that in 1986, the average home business claimed more than $5,000 in deductions.

THE ANATOMY AND PURCHASES OF HBEs

The underlying reasons why HBEs buy and what they buy can be traced to some basic factors. The economic situation, (ie., getting laid off or terminated), the presence of influentials—friends and associates who affect the buying process, habitual purchasing patterns, a strong dependence on reliability, and, to a lesser degree, the tax deductions associated with home-office purchases.

Let's explore these factors through actual examples and anecdotes.

From Laid Off to Growing Business

Gerry Granville's history as an HBE helps one visualize the many products HBEs purchase, and how they approach buying them. Gerry spent $5,400 in the first nine months that he started working from home. Let's follow the first nine months of his home-based business by tracking the growth of both his business and his purchases.

Gerry was laid off from his advertising job in February of 1989. His employer provided him with three months severance pay and out-placement counseling. The counseling helped Gerry decide to start a home-based business as a freelance ad copywriter. He wrote a brochure promoting his services and hired a marketing consultant to help him draft a business plan.

Gerry already owned a computer, an old Compaq portable from the early 1980s when portables weighed over 20 pounds (today's weigh as few as three pounds). His first major purchase was a printer. He chose the Canon Bubble-jet, which produces output that is close to laser quality at a lower price. It is small enough to fit in a briefcase and light enough to transport.

Portability was important to Gerry since he would be moving the printer onto his kitchen table every day. He also wanted to stay with a major manufacturer. He knew that the Canon print engine is used in a host of other manufacturer's printers, and was impressed by the Bubble-jet's product reviews.

Gerry bought the printer at a computer store. He also bought a cable to connect the printer to the computer and a surge protector. He had done without the surge protector when he used the computer only to track the family budget. Now that he would be having clients, he wanted to protect himself from losing files during a voltage surge. On his way home from the computer store he stopped at a hardware store for a screwdriver and a heavy-duty extension cord.

In the next few weeks Gerry made several trips to a local office supply *superstore* geared to the small business and home office market. He had to stock his office from scratch. He bought the following items, spending about $400:

- binder clips
- calculator
- computer diskettes
- computer paper
- 9 × 12 envelopes
- file box
- file folders
- file folder labels
- halogen task light
- legal pads
- letter stand

- paper clips
- pencils
- pens
- Post-it® notes
- scissors
- stationery and envelopes
- tape
- tape dispenser
- task chair

Gerry's first client turned out to be his former employer. Shortly thereafter, Gerry added three more clients, thanks to his marketing efforts. He loved the work, but was finding the kitchen table less and less useful as an office. Although he had worked evenings at the kitchen table on his family's finances, he was now finding it difficult to work there all day. The hum of the refrigerator bothered him, the kitchen lighting was uneven, and once he nearly lost an entire project when he tripped over the computer's extension cord. When his two children came home after school, they headed straight for the kitchen, making it difficult to concentrate there after 3:30.

Setting Up the Home Office
Gerry's solution was to move his office to the basement. He bought two two-drawer filing cabinets and made a desk by propping lumber from the hardware store across them. Gerry now had seven clients. He decided to buy a business-accounting software program to save him time on book-keeping.

He went to a local software retailer that stocked the most popular business and entertainment software and sold it at competitive prices. After viewing the displays, Gerry settled on DacEasy®, a small-business accounting package. While in the store, he also bought a diskette case, a keyboard drawer to mount under his new desk, and a computer mouse.

Gerry's new basement office was shaping up. It was a great improvement over the kitchen. He installed DacEasy and put all of his expense and income records on the computer. He felt that this gave him a much better picture of how he was doing. He discovered that he needed to increase his marketing efforts to make the income target he set. To help with this, he joined an association of marketing professionals and began to buy books and attend seminars on marketing consulting services.

After five months, Gerry hit a business slump. He was up to 11 clients, but he felt frustrated and underequipped. He made a list of what seemed to be amiss:

- The computer had an old-fashioned, small screen that was beginning to bother his eyes.
- He was nearly out of space on the computer's hard disk.
- He was running down to a local stationery store which offered fax service whenever a client asked him to fax something. This was getting expensive at $2.00 per page and cutting into his productive time.
- He disliked spending all day in the basement.

Gerry was confident he would be successful as a freelancer. He, his wife, and two children began to talk about how to set up a better permanent office for him. They agreed to make part of the basement into the home entertainment center, freeing up the first floor den to be Gerry's home office.

After a few weeks, Gerry's family moved the television, VCR, stereo, and most of the furniture out of the den, and Gerry took it over. He was ready to set up an office that better supported his efforts. His list of necessary items this time included a new computer, computer desk, printer table, fax machine, telephone answering machine, bookcase, and credenza.

Over the next few months, Gerry and his wife shopped for these items at some of the area software and office supply superstores, and at two local office furniture stores.

They also perused computer catalogs and a home-office supply catalog.

They moved slowly on everything but the computer. Gerry qualified for a *store charge card* with Eastwood Computers, one of the leading mail-order computer firms. He was able to charge a $3,200 computer on the store's credit card, which freed up his personal credit cards for other purchases. Eastwood has an excellent reputation for quality and service, but their credit program really sold Gerry. Soon, he had purchased everything on his list except the credenza.

Now Gerry was set up in an office where he was comfortable and productive. As a result, he got more work done and could feel the difference. He soon discovered other benefits of his more sophisticated office. He found he could use his new fax machine to help his marketing efforts. He faxed his promotional materials as an immediate follow-up to marketing phone calls.

In nine months, Gerry, whom you may recall had been laid off, had spent about $5,400 on his home office. Gerry's next roster of needed items, about $2,300 in goods, included the following:

- New carpeting for the den.
- A two-line telephone.
- A personal copier.
- A computer modem.
- A scheduling calendar for the wall.
- A laser printer.

A Somewhat Predictable Sequence

Gerry's experience is typical of the buying habits of many HBEs. Most start out small and increase their purchasing as they begin to generate revenues in their businesses. Rather than save early revenues, many will immediately plow them back into the business recognizing that moving up the growth curve is more important in the early years than amassing profits.

The first purchase made by most of those setting up a home office is a desktop calculator. A telephone answering machine typically is the second purchase, with the personal computer coming in third. Let's take a further look at other typical HBEs to see what they buy and why.

Influencing Factors

Don Wareham

A former claims supervisor in a large insurance company in Hartford, Connecticut, Wareham left the traditional workplace at the start of 1989 to launch his own home-based business venture. Don had always had an affinity for microcomputers and was something of a PC guru to his friends.

Time and time again, Don had observed people who weren't getting much of a return out of their computer investment because they didn't know what else could be added to their system to make it work best for them. Don decided to launch a business entitled the "PC Doctor" and used his own desktop publishing equipment to produce an attractive brochure and flyer.

Operating out of a second-floor bedroom that has since been converted into an over-cramped office, Don now helps clients with everything from installation of internal modems and fax boards to the design and installation of entire systems, plus training and follow up. Because of his limited amount of space, Don, like many HBEs, places a premium on products that are compact, lightweight, portable, and powerful.

Don gathers information about new products and services through a variety of means. He does not subscribe to but intermittently reads various PC-based magazines, such as *Home Office Computing,* and HBE-related articles. He also reads specialized newsletters published by home-based business networks, special interest computer groups, share-ware vendors and other like sources.

Because he orders frequently by mail, Don is on the mailing list of many national product distributors. Don carefully sifts through product catalogs and product and service literature. He is always on the lookout for the latest breakthrough in laser printers, hard disk managers, software, disk backup and storage devices, and so forth.

Don rises about 6 A.M. every morning and doesn't retire until 12 or 1 A.M., often reading software manuals and instruction guides late into the night. He finds the technology explosion for HBEs to be fascinating and is glad to be a part of the revolution.

What Does He Look For? Don is interested in products that represent true systems. For example, he shunned buying or recommending to his clients a very popular brand of laser printer because once installed, the printer required several very expensive font cards before users could have available a variety of desktop publishing options.

When an established vendor introduced for the first time its own line of laser printers, complete with a variety of fonts at no extra charge, Don bought the unit the next day and induced two of his clients to do the same. Similarly, as he learns of new support devices or software, Don is inclined to give them a hard look.

Don is not only a progressive HBE, but is also an opinion leader and conduit to selling to dozens of other HBEs. The good news is, there are tens of thousands of Dons throughout North America who serve as opinion leaders, gurus, and life-lines to the clients they serve (see Chapter 8, page 174 on PC users groups).

Before Don recommends anything to his clients he checks it out and makes sure it works for him. A shrewd shopper, he looks for 800 telephone ordering numbers, fax numbers, acceptance of major credit cards, easy return policy, and supporting hotlines. For larger purchases, particularly of hardware and high-ticket items, he prefers to buy from local or regional vendors, especially those with a store front.

"I don't mind shipping small parts or software back to Arizona," says Don "but when it comes to hardware or large items I want to be able to easily drive to the vendor's location and iron out the problem."

How to Sell to Don. To sell to Don, offer a complete or comprehensive system that offers a combination of features necessary and vital to get a particular function or job done. In the case of the laser printer, for example, Don would not plunk down an extra $400 or $500 for font cards nor would he recommend his clients to do so. He waited a year before buying his first laser printer until a vendor came along who was willing to offer a complete package at an attractive price.

Appeal to Don's intellect. Don has no interest in grand claims or in ad copy inundated with hype. He wants the straight dope on what your product or service can and cannot do, the cost, and what is included.

Like other PC gurus, Don belongs to at least one computer users group, subscribes to one of the on-line data bases such as CompuServe, BRS, GEnie, or Dialog, and attends one or more computer exposition or trade shows a year. In short, his name appears on one or more readily available mailing lists compiled by the national mailing list houses, and HBE industry support groups and publications.

Because Don makes purchases for his clients, he is constantly seeking relationships with retailers and distributors. For example, Don may suggest for the client the purchase of a large system. He then buys all of the components, then picks up, delivers, and installs the entire system. He makes a couple hundred dollars for this service, and additional revenue for training the client.

In the course of a month, Don might install three or four systems of $3,500 or more. Once he knows he can get a good price from a local vendor, Don will go back to that vendor again. Both Don and the vendor benefit. The vendor enjoys several large system sales that might not have otherwise occurred. Don talks the vendor's lingo and takes care of the end user, thus sparing the vendor countless hours dealing with PC neophytes.

If you operate your own retail or wholesale outlet, purchase qualified mailing lists, begin attending the local computer users group meetings, and regularly exhibit at PC expositions and trade shows. You will meet two or three conduits like Don nearly every time. In a short time you'll have a bevy of "PC doctors" ordering systems for their clients, through you.

Let's follow the chain of Don and his clients for a while to further understand the influencing factors behind HBEs purchasing decisions.

Dave Beresford

Dave Beresford is a marketing consultant to small- to medium-size businesses in the Hartford area. He is also one of Don's clients. Like Don, Dave intermittently reads a variety of PC and home business office–based magazines, scans a variety of newsletters, attends computer expositions and conferences, and receives catalogs from national suppliers.

Unlike Don, Dave doesn't have the depth of knowledge or patience to carefully read and digest most of the new product information he encounters. Instead, he often clips such materials and keeps them in a file marked "discuss with Don." Dave's business has grown dramatically in the last two years and without hesitation he is inclined to acquire any office support device that increases his productivity, be it PC-related or not.

Like Don, Dave also has limited space; he uses a converted den on the bottom floor of his split level home in suburbia. Under Don's guidance, Dave has upgraded his computer system in the last 18 months from 256K dual floppy system to a 40 mega-byte hard disk, to 160 mega-byte hard disk with three- and five-inch floppy slots. He also has a cassette tape backup system and three additional slots, all encased in a tower.

Dave hasn't caught up to all the hardware and software he's had installed. In many ways, he still uses his system as if it had less capability. Nevertheless, he is happy with his progress and is steadily gaining proficiency with each passing week.

Dave places a high premium on time and space. On the time issue, Dave likes to purchase anything that maximizes his use of time. For example, once he decided to upgrade to a 160 mega-byte hard disk, he was not looking forward to backing up the hard disk each day. Concurrent with the purchase of the hard disk, Dave asked Don to include a simple backup system, for which Don recommended a high speed cassette backup.

Whether the cost had been $100 or $300 ($300 was closer to the mark) was of no concern to Dave. He had no intention of devoting five or ten minutes a day to a ritual that could be handled automatically by making a one-time purchase.

Conserving Space. Dave wanted a modem to send and receive data from others, but didn't want another device with more wires on his desk. He asked Don to include a built-in modem into his system that was accessed entirely by software. Similarly, whenever Dave adds to his system he primarily explores built in functions. External switch boxes or other devices will simply never find their way into Dave's office, regardless of their utility.

Dave attended a lecture where he was advised to build change into his long-term plans. Hence, while Dave's current system represents overkill for him, he is unconcerned. His goal was to purchase a system that would last several years. Though he does not understand the technology, Dave senses that in the coming year he may step up to a CD-ROM drive, have a fax board installed, and perhaps add a second hard disk.

What Does He Look For? While Don will sit for hours and read detailed product descriptions and instructions, Dave prefers simpler print with graphics and illustrations that make the same point. While Don is building relationships with vendors, Dave has no loyalty to vendors whatsoever. Whatever appears to do the job faster, and with less bulk, or whatever Don recommends, is of interest to Dave.

Consequently, Dave doesn't care to be on mailing lists or regularly receive catalogs. What literature he does receive, he flies through in record time, extracting the few pages or product descriptions that may be of interest, and inserts them in his "Don" file.

Clearly, Dave is time and space conscious. Price, ease of installation (because he has Don), and brand name (again he has Don) mean little to him. For non–EDP-related items, Dave also is conscious of time and space. He shops for office supplies himself, usually on the way back from some other trip rather than delegating the task. He wants to see and feel what is available and be certain that what he buys will subsequently be consumed.

Dave doesn't have ample storage room and so, in essence, he has created a self-perpetuated, just-in-time inventory system. Shelving, related items, and anything that "stacks" finds favor with Dave. He uses the vertical spaces in his small office with great efficiency.

Dave only shops at superstores so that he may choose among a wide assortment and selection of goods. For this reason, he will drive past smaller, limited-line retailers. Dave is also an environmentally aware consumer. He loathes products that contain excess packaging. The terms *recycled, biodegradable, environmentally safe, nontoxic, no hydrofluorocarbons,* and the like, appeal to him.

How to Sell to Dave. The three keys to selling to HBEs like Dave (other than appealing to Don first!) is to stress how your product or service saves time or space, or supports the environment. Time savings could be expressed in terms of minutes or hours saved per time used—day, week, or month. Or, in terms of what other users achieved over a particular period.

Space saving can be accented through wording such as, "fits neatly into a letter-size file folder," "fits neatly in your brief case," or "contracts into a width of 2 inches." Stressing any elements of your products or packaging that help to support the environment also gains favor with Dave.

Richard Carlson

Continuing in the sphere of Don Wareham's influence, let's profile Richard Carlson. Richard is a trainer who has several large corporate clients in Boston, Providence, and New Haven. He has been on his own since 1986, grossing more than $175,000 for his one-man practice.

In contrast to Don or Dave, Richard has ample space in his home office which is located in the basement of his 2,800-square foot home. The basement floor is completely finished and includes a large den and TV area, a laundry area, a bathroom with a shower, a 360-square-foot office, a storage room, and another room that serves as a spill-over storage area for Richard's office.

When it comes to EDP equipment, Richard does no reading or reviewing. He relies totally on the input from others, including primarily Don, and other associates and fellow HBEs who share their information about what works and what doesn't.

Richard is technology phobic. Since he has ample space, particularly counter and shelf space, he often devises the most basic of systems to support his business. For example, rather than having one phone system with several different lines, Richard has four distinct phone lines:

- Line one is his primary business line to which is also attached an answering machine for when he is out of the office.
- Line two is a dedicated fax line.

- Line three is a nonbusiness line to which an answering machine is also connected.
- Line four is an extension line for his wife's business, also located at home on an upper floor.

To Richard, devices such as internal modems are scary and confusing. He wants to see what he is working with and to be able to push familiar buttons.

What Does He Look For?   Across the board, be it PC support devices of standard office equipment or supply, Richard looks for basic, no frills, "this is how you do it" products. While space is not at a premium with Richard, time is, and as we've seen, simplicity even more so. He will buy, and buy in quantity when convinced or shown that the acquisition can be readily put to work.

Richard will also pay for services in support of what he has purchased. For example, after installing a fax machine, if he doesn't understand one of the functions, he has no qualms about retaining a telecommunications consultant at $50 or $60 per hour for advice on how to make the equipment do what he wants it to do. Also, like many HBEs, Richard appreciates brand names but will readily abandon name recognition for performance, durability, and ease of operations.

How to Sell to Richard.   Retailers and national product distributors beware. Richard and HBEs like him are not likely to read your literature, send or write for your goods, or visit your place of business. Since Richard doesn't tend to go to shows and his name doesn't show up on lists, there are several ways to identify and encounter more like him: through professional and civic trade groups, simple advertisement in local papers, flyers and newsletters, direct mail coupon packs, door-to-door hand bills, and limited, targeted mailings.

Service providers can make an immediate splash with him by appealing to his needs, wants, and fears. Perhaps the best way to penetrate his defenses are to simply *call* him during the middle of a business day and quietly explain your service and what it has done for others like him.

For example, a copy repair service made a shotgun call to Richard and was effective using this approach: "Hello, I'm with XYZ Copy Repair Service and the reason I'm calling is we've found that many personal copier owners appreciate our $75 one-time dynastic review, maintenance, and cleaning." Once he has found someone he trusts and with whom he has a good working relationship, pretty much independent of fee, Richard will maintain the connection for months, or even years.

Observable Purchasing Patterns

Gladys Sansing

Gladys works from her home as a sales representative for a photographic supply company in Fort Mitchell, Kentucky. Divorced five years ago, Gladys has two children; one lives at home and the other is married and lives in the next county. She is on straight commission, has nearly complete independence in her work, and considers herself to be self-employed.

She has been at it for 18 years. In all this time, she has never set up a complete home office. She simply uses her dining room table a couple days a week, retrieving carefully arranged files that lean against the dining room wall.

Gladys is a non-EDP type of HBE. While she gets most of her supplies from the company she represents, she does have a continuing need for pens, paper, pads, paper clips, mail packs, tape, rubber stampers, and other traditional office support items, plus express and delivery services.

Gladys's overwhelming need, however, relates to her car. She regularly stocks Post-it® pads, pop-up Wet Ones®, maps of the local area, cassette programs, portable paper files, and all manner of emergency supplies. To remain stocked in these vital items, Gladys must visit as many as eight different stores. Few retail establishments in her area seem to recognize that there is a growing number of HBEs who rely on their vehicles and that such entrepreneurs have continuing needs in highly identifiable areas.

What Does She Look For?   Gladys tends not to do too much ordering by phone. Instead she makes stops on the way back home from prospect visits. She either patronizes the same basic locations, or when caught short for some vital supply, will patronize a new retailer if the store appears to be rather clean, well-lit, in a highly visible location, and has easy access and easy parking. She looks for bulk purchase discounts, acceptance of personal checks or credit cards, and friendly service.

How to Sell to Gladys.   There is a tremendous opportunity for vendors to sell to Gladys; her consumption patterns and continuing needs are well established. Rather than making the rounds as each item declines in number, the vendor who convinces her of the practicality and utility of sending her a periodic shipment of the supplies she needs will gain a long-term customer and bypass getting to sell to her only when she makes her rounds.

Sabrina Velenza

Sabrina is an export consultant who assists firms in the United States who want to sell their goods abroad. She is also married and the mother of three children, ages eight, five, and one and one-half. Her long-term goal is both to build a career working at home and to stay with her children. Particularly with the youngest one, her hours are not her own, so she takes every opportunity she can to be at her desk.

Some mornings she may get up at 5 or 6 A.M., before everyone else, to complete tasks on her computer, check for voice mail messages, scan computer bulletin boards, and respond to mail. "I walk in and out of my office dozens of times each day," says Sabrina. "If I can, I work for 15 minutes at a clip."

She finds that with continual interruptions the biggest task is regaining focus on the task at hand before she was interrupted. "You can do a lot in 15 minutes, if you can swiftly regain a sense of what you were doing. I can send four or five faxes or a couple of express mail packs overseas by quickly jumping back into my routine," she says.

Her office is equipped with a PC and modem, answering machine, fax, pocket dictator, laser printer, a cordless telephone, and intercom. "The cordless phone is a godsend," she says. "If the kids start to get noisy I can keep talking while I head for a more quiet place." Overall, Sabrina finds that office technology greatly assists her in managing her part-time business, being with her children, and building her future.

What She Is Looking For.   Sabrina seeks portability in the equipment she buys, as demonstrated in the use of her cordless phone and pocket dictator. She also seeks greater control over the timing of her transmissions. Her fax machine either does not allow delayed transmissions, or she is not aware of its capability to do so. Since she sends transmissions around the world, timing is critical to her. Similarly, she is apparently not aware that modem transmissions can also be scheduled at the discretion of the sender.

How to Sell to Sabrina.   As a full-time mother and part-time HBE, Sabrina has no time to attend outside meetings. She gets most of her new product and service information in phone conversations with friends and associates, through computer bulletin boards, and direct mail.

The most effective approach to sell to Sabrina is to first understand what she faces as an HBE and mother, and then provide products and services that enable her to stay focused amid disruptions and to maintain discretion over the timing of communication transmissions. Advertising copy and product description that address these needs would find immediate favor with the Sabrinas of the HBE market. There is also good potential for nontechnical items such as flip charts, erasable calendar wall charts, custom Post-it® pads, and the like.

Eliana Lewis

Eliana operates a three-person career counseling business out of her home. Located in Portland, Oregon, Eliana's house is large and contains a wing for her business. In all, the business occupies about 580 square feet. To counsel her clients effectively, Eliana first collects comprehensive information and stores it in large legal-size files.

Eliana uses a box number for her business address. Because of that, most catalog mailers don't realize that she actually operates a home-based business. As more entrepreneurs begin operating out of their homes and using post office address boxes or other addresses to disguise their location, it will become increasingly difficult for non-astute vendors to recognize this distinction.

Eliana's part-time secretary/administrative assistant is responsible for routinely purchasing office supplies. The secretary maintains product and supply catalogs, a file of vendor phone numbers, and other files organized by product or product category. Eliana makes the big purchase decisions such as desks, chairs, terminals, faxes. Eliana and her secretary order almost exclusively by mail and telephone. Eliana has no time to be traipsing around town purchasing goods, nor does she want her secretary doing the same.

What Does She Look For?   At Eliana's office, they hang on to circulars, flyers, and product catalogs. Increasingly, Eliana's office orders by fax—these purchases can be made more quickly, and efficiently, and can be organized more easily. Finding that ordering over the phone is a waste of time, they have designed their own fax purchase order which includes all the information a vendor would need to proceed with their order.

Because they have storage space, Eliana will buy in quantity if the price is right. She regularly consumes copy paper, fax paper, file folders, copy cartridges, printer ribbons, laser printer cartridges, stamps, envelopes, mail packs, and wrapping supplies.

How to Sell to Eliana. Because her office does so much ordering by phone and fax, any vendor literature that identifies these ordering options find favor with Eliana. While some vendors provide 800 fax numbers, this is of no particular advantage to Eliana Lewis since most fax purchase orders can be sent through in under a minute (less than 20 cents). Eliana will not give a vendor the edge for an 800 fax number. A regular 800 number is another thing, however. If Eliana or her secretary needs to call to discuss an item or to follow up, the vendor with the 800 telephone number who also takes fax orders has a distinct edge over others.

There are many small business entrepreneurs who, whether or not they maintain a box number, and despite the fact that they may maintain a commercial office, still do some work at home. A catalog that appeals to both commercial and home-office entrepreneurs will succeed with HBEs like Eliana.

Reliability More Than Price

As with most of the HBEs discussed above and many HBEs in general, price is not the primary concern when contemplating a purchase. Reliability is (see Table 3–1).

Inexpensive equipment that breaks down at a critical moment is no bargain for the HBE, whose strong reliance on equipment is easily understandable. The majority are willing to spend the money to get high-quality office products, and to have the security of first-rate, dependable service after the sale. Their businesses depend on it.

TABLE 3–1
Purchase Decision Factors for the Home Office Consumer

Decision Factor	Extremely/Very Important
Reliability	96%
Service	83
Cost to acquire	79
Manufacturer's reputation	75
Support by manufacturer	72

Source: *Home Office Computing*, 1990.

The HBE, like any other business customer, spends money to solve problems. Productivity is frequently a concern. While many HBEs hire assistants to help out, the major gains in profitability come from first fully equipping their offices with equipment that improves the HBE's personal productivity.

Tax Advantages

Self-employed HBEs can deduct their office expenses from their taxes. They pay no federal, state, city, or business taxes on their earnings, which are put back into their businesses in the form of purchases.

The impact of this tax treatment on purchase decisions can be substantial. Take the case of Sarah Tannen, a self-employed word processor. Once Sarah's income crosses the threshold of about $20,000, her marginal tax rate becomes a very substantial 49.9 percent. Here is how her tax situation breaks down:

- 28 percent Federal income tax
- 15.3 percent self-employment tax (Sarah pays both the employer and employee share of Social Security taxes)
- 6 percent state income tax
- 49.9 percent marginal tax rate

What this means is that every business purchase Sarah makes is, in effect, marked down by 50.1 percent. This leverage differentiates HBEs in the mass market of consumers. The $3,000 computer system Sarah wants to buy will only cost her $1,497; the remainder is money Sarah has now paid in taxes anyway. Likewise, HBEs proceed with many purchases fully confident in their ability to expense the sum in figuring tax liabilities.

TO BUY, THAT IS THE ANSWER

Influenced by peers and readily available, enticing literature, motivated by a constant desire to increase productivity, and spurred on by tax incentives, many HBEs are on a buying binge. A recent readership survey conducted by *Home Office Computing* magazine confirms this trend (Table 3–2).

The use of fax machines is clearly on the rise among HBEs. Fewer than 8 million fax machines are now in use worldwide, with half being used in Japan. As disgruntled postal patrons search for alternative means of sending a printed message, and as the price drops, fax machines will become standard home-office equipment, much as personal

TABLE 3–2

Office Products and Accessories	Currently Own	Plan to Purchase in the Next 12 Months
Fax machine	7%	54%
Copier	23	53
Telephone answering machine	76	29
Computer furniture	71	29
Video equipment (camcorder)	55	21
Postage meter	4	14
Calculator	86	8
Electric typewriter	46	8
Dictating equipment	9	8
Dedicated word processor	10	6

computers and printers are now. By next year there will be 10 million fax machines in operation in the United States alone, with predictable growth thereafter.

Most of the readers surveyed already own computers. For a substantial number of HBEs, however, a computer heads the list of planned purchases. Many have owned their computers for a few years and have watched as newer computers become faster and more powerful. They are eager to upgrade their machines and run all the latest software. In fact, home offices will drive growth in the personal computer market in the 1990s (see Figure 3–4).

Shipments of personal computers are growing by an average of 7 percent annually, and will reach just under 13 million by 1993. Sales to the small-business market will

FIGURE 3–4
Home Office Fastest Growing Segment of Personal Computer Market

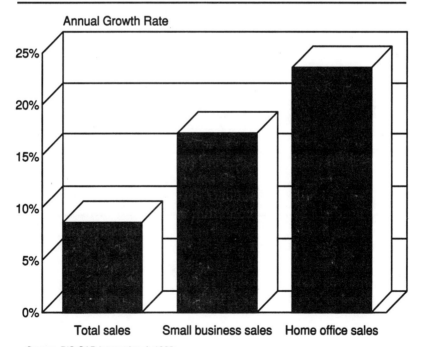

Annual Growth Rate

Total sales   Small business sales   Home office sales

Source: BIS CAP International, 1990.

grow at over twice that pace, at 16 percent. *Modern Office Technology* forecasts that sales to home offices, though, will grow even faster, more than three times as fast as the overall market, at 23 percent annually.

While the cost of computing power is constantly falling, the price of home computers is holding steady. A growing portion of these PCs are sold through the mail. There is even a magazine specifically for the home-office computer buyer, *PC Sources*, that provides advice on mail order buying.

The home office buyer is keeping the average purchase price up because he is demanding more advanced features. VGA color monitors, large hard disk drives, modems, and expanded memory are features that more home office buyers are including in their purchases.

A *Home Office Computing* reader survey, shown in Table 3–3, reveals that respondents who plan to upgrade their personal computers have a preference for IBM compatibles, which are PCs that offer the power of more expensive equipment at far less cost.

Accessories

More computer owners means more business for those who sell computer hardware accessories, software, printers, and supplies. Both new and seasoned computer owners invest

TABLE 3–3

Personal Computers	Currently Own	Plan to Purchase in the Next 12 Months
IBM compatibles	65%	76%
IBM	20	32
Laptop (portable), any brand	10	30
Compaq	2	17
Tandy	21	17
Macintosh	4	15

hundreds of dollars in additional hardware and software. The purchasing plans for PC accessories of *Home Office Computing* readers are shown in Table 3–4.

Software Purchases

Software is one of the major productivity tools for the HBE today. Personal organizers, accounting programs, and word processors all enable the home office to run more smoothly.

One major development is the widespread acceptance of the computer program Microsoft Windows 3.0. This has prompted HBEs to spend hundreds of dollars on software compatible with Windows 3.0. Windows™ 3.0 allows a computer user to work on several programs at once, swapping data back and forth between graphics, word processing, and spreadsheet programs, for example, or allowing a user to print and then continue working.

Table 3–5 shows the types of programs that the *Home Office Computing* readers indicated they will be buying.

TABLE 3–4

PC Accessories Wish List	Currently Own	Plan to Purchase in the Next 12 Months
Modem (internal and external)	72%	72%
Accessory boards (memory expansion, graphics, and multifunction)	68	59
Hard disk (internal and external)	62	42
Mouse	40	34
On-line services	29	31
Scanner	7	30
Tape backup system	4	20
Surge protector	81	15

TABLE 3–5

Computer Software	Currently Own	Plan to Purchase in the Next 12 Months
Graphics	48%	41%
Accounting	61	41
Word processing	94	38
Desktop publishing	31	37
Communications	42	31
Database	63	30
Entertainment	36	21
Spreadsheet	64	19
Utilities	44	17
Education	26	15
Integrated package	21	6

Crying Need for Improved Communications

Vendors and telecommunication consultants take heed—
one of the weak links in the marketing chain for the HBEs
is use of the telephone. Common usage problems include:

- Not having the right equipment.
- Not being proficient in using the equipment.
- Not having adequate telephone answering service.
- Not capitalizing on calls that represent new business.
- Inability to coordinate phone, fax, modem, answering
  machine, and answering service.

Opportunities exist in:

- All types of telephone and telecommunication equipment support.
- Training, instruction, guidance, and consulting.

Insure We Must

Home-office insurance will be a hot item among HBEs, especially home-office riders to the homeowner's or tenant's
policy, or separate business coverage.

A home office represents a large investment in time and money, as well as in inventory—an investment that needs to be protected. Most HBEs will be surprised to learn that their standard homeowner's policy doesn't cover dwellings not used principally as a residence, separate structures that are used in whole or in part for business purposes, or business property used in conducting a business on the premises, including all furnishings and equipment in a home office.

The standard homeowner's policy also does not cover business inventory or samples stored on the premises, losses from stolen business credit cards or checks, or accidental damage to business or personal equipment due to electrical surges. Neither personal liability nor medical payments for injuries to others, whether they are eligible for workers' compensation or not, are covered under a home business.

Because of the deficiencies in standard homeowner policies, opportunities to market insurance to HBEs are great. Included are policies covering workers' compensation; computer and software insurance; business inventory insurance; interruption of business insurance; health, life, and disability insurance; and malpractice and products liability insurance.

Other Products and Services

Products based on information technology comprise most of the spending on the home office. Still, there is a growing market for other products and services that make the home-business owner more productive:

Accounting
Business planning
Database technology
Daycare
Delivery

Electronic mail
Furniture
General office services
Graphic arts and design services
Marketing consulting
Mobile car care
Telephone answering service
Toll-free calling
Videotext

Let's briefly walk through each area of opportunity that is likely to grow in demand as the HBE trend accelerates in the 1990s:

Accounting
Keeping track of finances is a continuing challenge. The tax situation today for HBEs is far more complicated than for salaried employees. Though they don't all recognize it, every HBE and anyone who plans to deduct any home-office expenses needs an accountant. Some accountants have launched "mobile bookkeeping services" that consist of vans outfitted with a work space in the back, including a computer. The accountant comes to the HBE, bringing his own office with him.

Business Planning
Many home-based businesspeople fall into their working arrangements, like Gerry, and never actually sit down to compose a business plan to shape their ideas into a coherent, strategic format. HBEs need help in this area, be it via a consultant, business planning software, or both.

Database Technology
While many HBEs have specialized customer files, they may not be tapping the valuable marketing information that these files contain. Relational databases will gain in popularity as PCs become exponentially more powerful.

Daycare
HBEs with young children need in-house caretakers during working hours. This allows HBEs to be near their children during the day but frees them to concentrate on work.

Delivery Services
Any store that delivers HBE's phone orders, particularly on short notice, stands to win big. Major delivery services such as Federal Express® are doing an increasing share of business with home offices.

Electronic Mail, or E-Mail

While this may be a decade-old technology, HBEs are just beginning to realize its value. Close to a billion electronic messages were transmitted in 1988 alone. HBEs will respond to the ability to record and transmit computer formatted files and messages to individuals or groups easier, faster, and cheaper than the ever-costlier postal mail.

Furniture
Many home-office workers will be upgrading desks, tables, chairs, bookcases, and more. HBEs often like their office furniture to blend in with their home decor. A number of stores, Sears among them, now offer attractive, inexpensive home-office furniture. Generally, such furniture has all the functions of office furniture but is smaller in size.

General Office Services
On an as-needed basis, some HBEs will seek answering services tied into general office services such as courier services, and access to office equipment and conference rooms on a time-share basis. These will have to be tailored packages to meet their specific requirements.

Graphic Arts and Design Needs
Literature is often the first inclination prospects have of HBEs services or products. Many HBEs lack the time or

capability to design and produce their own stationery, let-
terhead, logos, brochures, fliers, and business cards. Many
opportunities exist for those proficient in design and
graphic arts.

Marketing Consulting
Marketing from home requires a new set of strategies. Marketing provides the lifeblood of any business, and many
home-based entrepreneurs have not marketed before. Consultants in this area are doing very well.

Mobile Car Care
HBEs lose time and money when they take their cars to
repair shops. Mobile tune-up services and mobile tire dealers are two of several auto-related services that HBEs find
attractive.

Telephone Answering Services
Many HBEs still prefer to have a human being answer the
phone for them. Such services can make the HBE appear
more professional. For HBEs, using an answering service
combined with a mobile pager can supply immediate action
on emergency calls.

Toll-Free Calling
For HBEs who want to encourage out-of-state clients and
prospective customers to call them at home, a toll-free 800
number will be a viable solution. HBEs will be attracted to
the savings, currently about 60 percent in per-minute
charges over collect calls, 45 percent over credit card calls,
and 30 percent over some 1 + calls. HBEs who travel will
use their own 800 number to call in.

Videotext
Literally thousands of videotext services exist in the
marketplace, varying in size and focus, but many HBEs are
unaware of the possibilities. Before 1995, this is likely to
change. Some HBEs may be interested only in a passive

service, such as a reference database. Others will be drawn to interactive videotext services, which include electronic mail and electronic bulletin boards. They will take active roles in communicating with associates, clients, and vendors through their computers.

Below is a roster of six myths and corresponding facts about selling to HBEs.

Six Myths of Selling to the Home Office Market

Myth #1   The HBE is a low-end sale.
FACT: HBEs are not primarily motivated by price; they want quality and reliability and are willing to pay for it.

Myth #2   Selling to the home office means developing a new product line.
FACT: Minor changes in packaging, store displays, or distribution channels can make your product appealing to this market.

Myth #3   The home-office market is too loosely defined to work as a target market.
FACT: Distribution channels to the home-office market are rapidly solidifying. Magazines, trade shows, conventions, direct mail, superstores, and catalogs are rapidly becoming solid sales vehicles.

Myth #4   The home-office market is inferior to and presents less opportunity than the corporate market.
FACT: If you sold 100 units to each of 30 percent of the Fortune 1200 market, you would only sell 36,000 units of your product. If you sold one unit to just 5 percent of the home-office market, you would sell 1 million units.

Myth #5   Sales costs are too high when selling to the home-office market.
FACT: The home-office market offers a shorter sales cycle than corporate markets because decisions are

made quickly and by one person. Often, a sales force is not needed; this market is sold by advertising which works faster, sells quicker, and costs less.

Myth #6   The home-office market is not significant at the retail level.

FACT: Home-office workers shop in retail stores in large numbers. They respond well to in-store promotion. They frequent computer superstores, office supply stores, consumer electronics outlets, office equipment and stationery stores, hardware stores, and department stores.

Hot Tips and Insights from Chapter 3

• The purchasing power of home workers in general and home-based entrepreneurs in particular has risen dramatically in the last four years. In 1986 new home–and existing office–related purchases totaled $15 billion. In 1990, the total was more than $30 billion.
• As the number of individuals who establish working space continues to rise annually, for at least the early part of the decade, home-office purchases will continue to increase markedly. Any leveling off of total purchases is not likely to occur until the mid- to late 1990s, if at all.
• Purchases of many products and services by HBEs remain on course even in the face of an economic slowdown.
• In many ways, home offices often represent a response to economic trouble. Laid-off employees are a significant source of home-based business start-ups. They invest in their home offices to help them earn an income when finding another job may be arduous, and many keep their businesses as permanent arrangements even after the economy recovers.
• HBEs can be counted on to make a sizable minimum number of purchases annually, almost despite their financial footing. A study conducted by Sharp reveals that the home workers it surveyed (not necessarily HBEs) had

planned to spend an average of $2,203 on office equipment in 1989.

- The underlying reasons why HBEs buy and what they buy can be traced to economic situation, i.e., getting laid off or terminated; the presence of influentials—friends and associates who affect the buying process; habitual purchasing patterns; dependence on reliability, and, to a lesser degree, the tax deductions associated with home-office purchases.
- The first purchase made by most of those setting up a home office is a desktop calculator. A telephone answering machine typically is the second purchase, with the personal computer coming in third.
- Because of their limited amount of space, HBEs place a premium on products that are compact, lightweight, portable, and powerful.
- HBEs look for 800 telephone ordering numbers, fax numbers, acceptance of major credit cards, easy return policy, and supporting hotlines.
- For larger purchases, particularly of hardware and high-ticket items, many prefer to buy from local or regional vendors, especially those with a store front.
- They appreciate complete or comprehensive systems that offer a combination of features necessary and vital to get particular functions or jobs done.
- Knowledgeable and/or extensive PC users often belong to a computer users group, subscribe to one of the on-line databases such as CompuServe, BRS, GEnie, The Source, or Dialogue, and attend one or more computer exposition or trade shows a year. In short, their name appears on one or more readily available mailing lists compiled by the national mailing list houses, and HBE industry support groups and publications.
- A growing number of HBEs are environmentally aware consumers who dislike products that contain excess packaging. The terms *recycled, biodegradable, environmentally safe, nontoxic, no hydrofluorocarbons,* and the like, appeal to them.

- Many HBEs like brand names but will abandon name recognition for performance, durability, and ease of operations.
- The most effective approach in selling to HBE mothers is to first understand what they face as HBEs and mothers, and then to provide products and services for them to stay focused amid disruptions, and maintain discretion over the timing of communication transmissions.
- HBEs love to order by fax—these purchases can be made more quickly, more efficiently, and can be organized more easily.
- One of the weak links in the marketing chain for the HBEs is use of the telephone. Common usage problems include not having the right equipment and not being proficient in using the equipment.
- Home office insurance will be a hot item among HBEs, especially home office riders to the homeowner's or tenant's policy, or separate business coverage. Most HBEs don't know their standard homeowner's policy doesn't cover dwellings not used principally as a residence or separate structures that are used for business.
- Despite the magnitude of the market, myths about marketing to HBEs have kept some vendors out of the game.

CHAPTER 4

SUPERSTORES: THE BIG STICK APPROACH

The toughest thing about
success is that you've got to
keep on being a success.
Irving Berlin

The rise of the HBE has spurred the growth of national retail chains, dubbed "superstores" by the business press. They offer a vast assortment of goods with a supermarket type of approach. The Price Club, Office Club, Staples, Hechingers, MicroCenter and The Soft Warehouse, among others, cater to a market that simply will not be denied. While none of the super retailers specifically restrict their appeal to HBEs, a simple analysis of their operations reveals that HBEs do represent a healthy, if not dominant, share of total revenues.

Physically Superior Stores

- More square footage
- More checkout counters
- More selection
- Extended business hours
- More parking space
- Clear return policies
- Extensive, updated product catalogs
- Superior shelf talkers and displays
- Superior lighting

THE OFFICE SUPERSTORE

While the home-office customer is willing to pay handsomely for sophisticated, technology-intensive products, he wants to do two things: cut costs on office supplies and shop in the least amount of time possible.

Those two needs have driven the growth of Staples, the office superstore. Staples has done for office supplies what Toys-R-Us has done with children's toys—made it difficult to justify shopping anywhere else.

Staples and Southern: A Tale of Two Office Suppliers

In my hometown, Falls Church, Virginia, in the Bailey's Crossroads section, Staples set up shop in January 1989. Prior to that, Southern Office Supply had been the premier office supply store throughout the 1980s. Southern was well located in the L-shaped shopping center at the intersection of Columbia and Leesburg Pikes. Both roads were major commercial highways and commuter thoroughfares. There was ample free parking in front of the store. The store itself was appropriately located next to a low- to mid-level quality department store and high-volume chain drugstore.

The interior of Southern Office Supply was adequate for its day, approximately 1,000 square feet. As office supply stores go, Southern was doing reasonably well. Over the years it had built up a mailing list and distributed a high quality four-color, four-page monthly flyer announcing specials and bargain buys. The personnel were helpful if not entirely knowledgeable about the products offered.

The atmosphere was one of benign indifference. You came, looked around, made your purchase, and left. A trip to Southern Office Supply blended in with the rest of your errands. It was one stop along the way. Except for the advertised monthly bargains—which were true bargains—one would consider the store's prices to be competitive.

Through January 1989, Southern's major competitors were Miller Office Supply, Ginn's, and Jacobs-Gardner. All three companies had numerous outlets throughout northern Virginia. The latter two chains largely served the office market. Southern had a much higher percentage of HBEs, though they probably didn't know to acknowledge the difference between customer segments.

Out of Nowhere?

From what must have seemed out of nowhere to Southern's management, Staples arrived in town. Staples took the corner space on the far right of the L-shaped shopping strip. The location's previous tenants had included Circuit City, which moved to an even larger location, Warehouse Foods, which failed miserably, and Bill's Carpets.

From its first month of operation through the end of the year Staples caught on like wildfire. The store was easily four times the square footage of Southern, as was its inventory. The selection was vast and deep. It is doubtful that any office supply purchasers in the area had ever experienced anything like Staples. It was clean and bright and bustling. The sign said "The Office Super Store," and the outfit lived up to it in every way.

When you first entered, you had the magical feeling that it was no ordinary office supply store. A large sign indicated that Visa, Master Card, Staples credit card, check, and cash could all be used for payment. Shopping baskets such as those used in supermarkets were available inside the entrance. All traffic was directed to the right so each shopper would have to walk a minimum of two aisles to get back to the cashier.

Staples's prices were unlike anything the area had experienced. Notebooks, pads, paper, and computer supplies—many items sold for as much as 40 percent less than at other office supply stores. If you happened to have a Staples card, and this was encouraged at all checkout counters by all employees, you could save another 10 percent. From week one, Staples's policy of issuing Staples credit cards to all customers helped them to build an enormous share of the traditional as well as HBE office market.

In addition to the traditional items one might expect, Staples also provided accessory office products. Bargains were offered on coffee, juice, business magazines, business literature, reference books—Staples was a one-stop center. Along the left side of the store were placed office copying machines so that you could make your own copies. There were also engraving and other related services.

Superior in Every Way

Staples was a physically superior store both inside and out, having show room lighting, attractive displays, and shelf talkers that said "buy me." Shopping there the first few times was a memorable if not pleasurable experience. Each time you entered the store you felt as if you were in partnership with the store. For the price-conscious HBE, the prices for some goods were so low that they wanted to stock up as much as possible on the first few trips. They wanted to make sure that these kinds of bargains, whether they lasted or not, were experienced now. There had been nothing like this before. In fact, the availability of Staples low-cost supplies actually enhanced the viability of many HBEs in the immediate area.

Along the wall facing customers, just after they finished checking out, was a six-by-twenty-foot bulletin board with clear plastic pockets to hold business cards. Across the top were major categories such as real estate, secretarial services, consultants, temporary services, and so forth. In a few months, hundreds of patrons had put their card in the plastic sleeves, becoming part of the Staples family. Most cards revealed a home-office address.

Southern Office Supply at one time actually had a similar technique. Their bulletin board, however, was two-by-two and one-half feet and cards were held in place by a pin or thumb tack. During its heyday, there were never more than 60 to 70 cards on Southern's bulletin board. By contrast, Staples displayed well over 1,000 cards in an organized, helpful manner. The bulletin board instantly became a one-stop center to enable HBEs to quickly find one another.

Various activity checks throughout the day showed that Staples averaged between 8 and 16 patrons in the store at any given moment, while Southern had fallen off to fewer than 2 patrons at any given time. By the year end, the surrounding Ginn's and Jacobs-Gardner, as well as Miller's Office Supply, were feeling the impact of Staples's methods and distribution of marketing capabilities.

Who Was that Masked Man?

Let's step back and examine how Staples positioned itself for success in northern Virginia and came to completely dominate the growing HBE market while old line vendors, such as Southern Office Supply, maintained business as usual, with inevitable results.

Staples was already successful throughout the New York metropolitan area: New Jersey, Philadelphia, Boston, and Long Island. Their expansion into the Washington, D.C., area was logical and perhaps even predictable.

Prior to opening in the Bailey's Crossroads area, they visited each of their potential competitors and examined how the shelves were stocked, their prices, ambience, the quality of employees, and many other factors. They determined that there were more than 15,000 workers within a two-mile trade radius and thousands more residents who demographically fit their target niche.

Among office supply customers, particularly HBEs, Staples learned that there is no real brand loyalty for office products—a note pad is a note pad and a computer printer ribbon is a computer printer ribbon. Significant price savings separated Staples from its competitors.

Staples placed full-page ads in the back of community newspapers and journals that highlighted some of their best bargains. Experience in other store openings showed significant word-of-mouth advertising could be generated. In every way, Staples was more customer-oriented. It opened earlier and closed later. Phones were answered within two rings. A store layout map detailing where each item in the store could be found was distributed to all customers, and staff directed customers to appropriate aisles.

Southern and many of its competitors, by contrast, were woeful in orienting themselves to the customer. Clerks were frequently put off and even acted as if they had been disturbed when asked about the location of specific items.

In leaving Staples, one had a choice of six different cash registers, including an express checkout line. When exiting any of its competitors, with their retail checkout counters designed in the 1970s and loaded up with notions and impulse buys, there was no room to set down your goods. These checkout counters took up everyone's time.

One could go on and on about the superior distribution and marketing techniques employed by Staples. Their ability to move into the market, meet the needs of a growing population of HBEs, and quickly position themselves as the dominant office supplier is now a matter of record.

While Rome Burned

What of the top management at Southern Office Supply and others like them who failed to acknowledge the changing needs of changing markets? Without insight as to management's strategies and activities, based on the fate that befell their stores, here is what they apparently did *not* do:

- Attend trade shows and conventions, and pay attention to the latest developments in the industry. It's hard to believe that Southern's top management had not heard of Staples or had any inkling that the company was in an expansion phase.
- Subscribe to and read industry journals, insiders' newsletters, and association reports. An organization

as well run and well functioning as Staples does not, and in fact cannot, go unnoticed within its industry. Indication of its existence and progress included its own PR releases, endless reports, and series of grand openings.

- Tour Staples and other competitors' stores. On a regular and ongoing basis, Southern's management might have been visiting the competitor stores and showrooms within its own region and beyond. The fact that Staples was not present in the northern Virginia area before 1989, but was operating successfully in the New York and New Jersey metropolitan area, was cause enough for alarm among Southern's top management.

Today, particularly in retailing, but also in services, an operation that is extremely successful in one part of the country *can be counted on to expand.*

- Communicate with the original equipment manufacturers, wholesalers, and distributors. Many of the items offered in Southern's outlets also appeared in Staples's outlets. In many instances, the two chains were served by the original equipment manufacturers and/or their distributors. Staples's expansion outside of the New York metropolitan area was known within the industry long before the actual grand opening in northern Virginia.

    Southern's top management, its business analysts, indeed, anyone above the clerical level, would have access to this information via the host of distributors and suppliers with whom they may have come in contact at least weekly.

The Southern Strategy

Suppose for a moment, *though one hardly could,* that Southern was aware of Staples's expansion, particularly expansion to the Bailey's Crossroads area. What could

Southern have done in the short-term and long-term to try to compete and protect their market share?

On a short-term basis, Southern could have advertised selected items at bargain prices and competed head on with Staples, vigorously promoting those items. Through its monthly circular to customers, Southern could have announced a price-slashing or a "we meet the competition head on" campaign, thereby increasing store traffic, temporarily. With such a campaign they might have encouraged bulk buying.

It would have also made excellent sense for Southern's managers to visit Staples to determine what the other store was lacking and become especially proficient in stocking those items. As a long-term strategy, Southern could have billed itself as home business office supplier, gearing its ads and copy specifically to the HBE market or other desirable target markets.

While store renovation is costly, in the short-term Southern could have enhanced their lighting so that the store would not seem like a cave compared to the professional showroom atmosphere that Staples offered. In addition, Southern could have redesigned its storefront displays, changing them from the sleepy, tired array of unexciting products to an eye-catching, customer-drawing, professionally crafted and designed display.

Last, and requiring even less ingenuity, Southern could have made use of in-store shelf talkers: signs that say "bargain," "buy me," "X percent off," "sale today," "red tag special," etc., and then made it easier for cashiers to ring up customers goods—but they did not.

Crushing the Competition

By mid-year, Staples was often ringing up more business in an hour than Southern was generating in a day. HBEs who had intermittently made frequent volume office purchases before Staples arrived (because no other office supply store offered shopping carts, wide aisles, and so forth) were now checking out of Staples with loaded shopping carts and purchases of $200 to $300 or more.

While Staples was advertising for more help, Southern had cut back its staff. Staples's entire product offering was discounted, while Southern continued to distribute the same monthly flyer that generated less and less response. Even with its neighbor a mere 200 feet away, and more visible marketing clues than one could ask for, Southern continued set in its ways, refusing to adopt *any* of the high-power marketing techniques Staples had mastered. It virtually handed over its base of HBE customers, in part because it never segmented their customers and appealed to specific needs.

It is easy to regard Southern's management as inept or out-of-step with the times. Yet, increasingly throughout the 90s, even those operations that take great pains to be aware of what is happening in the industry and how they should position themselves may encounter a surprise move by a Staples.

The key to survival and prosperity will be to continually seek a market position that sets your operation up as different or special, even if it's only for a particular commodity or service.

Faced with outrageous competition on all sides, as we'll discuss in Chapter 5, there are always options for profitability providing products or services in a manner that outflanks the competition, even the superstores.

Staples: Novelty, Choice, and Adventure Down Every Aisle

Loss Leaders:

The front of the store is filled with the store's loss leaders. These change, in response to their analysis of check-out data, and have recently included paper and file folder specials; packs of 10 legal pads; a "quick-start" filing system for home offices; a desk lamp, an attractive brass banker's lamp that would look good in any home, $19.97; a box of 100 file folders; and a ream of copier paper (used for draft printing in home-office laser and ink-jet printers).

Forced Traffic:

You enter at the middle of the store and are forced to the right where you are exposed to many more goods than just those you came in to buy. Staples has already let you know it expects you to buy a lot.

A Member, Not Just a Customer:

Staples membership is free and entitles you to the "member price" on certain advertised specials. The member prices are a good deal, but they are even a better deal for Staples. The cards are bar-coded, and the clerks scan them, along with your purchases, at the checkout. This gives Staples daily sales data from their most frequent customers.

Staples is building a valuable database that it uses to develop customer profiles and further refine its product mix and inventory levels. This will ultimately benefit the home-office purchasers, who are a major part of Staples's customer base. Stores that lack this kind of customer feedback will lag behind the curve in meeting customer needs.

Down the Aisles:

Aisles are lined with floor-to-ceiling shelves. Products are stocked as high as you can reach. Staples's staff is frequently restocking from this inventory.

The first aisle has paper, one of the major repeat purchases for the home office. Paper is available in a rainbow of colors; using colored paper is one of the least expensive ways for the home-office worker to make his materials stand out. High-quality bond stationery is sold across the aisle.

Aisle two has file folders, labels, and desktop supplies, such as tape dispensers or staplers. There are almost always member-only specials.

Aisle three brings you to electrical supplies, desk lamps, and more. Aisle four has computer supplies, including diskettes from more than 10 manufacturers.

In-House Services:

Staples offers in-house copying, collating services, and faxing.

Special Promotions:

Bins are stocked with special sale items, i.e., staple removers, key chains, thumb tacks, pencils, and tape and are available in multiple packs.

Office Furniture:

At least 10 varieties of file cabinets are available, ranging from a low-end two-drawer model to a sturdy four-drawer lateral file cabinet. Other products include all grades of desks, desk chairs, credenzas, visitor chairs, computer desks, printer stands, and fax tables.

Staples is catering well to the diverse home-office market, and getting upgrade business as well. The tax-savvy home-based entrepreneur may buy better quality goods for his home office than for the rest of his home because the home-office purchases are tax deductible.

Books and Tapes:

All manner of business books, motivational tapes, and a host of magazines are displayed.

Business Equipment:

A good assortment of copier and fax machines is offered, along with the cartridges, toner, and cleaning supplies that enhance your purchase. Other goods include paper shredders, desktop calculators, electric staplers, telephones, answering machines, cellular phones, and laptop computers.

Inventory Adjustment:

If typing stands are selling in Long Island, but not in Boston, Staples can make inventory adjustments accordingly.

AN IMMEDIATE SPLASH

For PC-related goods, wherever HBEs shop, they are attracted by service and convenience factors such as:

- Technical support for electronics and software.
- Manufacturer's warranties of at least one year.
- A no-questions, money-back guarantee of 30 days.
- For mail order, a toll-free number.
- No-hassle credit availability.

For these features and much more, the Soft Warehouse is a super retailer making an immediate and lucrative splash catering to commercial offices and HBEs. The catalog the Soft Warehouse distributes is an upscale, four-color, high-quality production geared to appeal to traditional office products buyers, small-business entrepreneurs, and HBEs who comprise about 25 percent of their market.

Located in Atlanta, Chicago, Dallas, Denver, Detroit, Houston, Los Angeles, Miami, Palo Alto, Philadelphia, San Diego, and Washington, and more major metro areas each month, the Soft Warehouse bills itself as the "computer super store." The chain advertises 30 to 80 percent off retail prices on a large selection of microcomputers, software, computer peripherals, computer systems, accessories, business machines, furniture, and supplies.

In six short years, the Soft Warehouse has experienced remarkable growth. The typical store ranges anywhere from 17,000 to 35,000 square feet, with the average around 25,000 square feet. Each store stocks more than 5,000 computer-related products, including a wide assortment of name brand PC compatible printers, monitors and related hardware, lap tops, disks, papers, supplies, storage equipment, and communication devices, as well as 2,000 different software packages.

The Soft Warehouse provides shoppers with wide aisles to stroll through with shopping carts much like shoppers do in a food supermarket. The difference being that customers ·

may use credit cards, and frequently charge sums of $500, $1,000, $5,000, and even $10,000 in purchases. Annual revenues in most locations top $40 million and in some stores, $50 million.

To be sure, the Soft Warehouse does not offer prices competitive with those of direct mailers advertising in the back of *PC Magazine* or *PC World*. The giant store front, however, has its advantages. Many people are still leery of purchasing equipment that must be shipped across the country, particularly sensitive items. When you can see an item, feel it, take it out of the box, talk to somebody about it, and even return it if you need to, you are willing to pay a bit more. The marketing strategists at the Soft Warehouse know this too well.

A full technical department offers everything from total system configuration to support along with maintenance and repair on the premises. Surrounded by available, convenient, and qualified support, the confidence factor of the typical shopper is indeed high, particularly the HBE who tends to value in-store support.

Like any good retailer, the chain employs effective retailing techniques such as loss leaders (i.e., Microsoft Windows sells for an attractive price). It also offers a convenient return policy, several ways to pay, extended hours, and ample parking.

Actually, a Friendly Place

When you first enter a Soft Warehouse store you are immediately struck by its consumer-friendly appearance. Large sliding glass doors welcome you and your shopping cart. As you enter to the right, you notice to your left several checkout stations, most serving customers, though there never seem to be long lines.

As you proceed to the right, the latest Soft Warehouse catalog and local ads are on display for your review. This is nothing new in retailing, however, added to a TV monitor showing new products, bargain items, and simply saying welcome, you find yourself in the mood to buy.

Each store is kept very clean. The aisles are wide. All around you are other shoppers seemingly encouraged by what they, too, perceive to be an extremely supportive environment. Shelf talkers abound. It is not difficult to make your way through this store, despite its mammoth size. Yellows, grays, oranges, blues, whites in displays, packaging, and signs dazzle your eyes.

The store is staffed with knowledgeable salespeople. Even at peak time on Saturday afternoon, help seems to be in abundance. If a salesperson can't answer your question, he immediately leads you to the person who can. In short, the salespeople at the Soft Warehouse have obviously gone through well-designed training programs.

Each staff member, when questioned, stops, looks directly at you, reflects on your problem, speaks to you, stays with you, and helps you. They don't dash off, they don't have clipboards in their hands, and they don't seem too busy to provide service.

The store need not dote on its customers, however, because it draws the half of the market that pretty much knows what it wants. About three quarters of the customers are from commercial offices and about a quarter are home-based PC users.

As you proceed down the aisles, you are immediately struck by the fact that some 40 percent, maybe even 50 percent, of the customers are female. Yes, the Soft Warehouse has found the key to drawing out the female buyer, whom many others mistakenly suspected had no role or interest in the PC revolution.

A Clear Focus

As if a fresh approach to retailing wasn't enough, the Soft Warehouse has also developed a system called the Flexible On-Sight Computer Users Support. As billed, F.O.C.U.S. is designed to serve anyone who "buys a system at the Soft Warehouse."

Created in partnership with Intel, the F.O.C.U.S. support staff includes factory trained specialists, seasoned PC experts, and Intel support organization. F.O.C.U.S. is available for an entire system, from keyboard to power cord, regardless of the manufacturer.

F.O.C.U.S. also offers a toll-free hot line backed by knowledgeable microcomputer experts who very often can help you right over the phone with the system that you purchased at the Soft Warehouse. For more involved problems, an Intel customer engineer employed by the Soft Warehouse will go to your office or home (indeed, their literature says, "home,") by the next business day. F.O.C.U.S. is offered at four different levels, depending on your needs and budget.

Pallets and Boxes

To maintain the image of a price-conscious retailer, many of the products offered by the Soft Warehouse remain on pallets or in neat stacks on the floor in their original boxes, unpacked. They are ready for you to wheel away in your shopping cart. Product turnover throughout the store is high. While most retailers stock the highest margin and fastest turnover goods in areas where there is traditionally high customer traffic, the Soft Warehouse has been designed to invite free and extensive roaming throughout the store. Hence, you are just as likely to examine products in the back as in the front.

With ample space available, an open service counter along one side of the store awaits patrons. Flanking the service counter is a wide assortment of working systems and peripherals for your exploration. Instinctively, you know that these may not be America's best prices, but they are close enough. Given all the other trappings of Soft Warehouse's delivery and support systems, you are willing to go ahead and make the buy.

A Final Surprise. In many stores, the checkout counter is their last opportunity to further disappoint you.

Not so at the Soft Warehouse. Even cashiers can answer last minute questions about the items you have collected. This provided help confirms your wise decision to buy here, to buy the particular goods in your basket, and to return in the near future.

WORKING THE SUPERSTORE CHANNEL

The HBE shops all over town, and through direct mail, all over the country. The distribution network that serves the home office is shown in Figure 4–1.

Major manufacturers and retailers are extending their distribution beyond their traditional network of authorized dealers or otherwise looking for new ways to reach the end-user/HBE. Newer manufacturers are including the HBE market in their plans from the start. Established manufacturers are seeking innovative ways to capture the lucrative HBE market. IBM is selling its new PS/1, a low-end computer designed for the home and retailing for under $1,000, through Sears office centers, which are located in Sears stores in major markets.

Dell Computer is the sixth largest PC manufacturer in the country. It grew by serving the Fortune 1200 market through aggressive telemarketing, superior quality, excellent technical support, and reliable on-site service. To penetrate the home-office market, Dell is also selling at retail through the Soft Warehouse.

Fuji Photo Film U.S.A., Inc. is one of the pioneers in effectively marketing to productivity-conscious HBEs. Fuji's market research showed that one of the big needs of the HBE was organizing their work for faster processing. Accordingly, Fuji made two changes in their computer diskette line.

First, they color-coded their diskettes so a home-based worker could use a different color for different business functions (i.e., orange for accounting, red for client files, blue for marketing, green for technical data, and so forth).

FIGURE 4–1
The Home Office Market: Served by a Growing Distribution Network

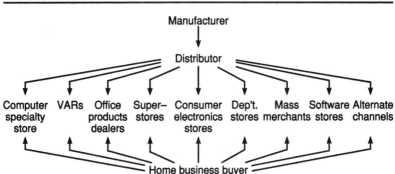

This proved to be an effective strategy. It also tapped into HBE's strong preference for colorful accessories, rather than the neutral ones preferred by corporate buyers.

In addition, Fuji started including free productivity software in its boxes of 10 diskettes. Offers included a demonstration version of Lotus' Magellan® and Spinnaker®. This arrangement benefitted both the software manufacturers and Fuji. Fuji has sold more diskettes and software manufacturers gain direct access to the home office market.

Hechingers Gets into the Act

Other super retailers not specifically offering home-based office equipment have caught on to the trend and geared their operations accordingly. For several years, Hechingers, a mid-Atlantic super retail hardware chain, has been featuring noncommercial grade desks, tables, chairs, filing cabinets, shelves, lockers, and other office accoutrements, presumably for the smaller business, or the HBE. The chain has recently expanded into New England, with further expansion on the front burner.

If you haven't shopped there yet, Hechingers is the be all and end-all of home hardware supplies and related equipment. Many of its outlets exceed 50,000 square feet. Like the Soft Warehouse, Hechingers is a model of credibility, convenience, and service—it meets all criteria an HBE could ask for. In most locations, the facility is freestanding, with its own ample parking lot.

Hechingers has always maintained an extensive array of hardware and electrical supplies, including telephone extension cords, couplers, answering machines, all manner of lighting, electrical extension cords, surge protectors, etc. Since mid-1989, many stores have been redesigned to include an extensive home remodeling division, complete with in-store design consultants armed with computer software and display terminals.

By giving a design consultant the size of your room and approximate measurements of your furniture, he or she can quickly demonstrate a variety of new designs, offering aerial and three-dimensional views. Much of the business Hechingers does in this area includes kitchens and bathrooms, with living rooms, dens, and home offices steadily gaining ground.

Here, You Need a Road Map
Like other giant retailers, room to roam within Hechingers is a key factor in your decision to shop there. The typical Hechinger's store is so large that one frequently must ask for directions. At the checkout counter, between 8 and 16 stations stand ready to serve you, although lines of even a few people can be slow, depending on what they have purchased and how bulky the goods may be.

The store provides many varieties of carts to wheel your cumbersome goods out of the store, allows convenient drive up, and does all it can to ensure that the goods can be taken away in your vehicle. They will tie down or arrange what you've purchased within the space you have available to transport it, or will lend you a cart to put on top of your car if you need it.

Hechingers's return policy is liberal by any standard. Nearly any item at any time can be returned if it proves to be ineffective for your needs, as long as you have the original receipt. Hechingers's prices, across the board, tend to be lower than those of competitors. The slogan "Nobody beats Hechingers's prices" accompanies most ads and can also be seen throughout the store.

Hechingers is open each night until 9 P.M., Sunday and most holidays. Like any good super retail outlet, the chain strives to make your shopping experience pleasant. Hechingers implants the notion that when you need additional goods and services which they can provide, their store is the only logical choice. In this way, the Price Clubs, Staples, Soft Warehouses, and Hechingers of the world predominate when it comes to serving the lucrative home-based business market.

There is room, however, for the smaller vendor, and that's the subject of Chapter 5.

Hot Tips and Insights from Chapter 4

- While none of the super retailers specifically restricts their appeal to HBEs, HBEs do represent a healthy, if not dominant, share of total revenues.
- While the HBE is willing to pay for sophisticated, technology-intensive products, he still seeks to cut costs on office supplies and shop in the least amount of time possible.
- Those two needs have driven the growth of Staples, the office superstore, which has done with office supplies what Toys-R-Us has done with children's toys—made it difficult to justify shopping anywhere else.
- For PC-related goods, wherever HBEs shop, they are attracted by service and convenience factors such as technical support for electronics and software, manufacturer's warranties of at least one year, and a no-questions, money-back guarantee of 30 days.

- To maintain the image of a price-conscious retailer, the Soft Warehouse leaves many products unboxed on pallets or in neat stacks on the floor for shoppers to wheel away.
- HBEs have a strong preference for colorful accessories rather than the neutral ones preferred by corporate buyers.
- While most retailers stock the highest margin, fastest-turnover goods in areas where there is traditionally high customer traffic, each Soft Warehouse store has been designed to invite free and extensive roaming throughout the store.
- Major manufacturers and retailers are extending their distribution beyond their traditional network of authorized dealers or otherwise looking for new ways to reach the end user/HBE. Newer manufacturers are including the HBE market in their plans from the start.

CHAPTER 5

CARVING YOUR NICHE

Life consists not in holding
good cards, but in playing
those you do hold well.
Josh Billings

Even with the rise of the superstores, Alvin Toffler sees great opportunities for smaller retailers and vendors. As home-office equipment becomes a commodity, a vendor's or dealer's ability to provide value-added services will become more important in both making the sale and building long-term repeat business. In this chapter we'll explore strategies for better understanding and capturing the business of selected HBE niches, and we'll explore the various types of offices from which HBEs operate.

First, let's consider what the small vendor can do to differentiate himself from the giant marketers.

Differentiating Factors for Smaller Vendors

- Offer added customer conveniences
- Compete on items where one has a cost advantage
- Offer extended credit terms
- Employ a helpful sales staff
- Practice after-marketing techniques
- Keep an eye on ways to innovate

Convenience

Suppliers serving HBEs can position themselves as stable, recognized businesses that facilitate the ordering of supplies by phone, through the mail, and by fax. Generally, these vendors produce a printed catalog and sell either recognized name brand goods or generic goods that are guaranteed.

The winners don't necessarily have the absolute lowest prices around, but like the Soft Warehouse, offer sufficiently low prices. As 7-Eleven stores thrive in towns with huge supermarkets, the smaller vendor can claim his turf amidst superstores. Combined with other outstanding attributes and service features, the smaller vendor can present an overall package that is extremely attractive to HBEs.

Cost

While they are not the least expensive, the winners give more for the dollar and consistently look for innovative ways to supply additional services. Some, like Staples, offer quantity discounts, and membership in preferred customer clubs. The successful smaller vendor can offer a loss leader—some desirable product, of a repeat purchase nature, that he's known for selling at the lowest price in town.

Egghead Discount Software stores now stock a few computer hardware items that particularly appeal to the home office purchaser. They offered a 2400-baud modem for $79.99, and they also sell hard-disk expansion cards (made by Plus), thereby offering cost savings and convenience. The expansion cards are the easiest way to extend storage space for data files; if you can use a screwdriver, you can put it in your personal computer.

Also, while many retailers advertise attractive prices for selected goods, a subset of those offer unadvertised, in-store bargains, which further prompt customers to return. The home-based entrepreneur has little or no staff, and precious little time to do comparison shopping. He relies on impulse, intuition, common sense, and whatever brief education the vendor can supply to determine why the prices of particular items represent a good buy.

Credit

Office supply vendors have always been a good source of credit for new businesses. With faster and faster devices for electronically verifying credit and account, more vendors are willing to open accounts with even small enterprises, and with a minimum of red tape.

Sales Staff

Who will represent your company? The superstores provide helpful service but they can't profitably offer extensive sales help with every customer—it would shrink their already low profit margins. Carefully examine the sales backgrounds and interpersonal skills of your sales help. The individuals representing you on the floor can be your strategic edge. Do they have the basic prerequisites to do the job? If not, can they be trained to do the job?

What types of training can you offer? Is your sales staff fully aware of the benefits and features of using your products or services and able to present them in a professional manner? Can they handle objections, use professional closes, and apply other selling fundamentals?

After-Marketing

This is a deliberate campaign to ensure long-term customer satisfaction and is of particular interest to the HBEs who are appreciative of support networks. After-marketing encompasses bulletins on new user applications, accurate and easy to understand invoices, and knowledgeable, committed, and skilled telephone representatives.

Innovation

Smaller retailers who are willing to offer extensive service will be better positioned to operate a thriving business. Toffler suggests that vendors examine new ways to serve this dynamic market. Retailers may yet emerge as mini-education centers offering in-store seminars and courses for customers.

Innovation may include serving as a recycling center both to help preserve the environment and to enable HBEs to receive credit for their old equipment. As more consumers are becoming environmentally conscious, responsive vendors are looking for ways to offer goods that require less packaging and less filler materials, non-PCP materials, and the like. The home-based entrepreneur in particular tends to be an environmentally conscious shopper, acknowledging the effects of what he buys and what he discards.

WINNING CATALOGS THAT BREAK THROUGH THE CLUTTER

Whether a multimillion dollar operation or a corner store, an international mail order supplier or a dining room table HBE, you can create a catalog that appeals to the HBE market and positions you for success. In doing so, first consider what the HBE faces each day and what it takes to break through the din. Then examine the best of the catalogs you receive and emulate the best parts of them.

The HBE Workday

In previous chapters we've reviewed some of the trials and tribulations of the home-based worker. Additionally, consider that the traditional 40-hour work week may be shrinking for the corporate set, but not for the HBE. Many spend a minimum of 53 hours per week on the job, particularly

during start-up and peak seasons. Added to other responsibilities, time pressure can become particularly acute to the
HBE, who has little or no staff and must be the chief cook
and bottle washer for virtually all aspects of his operation.

Winning Catalogs

- Appeal to HBE working styles
- Emulate the best in other catalogs
- Provide a toll-free 800 number
- Show comparison prices
- Provide quantity discounts
- Add color graphics
- Offer extensive product descriptions

Think of it. You're attempting to sell to an individual
who must quickly read and digest a large volume of product
and service information in short order, while keeping a
steady eye on bringing in revenue, satisfying clients, maintaining an orderly home-office, perhaps looking after a family, and perhaps feeling tired, upset, or undercapitalized.
Hence, the HBE needs to recognize the value or savings
that your product or service offers and be able to order it
easily and then go back to his business.

Traditionally insurance, home furnishings, magazine
subscriptions, and books have been most likely to sell by
mail. The PC revolution is vaulting software and office supplies as well as PC hardware items to the top of the list.

Emulating the Best

Among the sea of direct mail catalogs, including those of
Quill, Reliable Home Products, Global, and several others,
some common denominators surface.

800 Number for Ease of Ordering

The effective catalogs supply an 800 number that is prominently listed on the top or bottom of each page, along with information such as same day shipping, call us, or other encouraging words. Global, a software and hardware catalog distributor with locations in New York, California, Georgia and Illinois, uses (800) 8Global (800–845–6225) as its 800 number.

Any customer, HBE or not, is more likely to call you if you have an 800 number. HBEs in particular, who pay their own phone bill out of their own pocket, are particularly delighted to see 800 numbers. Before the end of the 1990s, not having a toll-free phone and fax line for placing orders will put vendors at a distinct disadvantage in marketing to HBEs.

Comparison Prices

The winning catalogs illustrate original price versus their price, often crossing out the original price with an "X" or slash. While this technique is nothing new in marketing, the frazzled HBE appreciates the comparison.

Quantity Discounts

Effective catalogs prominently show prices for quantity discounts using a stair-step function, for example 2 gets you so much off, 5 gets you more off, and 10 gets you even more off, to encourage multiple purchases.

Color Graphics

Direct mail firms rely on superior color graphics. Vendors and retailers with a store front, like Staples, may actually be visited by the majority of their customers and can get away with a less slick catalog, employing hand sketches and limited use of color. Forty years of television, with thousands of commercial messages bombarding the average individual each day, have taken their toll.

Consumers now have image-related expectations regarding virtually every aspect of the establishments with whom they do business. In a world where people are prone to make decisions based on a minimal survey of the situation, high-quality color graphics can be the make or break item in appealing to HBEs.

Extensive Product Description

This may seem to be a contradiction of sorts. On one hand, the HBE must do all of his own purchasing and has limited time to do so. On the other hand, as direct mail wizard Joe Sugarman of JS & A products in Chicago discovered long ago, extensive advertising and product descriptions, if well written, can capture the attention of the would-be buyer. Since the HBE tends to be well-educated, by all means, copy may appeal to the intellect.

When using any form of direct marketing, be sure to produce copy and layout that complement one another, answer questions that one would logically ask, and ask for an order.

Don't mail your catalog to HBEs unless you can afford to repeat the mailing at least three times at six-week intervals. Only a small portion of any list will even read your material, and only a small percentage of that number will take action. One way of building a strong HBE mailing list is to offer a discount or free item with purchases. Include space on catalog order forms for current recipients to write down the names and addresses of friends who might benefit from the catalog.

The Direct Marketing Association, Dun's Marketing Services, and several other industry leaders have developed a system, "2 +2 Enhancement," which expands the current four-digit classifications in the Standard Industrial classification system by two tiers and increases information about the businesses dramatically. New codes represent emerging industries and forms of enterprise. Ultimately, you'll be able to segment and fine-tune definitions of the HBE market, and select prospects with the greatest potential. For additional ways to obtain HBEs target lists, see Chapters 8 and 10.

TELEMARKETING TO HBES

Another edge you can gain over the giants in serving HBEs is the ability to call HBEs. The giants make considerable telemarketing efforts to land corporate accounts. With their slim margins, they have to go for volume. For smaller vendors, with wider margins, the economics may well exist to bolster your marketing efforts via the telephone.

If you find yourself reluctant to sell to HBEs over the telephone because you think your products or services are too unique or complex, let's look at the record. *The Annual Guide to Telemarketing* indicates that more than $115 billion worth of industrial products, ranging from fasteners to computer service contracts, were marketed by telephone in 1987 alone.

General Electric employs 2,000 telemarketers in 45 centers to sell a diverse product line. Other companies, like Goodall Rubber in Trenton, New Jersey, a $70 million manufacturer of industrial rubber products, has introduced telemarketing as a boost to sales.

One executive with a multimillion-dollar Chicago-based electronic and magnetic material distributor used marketing by phone to find out where the company stood with each of its 12,000 customers. Results allowed the company to take such actions as compiling a list of dormant accounts and putting the remaining accounts on a priority list.

When it comes to targeting HBEs, telemarketing goes where you can't—right into their homes. Often, it may not pay to send sales representatives to service HBE accounts. However, telemarketing is an excellent vehicle for reaching accounts of less than a few thousand dollars, or dormant accounts that could be reactivated.

For Telemarketing Success

- Find out when to call
- Determine in advance what to offer
- Create personal relationships
- Handle post-purchase concerns

When to Call

When calling the HBE, keep two obvious things in mind: when it would be convenient to them to receive your call, and when you can make a call that is most cost-effective to you. While the calling times suggested on the following list are not absolutes, they will help.

When To Call HBEs

Prospects	Best Time to Call
Accountants	Daily, but not between January 5th and April 15th
Builders and contractors	Before 9 A.M. or after 5 P.M.
Consultants	Before 8 A.M., after 6:30 P.M.
Dentists	Before 9:30 A.M.

(continued)

Engineers	Between 4 and 5 P.M.
Mothers	Between 10 and 11 A.M.
Lawyers	Between 11 A.M. and 2 P.M.
Professors and teachers	At home, between 6 and 7 P.M.
Word Processors	Between 11:30 A.M. and 1:30 P.M.
Stockbrokers	Before 10 A.M. or after 3 P.M.
Trainers	Any time

What to Offer

When you launch your telemarketing effort to HBEs, offer them only a few products or services at a time. One manager of marketing services at a computer supplies company learned this lesson the hard way when his carefully designed telemarketing efforts failed, not only once but twice, because he failed to focus the effort. His telemarketers were attempting to sell the company's entire product line. With his third campaign, the manager decided to tie the telemarketing program in with a direct mail campaign that featured only three or four products.

As we've seen in earlier chapters, all HBEs need basic equipment to start up their businesses, from phones to office furniture. Their most important piece of equipment is going to be a personal computer with communications software and a modem. Discover if the HBE you are marketing to has this basic capability. If so, find out to what communication services he or she subscribes. Then you can use that service to reach him or her in the future. From this basic equipment, there is a natural expansion of products and services that can successfully be sold by phone to HBEs. Some are quickly becoming as indispensable as the personal computer and modem.

CUSTOMER RELATIONSHIPS VIA TELEMARKETING

When you market to HBEs, you want more than a quick sale. You want to develop your relationship with your clients so that they become steady customers. More than placing orders, you want to manage their accounts.

To set up special or personal relationships with your HBEs, talk to them on the phone as you would a neighbor, someone with whom you would like to establish a give-and-take relationship, so that you literally watch out for each other's well-being and property.

Handling Post-Purchase Concerns

HBEs experience their share of post-purchase concern—after all, many of them reach expensive purchasing decisions on their own (other than the obvious influence of the seller). We all know how it feels. Suppose this evening you are going to pick up some new equipment that you just bought. You mention your purchase to a good friend who says, "Gosh, I wish you would have let me know before you did that. I could have gotten you a much better deal."

You're feeling down—it is called post-purchase concern. It shows up in many ways: Did I really make the right decision? Have I been taken? Will I regret this? Independent of the type of purchase, the bigger the price tag and the closer it impacts your personal and professional life, the greater the level and intensity of post-purchase concern. Experienced marketers are aware of this phenomenon and take steps to minimize its consequences:

1. They call the new customer with a bit of good news. "Just reviewed the system and thought you would be interested in knowing that the manufacturer is including three extra months on the warranty.

HBEs appreciate a phone call saying how much you relish doing business with them. Insurance super seller Joe Gandolfo always sends a hand-written note like the one below following a sale.

Dear Alex,

Tonight does not seem too soon to congratulate you on this afternoon's decision to purchase _____ . This is certainly a major step in establishing _____ . I hope that our transaction was the beginning of a long and enduring relationship . . .

2. They send something that relates to the buyer's interest. This could include a relevant article, a previous product review, or other item that solidifies the purchase.

The purpose of these types of actions is simply to reassure the HBE that he made a good decision to proceed. The subtle message that you are conveying is, "You chose the right vendor. We'll be here if you need us."

The balance of the chapter provides an inside look at HBE offices and the important role they play for their inhabitants.

HBEs and Offices

A key area of knowledge in marketing to HBEs is an understanding of their working environments. How HBEs feel about their home offices as well as how they function in them is very important. Most want an office that is comfortable and accessible and designed to support them. If they greet clients or customers at home, many HBEs would like to favorably influence them, or at least not offend them.

The key questions an HBE faces in working from the home are: "Does this office support me?" and "Can I use the space available, assemble the appropriate equipment and supplies, and arrange them so I can work in a highly effective and productive capacity?" As we've seen in earlier HBE profiles, it's difficult to work effectively from home in a less than sufficient work space.

HBE offices are found in detached single-family homes, high-rise condominiums, garden apartments, "hoffices," and other structures. If you offer any products or services that further enhance an HBE's productivity or comfort, you've got a customer.

A plethora of locations within the home include a den, semidetached apartment, attic, basement, and dining room table.

The Den Office. The den office (a spare bedroom counts just as well) is probably the most common among HBEs. It offers many advantages. Heating, cooling, and ventilation may be more easily controlled from the den office, although offices with southern exposure may experience a hothouse effect. Outside noise may also be a problem here.

HBEs who live alone can, of course, carve any portion of the home to set up a work environment. A den or spare bedroom office in a home with a spouse, children, or roommates may not offer the privacy and quiet one needs. A work-at-home graphic artist turns on a small fan located next to her office door. The gentle, rhythmic "white noise" of the fan's motor serves as a sound buffer to most of the sounds her husband makes in the rest of the apartment.

Marketing opportunities include:

- Polarized glass, shades, tinted mylar sheets, and awnings.
- Sound screens and room dividers.
- Cassettes with "white" noise, i.e., waves, or "Muzak" type.

The Detached or Semidetached Office. Particularly for lawyers, doctors, or dentists, the detached or semidetached office is mandatory. A semidetached office is a completely finished room that is otherwise not a part of the home. Ideally, the HBE has an entrance for clients and a passageway to the rest of the house from the detached office.

The detached office offers a great deal of privacy, can be decorated and furnished in complete contrast to the home, and affords most of the operating advantages of commercial offices. Especially for professionals who are reticent about asking existing clients for referrals, proper decor in the waiting room is just what the doctor ordered.

Marketing opportunities include:

- Coat racks.
- Magazine racks.
- Plants, indoor shrubbery.
- Aquariums.
- Custom wallpaper, tile, paneling, etc.
- Magazine subscriptions.
- Signage.
- Display plaques, laminated certificates, licenses, and awards.

Attic Office.   Many HBEs are refinishing their attics to locate their home office there. Bill Gengris, based in Madison, Wisconsin, did so. Except for excessive heat in the summer (heat rises) which he was able to control by a room air conditioner and set of fans, the attic office is more than adequate. He set up tables to handle projects in progress and installed a cot so that he could take quick cat naps during the day without going downstairs.

Soon, Bill found the distance to the kitchen and the bathroom was the problem. Every time he wanted a drink of water he had to make a trip downstairs. He started taking a pitcher of water upstairs, and soon installed a small refrigerator. Similarly, each trip to the bathroom and each time he forgot something, a sojourn down the creaky stairs was necessary.

Marketing opportunities include:

- Air conditioners, space-heaters, and fans.
- Mini-refrigerators.
- Carpeting.
- Phone lines and outlets.
- Lighting, light fixture, and electrical work.
- Plumbing.
- Carpentry—windows, sills, shelves, and stair rails.
- Interior decorating and refinishing.

The Basement Office. Alexandra is a small-business broker, helping clients to both buy and sell businesses. She lives in a seven-room, three-story townhouse in Wilmette, Illinois. The third level of her home is a basement that includes her office, a storage room, and laundry room. Because the door to the basement is adjacent to the front door to her home, Alexandra is able to easily meet and entertain clients in her basement office.

She has a second phone line, an answering service, and an answering machine so she is "covered" around the clock. Wall-to-wall carpeting and moderately priced furniture keep the room comfortable but not overdone. Alexandra maintains one chair for a visitor by the side of her desk, a four-seat circular table to the far left of her desk, a couch with a parallel coffee table, and some other chairs on the opposite side of the room.

With this variety of furniture groupings, Alexandra is able to comfortably meet up to four people at a time. To keep her office visitor-friendly, Alexandra stocks it with pads and pens, a copier and a fax machine, two hand-held calculators, and a phone extension a mere 20 feet from her desk phone.

Alexandra wants her clients to feel comfortable at her home office and see it as a meeting place that is highly conducive to doing business. Last fall she installed a finished half bathroom and next year will be installing moderate-color wood paneling.

Rick, another HBE, provides management assistance to professional service organizations. He also maintains a basement office, or more accurately, offices. The construction of Rick's home is such that as one proceeds downstairs from the upstairs hallway, to the right is a finished den with bookcases, a television, and a couch. To the left is a hallway that leads past the laundry room, then another small room that Rick uses for storage, supplies and files, and then his main office.

He keeps on hand only those few items that he is presently working on while housing large filing cabinets, a storage locker, portable files, and two shelving units in the secondary office. Though there is an outside entrance to the hallway leading to Rick's office, he practically never uses it. Instead, he leads the few clients who do visit through the living room to the dining room table where the appropriate materials, dictation equipment, pads, and pens await.

Jean represents a third type of home-based marketer operating from a basement office. She is located in Annapolis, Maryland, and provides EDP seminars and instruction to area firms, the Naval Academy, and branches of the federal government.

Jean uses her expansive basement to house her computer, printer, and several flip charts and drawing boards. She uses an intercom which is always left in the "on" position to monitor the activities of her child who stays in a sectioned-off playroom, also within the basement. On days when Joan works on site at clients' locations, the child and his nanny remain on the main floor of the house for meals, playtime, and bathing.

Marketing opportunities include:

- Heating and cooling devices.
- Humidifiers and dehumidifiers.
- Rodent control products.
- Phone, portable phones, electrical outlets, etc.
- Intercom.
- Closets and shelving.

The Dining Room Table.   The dining room table, other table, or corner of a home is the office of many start-up HBEs as well as veterans, including sales representatives for a company with headquarters elsewhere and part-time entrepreneurs and hobbyists. This type of "office" works best when a venture doesn't require a lot of paperwork, notes, files, materials, etc.; the HBE has only a few key accounts; and the work performed can be performed in a very small area; or the HBE is extremely organized and perhaps is supported by resources such as a hard disk or appropriate shelving.

Sheila is a sales representative for a photo and portrait studio. Through an agreement with national diaper services the studio offers a free baby picture to new parents. Sheila's job is to both deliver the free picture and attempt to sell reprints of the other proofs shot during the photo session. All of her business is conducted outside the home and, other than singularly writing up orders, Sheila does not maintain other records.

Using a list prepared for her, Sheila's task is to call the parents (usually the mother) and schedule an appointment. She makes follow-up calls when a couple is "thinking about buying."

Barbara is a sales representative for a nationally known insurance company. Barbara has a full-time receptionist/secretary and a well-equipped office in town. At home, Barbara maintains a dining room table "office," though her dining room is actually clear. She uses stacking plastic trays to maintain a healthy volume of files and work-related papers on the credenza to the right of the table.

Like Sheila, Barbara never greets clients at home and so the appearance of her home office substation is not important. Barbara has compromised the ambience and appearance of her dining room, but that is of no concern to her. She also maintains files in her upstairs bedroom in a two-drawer filing cabinet and on top of the cabinet. This combination of "outposts" is sometimes more disruptive than helpful. Barbara often spends considerable time searching through her files, frequently over copies, and has visible, growing clutter in all three locations.

Marketing opportunities include:

- All manner of portable equipment.
- Stacking trays.
- Flexible files.

Other Considerations.   Here is a quick review of additional needs HBEs may have depending on their location, type of business, and office setup:

- Adequate office and storeroom space.
- Available parking.
- Special lighting, heating, or cooling.
- External lighting.
- Insurance—renters, property, liability, and disability.
- Sufficient pick-up and/or delivery services.

THE RURAL HBE

In a world linked by communication technologies, some HBEs are opting for rural locations, particularly those whose revenues are not dependent upon face-to-face interaction with clients or customers. Their office setups could resemble any of those discussed above.

Rural HBEs can make purchases by mail, phone, and fax as well as the next guy. They tend to be as well versed in PC-related technology as their urban and suburban counterparts. What counts with them, perhaps more than anything, is service. Whether it be ease of operations, hot line or 800 number support, warranties, return policies, or pleasant telephone representatives, they seek products and services designed to enhance the quality of their professional and personal lives. They depend upon a level of customer service that enhances the same before, during, and after the sale.

Marketing opportunities include:

- Mailbox and address representation reflecting metro areas.
- Express mail and delivery services.
- Satellite dishes.
- All manner of strong-reception communication equipment.
- All manner of mail-order supplies.

In gaining a profound understanding of the needs of HBEs, or any target market for that matter, new marketing opportunities readily become apparent.

Hot Tips and Insights from Chapter 5

- As home-office equipment becomes a commodity, a vendor's or dealer's abilities to provide value-added services will become more important in both making the sale and building long-term repeat business.
- Suppliers serving HBEs can position themselves as stable, recognized businesses that facilitate the ordering of supplies by phone, through the mail, and by fax. These vendors produce a printed catalog and sell either recognized name brand goods or generic goods that are guaranteed.
- The winners give more for the dollar and consistently look for innovative ways to supply additional services. Some, like Staples, offer quantity discounts and membership in preferred customer clubs.
- The successful smaller vendor can offer a loss leader— some desirable product, of a repeat purchase nature, that he's known for selling at the lowest price in town.
- Extensive advertising and product descriptions, if well written, can capture the attention of the would-be buyer. Since the HBE tends to be well-educated, by all means make your copy appeal to the intellect.
- The giants make considerable telemarketing efforts to land corporate accounts. With their slim margins they have to go for volume. For smaller vendors, with wider

margins, the economics may well exist to bolster your marketing efforts via the telephone.

- HBE offices are found in detached single-family homes, high-rise condominiums, garden apartments, "hoffices," and other structures. If you offer any products or services that further enhance an HBE's productivity or comfort, you've got a customer.
- Depending on their location, type of business, and office set-up, HBEs may have problems with office and store-room space, parking, heating or cooling, external lighting, insurance needs, and delivery service.

CHAPTER 6

RESEARCH TO STAY
ATTUNED TO THE NICHE

It is not enough to aim for
the target. You must hit it.
Italian Proverb

Peter Drucker observes that of all the elements that make
up a business, the *customer* is the only one that is essential. To capture the HBE dollar, develop a detailed profile of
your ideal prospect. Stated differently, unless you can describe to a tee who your typical buyers/customers/cli-
ents/prospects are, and their ages, income, family status,
profession, dwelling, and so on, you haven't done the job.
The data provided in earlier chapters will get you off and
running. In local or regional areas, however, you'll need
highly targeted data.

One of the greatest pitfalls facing a marketer is developing the mind set "I already know who my customers are."
Armchair marketing analysis is characterized by those who
no longer scout the competition, don't continually examine
trends in the marketplace, and fail to keep close tabs on
their customers (or worse, don't listen to staff who have).

The armchair market analyst develops, or more accurately, maintains, strategy based on what happened in the
past, or on hunches and best estimates. None of these techniques individually or collectively are a substitute for accurate, reliable, timely data regarding what is occurring in
the marketplace. This problem is particularly insidious for
those marketers who have achieved success in the traditional business to business marketing.

A MARKET IN FLUX

In terms of selling to the HBE market, understanding of the market is still in its formative stages and the market itself is changing too quickly to allow resting on one's current knowledge. If your research effort is lax, the ability to accurately define, track, redefine, and retrack the target market is severely hampered.

For those serving HBEs, questions abound. What is the nature of the niche that you serve? How many are there? What are their operating characteristics? What are the trends? What is necessary to reach the market? If you have gathered all of this information, then there are more questions that need to be answered, certainly for local markets. When do they buy? Where do they buy? At what frequency do they buy? How much do they buy? What types of delivery and service do they expect? What type of quality and quality control do they expect?

Those effective in marketing to HBEs realize that no single marketing tool, or marketing strategy, over time is sufficient to continue to effectively attract them. Staples recently added next day delivery when it realized it was losing sales to large mail order suppliers like Quill and Reliable. Sound marketing management requires continual honing, modifying, and readjusting to the environment and the needs of the niche. What worked yesterday may work today, but not tomorrow.

Good marketers are forever seeking feedback: What attracted the customer? What seemed to be the most effective promotional vehicle? What are the successful vendors in my industry doing? Attracting profitable new customers and repeat business is a challenge that never subsides.

MEASURING YOUR MARKET AREA

G. A. "Andy" Marken is president of Marken Communications, a Santa Clara, California-based advertising and public relations firm specializing in high technology companies. Using the example of PC dealers, he outlines for smaller vendors how to measure a market area before creating the next advertisement or promotion piece.

In the early days of modern retailing, retailers of all types knew their customers personally, greeted them by name, understood them thoroughly and knew what products they wanted and needed. As businesses grew larger, extended their trading areas and became more complex, the day-to-day customer contact was lost. With an extended trading area and a larger potential customer base, the "personal touch" fell by the wayside.

Instead of catering to customers' specific needs, retailers made their buying and selling decisions based on intuition and hunches. Dealers ordered goods based on what they thought they could sell. They became selling agents for the vendor rather than buying agents for their clients.

This worked fine when the customer didn't have a wide variety of retailers with whom to do business. When it came to selling PCs, it was also acceptable in the early days when little was known about computers and people purchased what was available—and what the dealer recommended. Today, buyers are more sophisticated. This precipitated the emergence of the superstore, but it also presents new service opportunities for smaller vendors.

Suddenly, in spite of the fact that their knowledge may not be 100 percent accurate, customers are now able to compare systems, software, capabilities, and peripherals, along with all of the many parameters that dictate making "the right decision." Today, for a computer dealer to profitably attract HBEs and other business, he must use the kind of "personal touch" that made his early predecessor a success.

Dealer Needs to Know

This new buyer awareness (and freedom) means that to build a growing and profitable business, one needs to hold on to old customers while attracting new ones. Inventory must be based on selling probabilities rather than buying possibilities.

In today's increasingly competitive conditions, a dealer's success is directly proportional to his or her ability to identify and understand his or her present and prospective customer base. This is vital to devise merchandising service, support, and promotional policies. Questions include:

1. Who are the store's present and prospective customers?
   a. What percentage are HBEs?
   b. What are their group characteristics (whether companies or individuals and what is their influence on retail purchases?)
   c. How many prospects are in each group?
2. Where do the customers live and work?
   a. What is the store's present trading area?
3. What are the merchandise and service requirements of the customers?
   a. What are their buying habits?
   b. What are their service needs?
4. When may the store get in touch with these people most advantageously?
   a. Which is the best approach?

An understanding of the special circumstances that determined the value of an organized research effort is an essential prerequisite of a successful promotional program. As is knowledge of the methods in handling such research.

The value of research to a dealer is dependent to a high degree upon local conditions. The size of the city, character of competition, nature of the available media, and similar conditions determine the need for organized research. For example, while Countryside Computers in Marion, Iowa, may have few problems in knowing what, when, where, and how to advertise; Computer Wares of Houston, Texas, may find such selections much more complex.

---

12 Characteristics to Know

Your promotional plan should be designed to reach and influence those people in your market area. First on your list of things to do: determine the group characteristics of your present and prospective customers. Here are important characteristics to consider:

1. Age
2. Sex
3. Race and nationality
4. Religion
5. Family status: number and size
6. Social scale
7. Education
8. Occupation
9. Vocation
10. Present ownership of computers
11. Type of residence
12. Income level

Undoubtedly, dealers are less likely to need organized research when their stores or businesses are located in smaller cities where conditions and alternatives are dramatically simplified. In comparison, in larger cities competition is keen, advertising mediums are numerous and varied, and customers have a wide choice of buying locations.

Even in smaller communities, retailers may profitably undertake modest programs of systematic research to unearth facts on what to promote and to whom. When they rely on haphazard observations and unorganized experience, dealers are likely to overlook possibilities to increase sales and profits.

Cost of Retail Research

Marken found that most retailers believe that valuable data could be generated, but are unwilling to do organized research because they believe such programs entail elaborate, costly investigations. This, he finds, is a gross misunderstanding.

The scope of investigation and methods used depend on the size of the store and nature of the community. Small city stores, which maintain frequent contacts with customers, need only undertake the simplest and least expensive form of investigation. Large city stores may find it necessary to make more comprehensive studies since they do not enjoy close contacts with their clients. Even then, good research needn't involve large cash outlays.

Much of the information the store needs has already been compiled by agencies inside and outside the store. The chief requirement will be to assemble, analyze, and interpret data that has already been gathered. Then, on the basis of these findings, you determine your product mix and your promotional plans.

Stores that have made extensive use of promotional research have demonstrated that a large staff is not needed to secure satisfactory results. Simply by assigning the task to one or two of your best people and using the computer power you have in your own store, you are able to achieve outstanding returns.

Who Are the Present, Prospective Customers?

The dealer is not buying for his entire community (business or home), but for a segment of the community. If you are an established dealer, you should be most interested in finding out as much as possible about the characteristics of your present customers. If you make periodic studies of the group characteristics in your trading area, you can understand and forecast changes in the composition of the population. By keeping abreast of these changes, you can forecast changes that will be required in your product mix.

This information is available from a variety of sources. One of the best sources is *Market Research Sources,* which is published every few years by the U.S. Department of Commerce. This handbook lists all available sources of market data under such headings as: federal government; state governments; colleges, universities, and foundations; publishers of books and trade directories; and commercial organizations. By referring to these sources, you can avoid duplicating work that has already been done.

Population statistics tend to be outdated quickly, so they should be supplemented with all available current information. Income statistics, for example, can be brought up-to-date with current figures on tax payment, bank deposits and savings accounts, building and loan association assets, building permits, automobile registrations, local employment information, and average wages paid. All of this information is available from local, county, and state sources.

From Whence Do Your Customers Come?

Before you can determine your present and potential trading area, recognize that retail buying tends to be carried out in certain clearly defined geographic areas. Even the largest metropolitan department stores find that their business is concentrated in certain areas in the city.

There are three factors that dictate this concentration of business. First, the business is conveniently located to where the patrons live. Second, delivery of dealership facilities limits the area the store can profitably serve. Finally, people with common traits or backgrounds tend to patronize the same establishment. While the store should reach out to all areas that hold promise of profitable volume, you must establish territorial limits or your efforts will be haphazard, scattered, and wasted.

To determine the limits of your trading area, analyze sales and find out where you get your present customers.

Next, analyze your deliveries by frequency and volume. Keep in mind that this has two weaknesses: it fails to show relative importance by total dollar sales, and it doesn't include "take" transactions. Because of the size of sales involved in the computer outlet, you can also analyze your charge account records easily. This procedure shows the location of frequent purchasers. The best analysis is made by using a combination of three methods (deliveries, charges, and saleschecks). By comparing the results of the three you can get an accurate character of your business as well as the cost of sales in deliveries.

The location of your present customers is a valuable and often overlooked tool. After undertaking such a project you have a true picture of the extent and nature of the area you draw from; you learn more about the living, working and buying habits of the people in your market; and you can rate and prioritize the various market areas. In addition, you can determine with a greater degree of predictability the best method for reaching your customers, and can develop a true character of your business and cost of your sales.

Potential Market Areas

Once you have an understanding of where you are presently getting business, you can decide whether you need to cultivate more business in your present market area or if you need to reach out to other areas for business. A city's or community's trading areas define the maximum area you can normally hope to draw from. Before you extend your activities, you need a clear picture of your community's trading areas.

These areas are defined by:

- Topographical boundaries.
- Transportation and communications facilities.
- Distance from outlying areas.
- Business and social activities.

- Density and character of the community and surrounding areas.
- Other attractions and nature of competition.

To measure your community's trading areas, you can use:

- Volumes of traffic handled by transportation and communications firms.
- Circulation of papers and reception areas of radio and TV stations.
- Credit inquiries.
- And again, deliveries.

The efficiency of your business is the chief factor in determining your trading area. If your advertising and promotional activities do an outstanding job, they will attract people from outside your normal "market." For example, some larger consumer specialty stores draw business nationally and internationally. While the computer industry is too competitive to achieve such a draw, effective promotion can draw business and individual customers from other dealers in or near your market area. When you have a good picture of your present and prospective market areas, have determined your plan of action for growth (present customers or new outside customers), and have profiled the community, you may find new areas of profitable business. Once you have done this you can determine what, how, and when to promote your store, your operation, your character of business, and your products.

Information Sources
When it comes to getting the facts, there are literally thousands of sources available to you. Your approaches are divided into two categories—secondary or printed resources and primary or original resources.

Primary Sources. You must pinpoint exactly who you need to contact, whether specific buyers in companies, heads of certain companies, heads of certain types of households, or certain types of users. The use of these sources usually involves original research and more expensive, time-consuming research. If you elect to use these sources, you also have other work to do. It takes time to gather information, tabulate, and analyze the results.

Research data can be gathered by mail or phone surveys. Mail surveys have a far lower rate of response than phone surveys, but enable you to reach many more targets with far less effort. Moreover, those who don't respond still have received the message that you are conducting research. Calls directly to targets require considerable effort on your part but are likely to yield far greater information and often result in inquiries.

Secondary Resources. These resources include materials that are already available. They have been produced by your trade association, by publications, and by the government. It's surprising how much information has already been produced. You need only know who to ask and what to ask for. There is an excellent chance that someone has already been over that ground before, and recently.

Secondary Information Sources Abound

- The government
- Large banks
- Newspapers
- Radio
- Television
- On-line databases

The federal government maintains literally thousands of reports of all sizes, on every subject imaginable. In one way or another, you have paid for that research, so use it to the maximum. Because government is a bureaucracy, there is also a great deal of duplication and redundancy going on. As a result, similar reports and studies are carried on at the state, county, and city levels.

Only the largest banks have undertaken original research, but every bank has done a study of your area and can give you assistance. Go to your own bank's manager to find out what their market research department has available nationally, regionally, and locally. They have probably already studied, analyzed, and synthesized many of the other secondary reports you would research, making your work even easier. Don't reinvent the wheel. If they have done the work and developed the answers, use them.

Magazines are one of your best sources for research results as well as further research data. National, regional, state, and local magazines have studied their markets to determine how they can best serve those markets and the makeup of the markets. Most will be able to provide you with not only a breakdown of their circulation but also industry/market area trends and statistics. The same is true of other media—newspapers, radio, and TV. Local media spend hundreds of thousands of dollars annually to determine what their market area is doing, what its makeup is, and how it is changing. This is how they prove to you that they can deliver in your market.

Also, the growing list of on-line databases available to you is as close as your telephone and terminal. These include Dialog, Dun & Bradstreet, Dow Jones, and hundreds of other national, international, and regional databases that are cropping up to meet the needs of information-hungry customers.

Time Limits
Before you launch into research, determine exactly when your analysis will be over (for now). This will help put limits on the depth and breadth of your research. Time limits are important because the longer the research drags on, the less important the results become.

Because there are so many different sources of information, and the information is changing daily, you have to create an artificial stopping point. A deadline or due date gives you the cut-off to the research. It also gives you, and those around you, an action date—a point they can look forward to for doing something constructive with the new information. You've determined there is a need for the study, spelled out the possible actions that can be taken, determined your primary and secondary sources of information, and are ready to present your findings, alternatives, and recommendations.

Your market research could take a few days or a few weeks. The results will help you and your organization chart a safer course. The research won't ensure your success because there are too many variables in this business, but we can all use every safety net that is available.

Hot Tips and Insights from Chapter 6

- Of all the elements that make up a business, the customer is the only one that is essential.
- To capture the HBE dollar, develop a detailed profile of your ideal prospect. Unless you can describe to a tee who your typical buyers/customers/clients/prospects are, and their ages, income, family status, profession, dwelling, and so on, you haven't done the job.
- One of the greatest pitfalls facing a marketer is developing the mind set "I already know who my customers are."
- Those effective in marketing to HBEs realize that no single marketing tool or marketing strategy, over time, is sufficient to continue to effectively attract them. Sound marketing management requires continual honing, modifying, and readjusting to the environment and the needs of the niche.
- To build a growing and profitable business, one needs to hold onto old customers while attracting new ones.
- *Market Research Sources* is published every few years by the U.S. Department of Commerce and lists all available

sources of market data under such headings as: federal government; state governments; and publishers of books and trade directories. Referring to these sources, you can avoid duplicating work that has already been done.

- Here are important characteristics to consider when locally marketing to HBEs: age, sex, race, nationality, religion, family status, social scale, education, occupation, vocation, type of residence, type of computer, and income level.
- When you need data, there is an excellent chance that someone has already been over that ground before. Major sources include the federal government; the largest banks; the media: newspapers, radio, and TV; and on-line databases.
- Research never ensures success because there are too many variables in any business, so use every safety net available.

CHAPTER 7

SCOPING THE HBE MARKET IN CANADA

"I skate to where the
puck is going, not to
where it has been."
Wayne Gretsky

Jo Ann Austin, owner of Austin Tayshus Communications, has been working out of her Toronto home for more than three years. She started her business at home as a money-saving measure, but now she wouldn't have it any other way. "There is a lingering perception in Canada that home-based entrepreneurs are eccentric or underachievers," says Austin. "But that's just not the case."

Austin observes that about half the people who run their businesses from home in Canada have no desire to move from there. "They can be more productive in a comfortable environment, they have more flexibility in managing their household and family life and they don't have to drive to work," says Austin.

"It took about six months before I got adjusted to being home-based, so that I could ignore what was going on around me and concentrate on the task at hand," Austin says. "Now I love it because I can meet with my clients any time. It's a big advantage as far as providing service."

ENTER THE NHBI

Austin now puts her experience as a home-based entrepreneur to good use as executive director of the National

143

Home Business Institute Inc., an international organization that provides research, education, and consulting services in the home-office marketplace. With the help of Vancouver-based lawyer and NHBI President Douglas Gray, an expert on small business law and co-author of *Home Inc.—The Canadian Home-Based Business Guide*, the NHBI has built up a data-base of over 12,000 Canadian home-based entrepreneurs. That number is rapidly increasing as more data is collected.

Gray and Austin aim both to raise the profile of and serve entrepreneurs working at home through the NHBI. They've developed a package of services for association members that includes group rates on medical and dental insurance, a referral service to promote members' services, and discounts from office suppliers who wish to aim their products at the home-based market. They also feature how-to seminars, and literature and consulting services for marketing, operations, business planning, and technology purchases. The Association is working with a variety of major manufacturers, distributors, and retailers so that members can purchase equipment and services at rates significantly lower than if they were buying as an independent small business.

"The hope," says Gray, "is that we can set up a number of noncompetitive sponsorships and as the association grows, we expect regional retailers to jump on the bandwagon. We're not setting ourselves up as a distributor or as

---

Many Reasons for Canadian HBE Boom

- Cocooning
- Increased PC capabilities
- Increased computer literacy
- Re-emphasis on family values
- To save time
- To capitalize on free trade with U.S.

---

warehousers. Deals will be with manufacturers and/or distributors through their normal chains. We want to work with retailers, not against them, and obviously the local home business operators will want to go to local stores or outlets. In fact, retailers will be able to approach us and work with us." (See page 168 for NHBI addresses.)

Propelled by Social Trends

Gray sees several social trends contributing to the growth of Canadian home-based businesses. Cocooning, or the tendency to center one's leisure time on the home and family, is one major factor, along with the dramatic growth of the service industry, a common type of home-based business.

As in the U.S., computerization and the increased affordability of office equipment also make running a business from home more attractive. "More workers are becoming computer-literate, and with the prices of personal computers coming down, their skills can easily be transferred from the office to their home," says Gray.

"Perhaps it's the popular misconceptions about home-based business that have stalled the industry's active pursuit of these entrepreneurs," Gray says. All too often, Canadian HBEs have not been taken seriously until they've acquired "real" office facilities. Today, with computer and telecommunications advances, escalating commercial real estate costs, and the re-emphasis on family values, approximately two thirds of all home business owners want to stay home-based.

Time and Cost

Colleen Armstrong, who manages two companies out of her Scarborough, Ontario, home, believes that cost and time savings are the major considerations for every home business. Austin visited Armstrong Computer Products and found that the company sells a variety of computer products to the end-user. Armstrong's husband works in computer services for the Metropolitan Toronto Police Force and provides technical expertise for her ventures.

Austin sees the development of Armstrong's home-based operation business as typical. "I started the first business three years ago as something to do on a part-time basis, primarily when my children were sleeping," says Armstrong. For Armstrong, whose youngest child enters school this fall, the home-office may or may not be a permanent solution. Already the office and separate assembly and packaging area are testing the limits of the space available.

As a computer dealer, Armstrong is not the usual home-office buyer. She purchases her technology directly from manufacturers and distributors. Occasionally, when she runs out of an essential office supply item, Armstrong will visit a nearby local office supply retailer. For the majority of their office supplies and small business machines, the Armstrongs drive about 30 miles across Toronto to the Price Club, a giant discount retailer. Often the trip becomes a family outing and they do their "non-business" shopping at the same time.

"The Price Club is basically a warehouse-type operation that sells everything from food and office supplies to appliances based on a membership concept. We shop there for several reasons, price being the strongest one," says Armstrong. "For example, I can purchase paper, which I resell to customers for laser printers, for much less than I can buy the same paper, even in huge bulk orders, from the distributor. Also it's one-stop shopping for both my family and business needs, and it's open on Sundays for commercial members. We discovered Price Club through word-of-mouth." While it may seem like a small amount, Armstrong purchases over $5,000 in office supplies each year for her own consumption and resale to her computer clients.

Armstrong also works with mail-order houses and warehouse merchandisers. She makes computer technology purchases based on the supplier's support facilities and brand reputation for their consumable office products and furniture. Still, low prices, the convenience of one-stop warehouses or catalog shopping, and delivery are more important to her than brand names.

Recently, a new player has entered the Canadian HBE market to capture the patronage of HBEs like Colleen Armstrong. An Ontario-based franchise chain, First Class Business Stores, evolved around the home-office trend. Charles Landon, a principal in the growing chain, says his group spent five years developing its mix of services and products for the small business customer. Each franchisee stocks around $50,000 in office supplies and provides a range of business services. With four Toronto locations and 35 stores committed to the Ontario marketplace, First Class Business Stores may make an impact on the HBE market there.

CANADIAN HBEs: EDUCATED FREETRADERS

Successful growth-oriented Canadian entrepreneurs are typically 30 to 49 years old, have some post-secondary education, and keep setting higher goals for themselves and their companies, according to a report from management consulting firm Laventhol & Horwath, Toronto. Many have also held a previous managerial position. The experience and the mistakes they made in those jobs provided important knowledge when launching their own ventures, the report says.

Most successful Canadian HBEs are in the service industry. Canadian statistics for 1978 to 1985, the latest available, reveal that service businesses grew by 37 percent over the period versus 24 percent for small businesses as a whole. The service sector requires less start-up capital and equipment than manufacturing or retailing.

Free trade with the U.S. is also popular among the most successful entrepreneurs, according to the Laventhol

& Horwath report. To Canadian HBEs, "the free trade agreement offers expanded boundaries and an opportunity to outthink the competition in both domestic and foreign markets. They have more confidence of their ability to launch a successful entry program and the staying power to attain success in the near term."

Probing the Depths of the Canadian HBE Market

Linda Russell is a strategic marketing consultant in the computer and telecommunications industries who is developing an extensive market research program for the NHBI. Russell believes that the classic profile of the "cottage industry" home worker is dangerously off-base.

"Virtually every career-oriented Canadian is a potential consumer of home-office products, especially computers," says Russell. "Consider the bulk of the Canadian working population. They're individuals between the ages of 30 and 50, generally well-educated, and driven to work harder than ever before, to get ahead or just to stay employed. If you add in other factors, you've got the makings of the home-office phenomenon," says Russell. "First, this same working population now has families, thus the appeal of a home-based business or home-office for overtime work from a regular job. Second, like America, our economy is quickly becoming service-based and much of our work is done in a nonmanufacturing environment.

"It's a simple equation to add these factors up into a home-office market comprised of either full or part-time home-based entrepreneurs and corporate telecommuters with satellite home offices. The market can only grow. Young people who are educated with computers and are raised in families with home-offices will enter the work force and influence working styles and corporate policies."

Douglas Gray believes that Canadian statistics will show many parallels to the American market. "By the year

2000, 40 percent of the Canadian work force will be working out of the home." Russell concludes that "in the NHBA's market research, the challenge will be to determine the common denominators that influence purchases among this very diverse group."

THE CHALLENGE OF APPLYING
EARLY DATA

"Marketing statistics and databases can be such delicious and addicting stuff," Austin says. "We pick a customer 'type,' purchase a list of obvious prospects, and confidently take aim at our target." But what happens when the data compilation on the target market is still in the early stages? The Canadian home-office marketplace can present a challenge to marketers.

Dave Langdon, sales manager for Sharp Electronic's Personal, Home, and Office Division, agrees. "The very diversity of the home-office market has made the market research task a difficult one. One of the problems of researching the 'corporate-sponsored' home office has been that such arrangements are often made on a departmental, rather than a corporate-wide level.

"For example, an individual manager may provide a computer for a woman on maternity leave or a temporarily disabled employee. That same company's human resources department may have no knowledge of that arrangement."

While Sharp's advertising directly targets the home-office market with its "Know who's staying home these days? The Office." slogan, Langdon questions the concept of developing products specifically for the home office. He fears that home-office workers may see such products as low-end and not as powerful as those targeted for the corporate market.

Kevyn Cohamin, product manager for IBM's recent entry into the home-office market, the PS/1, disagrees. He asserts that this market was asking for a product that specifically addressed its needs and that the PS/1, with its ease-of-use, built-in modem and other "bundled" offerings, is that product.

"The Canadian home computer market has changed significantly over the past 5 to 10 years," says Cohamin. Three years ago, IBM, recognizing a significant growth in unit sales for homes, decided to take a close look at the market to determine why people were buying for the home."

IBM's analysis demonstrated a dramatic "evolution" of the home computer buyer. Research in the early 1980s indicated that over 50 percent of home computers were purchased for light applications in home entertainment. Only 16 percent of home computers were equipped for more serious applications: 8 percent for home-based business and 8 percent for work brought home from the office.

"Our recent research, almost a decade later," says Cohamin, "indicates that the primary applications have reversed. Now less than 25 percent of home computers are purchased for light applications. Sixty percent are installed for the more powerful applications, divided equally between telecommuters and home-based businesses."

While the computer manufacturers may differ in their analysis of the marketplace, both the comprehensive U.S. research and the preliminary data-collecting missions by the NHBI point to a common (and promising) denominator among the diverse home-office purchasers: they are willing to spend a higher overall purchase price for computers, software and peripherals, if it's justified by brand reputation, product functionality, and informed, timely service.

OFFICE SUPPLIERS CAN GAIN FROM HBE BOOM

"When no simple picture exists of a specific market, it may seem easier to dismiss it or hope you're catching your share of it through your other marketing efforts," says Austin. A smarter approach, especially considering the burgeoning Canadian HBE for office supplies, is to go back to marketing basics.

"With as many as two million home offices in Canada, each buying roughly $1,000 worth of equipment and supplies annually, the market could be worth as much as $2 billion," says Austin. Many office suppliers, unsure of how to target the home-based market, are losing a significant amount of this business to more consumer-oriented stores.

"The home-based market has been a challenge for office suppliers to pin down," says Austin. "The home-based entrepreneur is a sort of hybrid between the consumer and business shopper. This is a growing market, however, that office suppliers can't afford to ignore."

Austin found that some office-supply companies have recognized the potential of the home-office market and are targeting the area specifically. Toronto-based electronics distributor Beamscope Canada, Inc., for example, is marketing a line of facsimile machines, personal copiers, laptop computers, portable printers, and furniture designed to fit into the home-office environment.

"Home-based businesses are looking for products that are less expensive and smaller than what most offices would use," says Beamscope's marketing manager. "It really is a whole new area of the office market for dealers to service." Beamscope's approach is to reach the home-based entrepreneur through advertising in dealer, corporate and consumer publications, and at trade shows.

Austin confirms that the secret for office suppliers to reach the HBE market is developing a hybrid marketing program. Vendors need to track their customer base to determine the number of home-office customers, the areas they're coming from, and their general purchasing habits. After finding appropriate ways to communicate with the group, effective marketers to HBEs tailor their advertising specifically to the customer.

PENETRATING THE CANADIAN HBE RETAIL MARKET

How can smaller retailers specifically take advantage of the commercial possibilities offered by the growing home-office marketplace? "While his technology needs may equal those of his conventional office counterpart, his shopping habits may be strongly influenced by his family and home activities," says Gray.

"The electronics retailer's softsell approach has driven many home-business buyers into the arms of the mass merchandiser, whose broad-based promotional activities and competitive pricing can appeal to both sides of this hybrid consumer."

"While taking on K-Mart and Consumers Distributing in the mass media may be beyond the means of the typical electronics retailer," Gray says, "there are many ways that the astute marketer can attract and retain the home-office customer." The following checklist for creating one's own assault on the Canadian HBE market is based on NHBI's continuing Canada-wide research with home-based operators:

1. Seek out and/or demand manufacturer/distributor home-office programs. Many of the major vendors are gearing up to target home-office buyers and understand their purchasing habits.

Traditionally, electronics manufacturers have split their marketing efforts between commercial/industrial and consumer sectors. Within vendor organizations, task forces, with representation from both sides, are now actively researching and planning home-market programs. If your suppliers are not currently providing marketing direction, point-of-sale or merchandising displays and co-op advertising programs, ask for them.

2. Construct your own market data. As the market fragments into many smaller and more difficult to reach customers, such as the home business operators, develop ways to track each outlet's customer base. Determine the number of home-office customers by the geographic areas they're coming from. Then study their purchasing habits.

Are they buying only during special sales? Do your game/ software promotions—which may have better reach to the average consumer—bring in new home-based business? Stage mini-focus groups with your home-office customers and determine their special needs, such as delivery, packaging, and product support. Use this data to design your marketing programs.

3. Sell to the "home" in home-based business. Until you have developed a strong base of home-office customers, use the same advertising vehicles as the mass-merchandisers—radio, newspapers, and flyers. If you're able to determine which neighborhoods your current home-office customers are coming from, mail or walk a flyer to these homes.

In your mass media advertising or flyer, use a premium item that would attract home businesses only, perhaps a how-to book or an inexpensive software "learning" package. Track responses to the promotion and build a base of qualified leads for further marketing efforts.

4. Maximize your display areas to encourage walk-in trade, and identify home-office products. Demonstrate to the HBE that you recognize him. Ensure that he recognizes himself in your advertising copy. Statements like: "We know the home-office has special needs. We're here for you!" would make that clear.

Create distinct sections in your catalog, mailers, or retail outlet that talk directly to the home entrepreneur. Identify package pricing or bundling of products that meet the needs of start-up operations. Get the home-office buyer into the habit of purchasing from you by stocking small quantities of accessories and office supplies.

5. Work the associations, groups, and clubs. Find ways to communicate with groups in your community that may have home-office members. Research local resource centers, entrepreneur groups, and special interest clubs. If you qualify for membership, consider joining the associations. Research sponsorship opportunities, offer your people as event speakers, and provide special offers or information for association newsletters, etc.

6. Develop ongoing direct mail programs: direct mail is an excellent way to reach the home-based enterprise and maintain a personalized dialogue.

Augment your own mailing list by renting lists of vertical markets, from direct mail houses, trade magazines or associations in which home businesses might dominate, i.e., computer consulting, medicine, and services. Check the list for addresses in noncommercial areas and for post-office boxes which many home-based businesses use to avoid zoning problems.

MANUFACTURERS ZERO IN ON THE HOME-OFFICE MARKET

Austin interviewed a wide range of vendors and found that major Canadian manufacturers are gearing up to peg the HBE and his purchasing habits, and they're encouraging their distribution channels to do likewise.

"I think the dealers and retailers are looking to the manufacturers to provide direction," says Ben Webksi, Canon Canada's national marketing manager, Reprographic Products Group. "We're actively seeking data on the home-office market and fine-tuning the right mix of 'consumer' and 'business' message, and determining the right advertising vehicles in the vertical (trade) or mass media. As Canon owns approximately 90 to 95 percent of the Canadian personal copier market, the onus is on us to 'educate' the home-office buyer.

"Through a combination of product placement tracking, surveys, and other research, we're estimating there's a potential market for personal copiers in 600,000 home offices. Our challenge now is to develop specific market data and build databases of home businesses, both of which do not currently exist."

Austin finds that part of the problem for many manufacturers has been the typical division between their commercial/industrial and consumer marketing efforts. At Sharp Electronics of Canada, the Personal, Home, and Office Division is trying to bridge the split. "One of the difficulties in selling to the home office is identifying the exact market size," says Dave Langdon. "We feel the market is a lot bigger than it appears on the surface.

"Our marketing thrust is to portray our products as the total solution for the home office. However, we're not really altering the features of our products, because the home-office technology user requires the same functions."

3M Canada's Commercial Office Supply Division has been doing well in the home-office market because of their broad distribution in both mass merchandise and regular office supply channels, according to Rod Lacroix, general sales and marketing manager. "Based on our U.S. company's research into the numbers, buying patterns, and product usage of the home-office market, we determined that, by luck or by design, we are reaching that same market in Canada.

"At the same time, our retailers are coming to us with concerns about the market's fragmentation into many smaller and more difficult to reach customers, such as home-business operators," says Lacroix. For the past few years, we've been using more "bounce-back" opportunities in our advertising and merchandising to track our customers. We're working with our dealers to improve things like catalog and mail-order programs to attract the home market."

3M's success in reaching the home market through mass merchandisers is shared by Commander Business Furniture. According to the manufacturer's vice president of sales and marketing, Brian McCabe, discount retailers such as K-Mart and Consumers Distributing sell large volumes to the home-office market for two reasons.

"The first reason is that since home-office shoppers are buying for their own home, they're naturally oriented towards shopping where they make other household purchases," says McCabe. "The second reason is that mass merchandisers are more aggressive than traditional office supply retailers in terms of both promotion and pricing.

"Part of the key to selling to home-office buyers is to encourage walk-in trade with products and promotions designed for them. For example, the discount department stores do very well with our small, light-duty filing cabinets. Office supply and furniture dealers have realized the opportunity for marketing both lower end and traditional items to the home-office market."

DO YOUR HOMEWORK

As in Canada, the United States, and elsewhere, the secret to reaching the home-office market, says Austin, is "to develop your own hybrid marketing program." Demonstrate to the HBEs that you recognize them. Find ways to communicate with groups in your community that may have home-office members. Research local resource centers, entrepreneur groups, and special interest clubs. Capitalize on the home-office customers you already have. Run a special promotion or contest for all current home-office customers who bring a specific number of new customers to open new accounts.

Re-examine your catalog. Is there any way you can create a special section on the home-office that offers products especially designed for this marketplace? Small copiers, toner cartridges, multifunctional desktop fax machines, filing systems that make record-keeping easier, desk organizers, compact computer workstations, chairs, lighting, and other office items can lend themselves nicely to this potential customer.

Hot Tips and Insights from Chapter 7
- Several social trends have contributed to the growth of Canadian home-based businesses. Among them are cocooning, the dramatic growth of the service industry, the PC, and the increased affordability of office equipment.
- Successful growth-oriented Canadian entrepreneurs are typically 30 to 49 years old, have some post-secondary education, and keep setting higher goals for themselves and their companies.
- Many Canadian HBEs previously held a managerial position. The experience and the mistakes they made in those jobs provided important knowledge when launching their own ventures.
- Most successful Canadian HBEs are in the service industry, which requires less start-up capital and equipment than manufacturing or retailing.
- To Canadian HBEs, Canada's free trade agreement with the U.S. offers expanded boundaries and an opportunity to outthink the competition in both domestic and foreign markets.
- By one estimate, nearly every career-oriented Canadian is a potential consumer of home-office products, especially computers. The bulk of the Canadian working population consists of individuals between the ages of 30 and 50, generally well-educated, and driven to work harder than ever before to get ahead or just to stay employed.
- Canadian HBEs are willing to spend a high overall purchase price for computers, software and peripherals, if it's justified by brand reputation, product functionality, and informed, timely service.
- With as many as 2 million home offices in Canada, each buying roughly $1,000 worth of equipment and supplies annually, the market could be worth as much as $2 billion.

- Many office suppliers, unsure of how to target the home-based market, are losing a significant amount of this business to more consumer-oriented stores.
- To create one's own assault on the Canadian HBE market: seek out and/or demand manufacturer/distributor home-office programs, construct your own market data; sell to the "home" in home-based business; maximize your display areas to encourage walk-in trade; identify home-office products; create distinct sections in your catalog, mailers, or retail outlet that talk directly to the home entrepreneur; work the associations, groups and clubs; and develop ongoing direct mail programs.

CHAPTER 8

PENETRATING THE HBE MARKET THROUGH INSIDER GROUPS

A good plan today is better
than a great plan tomorrow.
General George Patton

Marketing to HBEs can be an expensive proposition, requiring substantial time and out-of-pocket costs. Yet, there are ways to effectively penetrate HBE niches that are less taxing than traditional marketing approaches. One effective way is by becoming an insider to the groups you've targeted. Your ability to sense, serve, and satisfy needs of targeted HBEs in ways in which *they perceive the value* will result in marketing success.

Developing an insider's reputation in targeted HBE groups yields at least two major benefits: (1) it minimizes the amount of rejection you will experience when marketing to the niche, and (2) it helps to prompt new business inquiries from those who know and trust you. When members of the niche regard you as one of them, you've built the trust and rapport necessary to be prosperous.

A CONTINUAL PROCESS

As Richard Connor and I elaborated in our book *Getting New Clients* (Wiley, 1988), becoming an insider to any group is a continual process. Ideally, you undertake some targeted marketing and selling everyday to penetrated the targeted niche. On one day you may be developing and strengthening relationships with key influentials in the infrastructure of the targeted niche, such as association directors; another day you may be planning an advertising or promotion campaign to reach prospects in the niche.

MAINTAINING AN INSIDER'S REPUTATION

Companies successful at marketing to HBEs by developing an insider's reputation employ at least four strategies, including:

- Becoming an active, accepted, visible, and working-serving member of the infrastructure.
- Creating, maintaining, and enhancing a favorable awareness of themselves, their firm, and its services.
- Stimulating inquiries from high-potential customers.
- Paving the way or gaining acceptance on the part of targets when making mailings and telephone contacts.

Perhaps the key to effectively penetrating a targeted niche and attaining insider status, however, is maintaining an image and reputation that you are different and/or better than the competition, and then living up to that reputation.

To gain this reputation, you'll need to develop and use an assortment of promotional activities. Such opportunities emerge by being involved in "forums"—organizations, networks, groups, and publications made up of and read by your targets. In this chapter, we'll focus on organizations and groups that serve or support specific segments within the HBE market. In the chapter that follows, we'll explore publications that address the HBE market.

The groups discussed below fall into three categories, including:

- HBE-focused groups.
- PC user groups.
- Small business groups.

HBE-FOCUSED GROUPS

Small Business Network (SBN)

The Small Business Network is an interconnected group of business organizations designed to develop and support small businesses in a free market system. The SBN provides several benefits for its member organizations: *(1)* marketing and management services, *(2)* import and export management services, *(3)* a business and consumer-marketing network, and *(4)* business evaluation for potential members.

Member groups of SBN include the International Association for Business Organizations, National Association for Business Organizations, National Small Business Institute, and National Association of Home-Based Businesses (described below).

For more information, write or call: Small Business Network Inc., Post Office Box 30220, Baltimore, Maryland 21270. (301) 581–1373

The National Association of Home-Based Businesses

The National Association of Home-Based Businesses is a private organization for individuals who own and operate a home-based business. The association consists of local and state chapters. Membership is open to HBEs as well as to professional consultants and service associates who provide support services to them. As such, professional consultants and support associates, such as lawyers, teachers, and accountants who provide consulting services, are among its members, as are graphic designers and printing companies.

The NAHBB was created to help small companies in their early stages when they are most susceptible to failure. The association encourages the entrepreneur to take a hard look at his or her business venture before investing a lot of time and money. Each business entering the NAHBB is evaluated through its business plan. For members who need a more in-depth analysis, the NAHBB can provide members with a "Business Profile." This analysis gives business owners a new insight into his or her business venture.

Association members sometimes jointly market their products and services to reach broader public and private markets. The group publishes the *Home Based Business Newspaper,* which contains advertisement and business opportunity sections. It also publishes annual state HBE directories, and sponsors trade shows and business expositions.

The Association frequently sponsors private seminars and workshops for members in authorized chapters. And it directs members to area community colleges and other institutions that teach small business courses. The NAHBB also has a direct mail service available that mails from 6,000 to 25,000 pieces per mailing to both local and national lists. To contact the NAHBB write to: National Association of Home-Based Businesses, P.O. Box 30220, Baltimore, Maryland 21270.

For American HBEs

The American Home Business Institute, Inc. (AHBI) is a research organization providing information and education for the benefit of people who conduct business at home. The Association helps HBEs achieve greater satisfaction in all phases of their businesses. Services and benefits include:

- A monthly publication, *Home BusinessLine,* which carries timely topics, such as "Should You Incorporate?" "How to Expand Your Business Profitably," and "Are You Charging as Much as You Should?" The publication contains articles by experts to help members reach higher profits and maximum efficiency.
- A comprehensive group insurance plan for major medical cost and hospitalization at substantial savings.
- A hot line advisory service—Experts on tax management; marketing and advertising; financing; time saving; fee-structuring; and all other areas are available by phone to assist members with any business problems.
- Buying Service—As with many HBE support groups, members can buy name-brand equipment, such as word processors, copiers, fax machines, telecommunications equipment, office supplies, and stationery at close to wholesale prices.
- Discounts on Avis Rent-A-Car, travel, and many other travel related items. Members reportedly receive an average discount of $2,500 on most American cars and about $1,500 off the sticker price of Japanese cars, $50 to $125 above dealer cost. One can get a computer print-out on all the options and standard equipment on any car for $9.95.
- A 15 percent discount on top of the lowest toll calls offered by the major long-distance companies.

For information write to: AHBI, 397 Post Road, Darien, CT 06820.

The New Working Mothers Work at Home

Mothers' Home Business Network (MHBN), a national organization with 5,000 members, was founded six years ago to help mothers become homeworking mothers. The

Network publishes the newsletter, *Homeworking Mothers* and other specialized material, providing a way for work-at-home mothers to reach out to each other for support, information, and collaboration. It is reportedly the largest home business organization for women in the United States today.

The Network has grown in numbers thanks in part to the editorial mention it has received in magazines such as *Family Circle, Woman's Day, Glamour, Parents,* and *American Baby.* After reading the recommendations of these magazines, young mothers write requesting home business guidance. The majority also purchase a sample issue of Mothers' Home Business Network's newsletter, *Homeworking Mothers.*

Georganne Fiumara, founder and president of MHBN, says the new working mothers, women who choose to work at home so that they can spend more time with their children, are a varied and growing group. "Some have started high-powered companies and use supplemental child care, even though they work at home," says Fiumara. "Others earn just enough income to allow them to stay at home full time and devote their days to their little ones. Homeworking mothers may choose different pathways, but they all share a dedication to family and career and the willingness to seek creative ways to handle both simultaneously.

"Even though a majority of mothers work outside the home, many continue to search for a workstyle that will allow them to spend more family-centered time," says Fiumara, a work-at-home mother herself. "In the past six years, we have received more than 100,000 letters from mothers who are searching for a way to mother their children while earning needed income. A home-based career can be the answer."

MHBN's members represent each of the 50 states. Membership cost is nominal and includes four issues of the newsletter *Homeworking Mothers;* two issues of the newsletter, *Kids & Careers: New Ideas and Options for Mothers;* a booklet, *"Mothers' Money Making Manual"* (containing 150 work-at-home ideas and basic start-up information); a copy of the annual resource guide, *Mothers' Home Business-pages;* and free classified advertising.

The Network is making available their list of 55,000 home-working mothers. The list not only targets women who choose to work at home, but each of them is also a young mother in search of ways to gain more family-centered time. They are interested in legitimate at-home money-making opportunities; home business and parenting books and other publications; home-office equipment and supplies; home furnishings; insurance; and products for women and children. Sales are managed by Advantage Line of Wolf Point, Montana. The cost is $90 per month and two sample mailing pieces are required. For further information, contact Advantage Line, Box 4038, Wolf Point, Montana 59201.

MARKETING TO MOTHERS: WOMEN DISCOURAGED BY OTHERS

Fiumara observes that some people try to discourage mothers from working at home. They say, "Why would you want to sit at a typewriter trying to work while balancing a baby on your knee?" These people feel that working at home puts a woman in the position of trying to do it all—all at once! Yet, according to the results of the first National Poll of Homeworking Mothers, a majority of mothers who want to work at home say it's their first choice.

"The poll was sent to our 3,000 members and the results are based on the responses of 527 members," says Fiumara. Take note: "98 percent said that they feel working at home is the perfect way to juggle the conflicting demands of work and family. The remaining two percent said flexible scheduling outside the home with on-site child care would suit them better."

Some 72 percent want to work at home so that they can be with their children while earning money. A vocal 22 percent use home as a place to start a business simply because it is an affordable place to do so. Starting a business at home gives these women a chance to achieve the personal fulfillment and income that business ownership can bring while avoiding the high cost of renting an office or store. Fifteen percent like having control over their own time and being able to work any time of the day or night.

"Homeworking mothers do feel that they need help, but only nine percent are seeking child care," Fiumara says. The most commonly cited need? "A maid! While 39 percent do say they need more help with housework, a greater percentage want business assistance; 30 percent want help with marketing their business and 10 percent are seeking wholesale connections. In other words, these are dedicated mothers and very serious business women!"

Having the time to spend with children (56 percent) and the flexibility to do all roles (27 percent) were cited most as the greatest advantages to working at home. Handling conflicting priorities (29 percent) and managing time effectively (23 percent) were shown to be the greatest disadvantages. Homeworking mothers also worry about projecting a professional image and making a profit.

Homeworking mothers buy home office equipment; 51 percent own computers and printers while 75 percent own an electronic typewriter! Answering machines (35 percent), office furniture (62 percent), calculators (85 percent), and photocopy machines (27 percent) are also in demand by entrepreneurial mothers. "Those who do not own all the equipment they need intend to buy it soon," says Fiumara. "The greatest percentage want a computer (32 percent) followed closely by a desire for a better computer printer; 29 percent want a laser printer. A second business line, computer software and a "comfortable chair" all appeared on the homeworking mother's wish list.

The survey also revealed:

- 50 percent of the respondents own a home business now; 38 percent want to start one in the next year.
- 2 percent currently hold positions as at-home employees but 9 percent are looking for jobs at home.
- Because 22 percent report that they are currently employed outside the home it is apparent that some work part-time, some work full-time but plan to start a home business, and others are juggling a job while trying to launch a successful home business.
- 41 percent of the respondents have two children; 38 percent have one and 12 percent have three or more children.
- One surprising finding: 9 percent of the members do not have children yet, but are interested in starting a home business so that they will already be home when they do have children.

For more information on MHBN or on marketing to mothers in general, write to MHBN, P.O. Box 423, East Meadow, NY 11554.

ORGANIZING MASSES OF CANADIAN HBES

The National Home Business Association (covered in more detail in Chapter 7) is a division of the National Home Business Institute, an international organization that provides research, education, and consulting services in the home-office marketplace and is Canada's first and largest association for HBEs. The Association offers a comprehensive package of benefits that include group rates on medical and dental insurance, a referral service to promote members' services, and discounts from office suppliers who wish to aim their products at the home-based market.

The Association also features how-to seminars, and literature in the areas of marketing, operations, business planning, and technology purchases. For more information contact:

NHBI
1070 West Broadway, #310
Vancouver, British Columbia, Canada V6HIE7

or

NHBI
615 Mt. Pleasant Road
Toronto, Ontario, Canada M453C5

or

NHBI
15 Veteran Way
Oakland, CA 94602

A UNITED FRONT FOR HOME OFFICES

A national association, United Home Offices, was formed for the purpose of helping home businesses grow and prosper by linking them together and providing benefits previously unavailable to home businesses.

One of the biggest challenges facing home businesses today is finding comprehensive group health insurance. The member benefit program endorsed by UHO, available to members, their families, and employees, is made up of term life, major medical, and dental insurance. Rates vary due to location, age, marital status, deductible, and so forth and are available only to members of UHO.

United Home Offices publishes *The Home Run,* a periodic newsletter featuring articles written by home business experts on topics including tax tips, time management, space management, new software, computers, and legal advice.

Like many HBE support groups, UHO offers a discount shopping club. This program offers UHO members substantial discounts on brand name office equipment, including computer hardware and software, modems, and other equipment. The UHO Discount Shopping Club gives the home business owner the buying power of large companies, with discounts of up to 40 percent off list prices.

UHO also maintains a Resource Database that includes electronic bulletin board systems worldwide, general and government resources available to small businesses, sales and marketing materials, special interest groups, newsletters, and books about small businesses. The databases are accessible directly by modem or one may call UHO for information about receiving a printout.

The UHO Information Exchange Network puts members in touch with a network of other home business owners. UHO members have immediate access to this network through a personal computer and modem. Simply by following the menus presented on this computerized bulletin board, one may communicate with other members to share ideas, information, and resources. Members without modems may take advantage of this network by calling UHO for information about obtaining printouts (for a small fee).

UHO's network can be used to gain access to other UHO members. For example, one may obtain a list of members by occupation, city, state, or key words. One may participate in conferences on topics of specific interest. Topics include computers, legal and accounting, women's issues, writers, arts and entertainment, and humor, with new topics added periodically.

Members also can conduct conversations via electronic mail. UHO also offers seminars on How to Succeed by Working at Home. UHO's New Regional Chapters at present include Westchester, Rockland, New Jersey, Pennsylvania, Connecticut and Massachusetts, with other chapters in formation across the U.S.

UHO's Advisory Board is in full effect for counseling and consulting, and helps members with problems that may affect their business. The Board is composed of a team of top professionals who can help members (one-on-one) resolve problems in many areas. There is a fee for this service, though advisory board consultants charge members significantly less for this service than they do their regular clients.

Non-UHO members have a 24-hour a day open invitation to a free visit to the Information Exchange Network by dialing (718) 898–5107 on a modem. The system is menu-driven and on-line help is available. UHO can be reached by writing United Home Offices, 88–43 62d Drive, Rego Park, NY 11374.

An Association for the Cottage Industry

The National Association for the Cottage Industry is another HBE support group providing a vast array of services and benefits for its members. Membership categories include individual, non-profit, and corporate, and the association continually monitors the background and interests of its members, particularly through its membership application form, which asks:

- Do you own a personal computer, and if so, what kind?
- Do you own an answering machine?
- Could you help start a chapter in your community?
- Which of the following committees would you like to work on: membership, zoning ordinance, publicity, conference, legislation watchdog, fund raising, or newsletter?

The application also asks members if they are interested in attending and/or exhibiting at the home business show sponsored by the Association each fall.

The Association publishes the *Cottage Connection,* a monthly newsletter that offers an open invitation to advertisers and suppliers. The newsletter accepts business-card size advertisements and classified advertisements, while reserving the right to reject any advertisement that isn't in keeping with the publication's standards.

The Association also advertises the availability of its mailing list, which contains some 36,000 names. It sells one-time rights to its list at a fixed minimum fee per 5,000 names. The names are supplied on pressure-sensitive labels organized by zip code. For more information, write to: Editor, Cottage Connection, P.O. Box 14850, Chicago, IL 60614.

A One-Stop Center for Family Business

The Center for Family Business has been serving family companies for more than 20 years. It was founded in Cleveland in 1962 by its CEO, Leon A. Danco, Ph.D. The Center is committed to helping family businesses succeed and grow, year after year, generation after generation. The Center offers publications and programs designed and refined through experiences to serve family business. Thousands of companies have attended the Center's family business seminars. Write to: The Center for Family Business, P.O. Box 24268, Cleveland, OH 44124.

Here are the addresses of other HBE support groups:

Family Firm Institute
P.O. Box 476
Johnstown, N.Y. 12095

Holds an annual conference with keynote speakers and dozens of workshops on effectively managing a family-owned or run business.

Mothers at Home
P.O. Box 2208
Merrifield, VA 22116

National Alliance for Home-Based Business Women
Box 306
Midland Park, NJ 07432

Provides seminars and workshops on being more effective in your home business and also maintains local chapters throughout the United States. Also provides group discounts, life insurance programs, legislative watch. Men may join as well.

National Association for the Self-employed
2324 Gravel Road
Fort Worth, TX 76118

With more than 350,000 members, this organization provides information for the self-employed and independent entrepreneur. Publishes *Small Business America,* an extensive monthly tabloid, and a variety of pamphlets. Has insurance, purchasing, and other group discount programs.

POWERFUL ELECTRONIC FORUMS, NETWORKING AND PC USER GROUPS

Many HBEs are networking through national, for-fee, interactive services, and among themselves. HBEs can subscribe to services such as CompuServe and join forums on home-based business. Here are some early leaders in electronically linking HBEs:

GO CONSULT, GO USEN, CO WORK
CompuServe Information Service
5000 Arlington Center Boulevard
Columbus, OH 43220

Interactive professional forums bulletin boards, serves as daily reading and communication for thousands of HBEs.

GEnie
General Electric Network for Information Exchange
401 N. Washington Street, MC5A
Rockville, MD 20850

Links 200,000 subscribers to a business and computer support network, including the Home-Office/Small Business Roundtable.

Prodigy
Prodigy Services Company
445 Hamilton Avenue
White Plains, NY 10601

Home business advice and software reviews, and on-line financial and business advice.

Other electronic networks are rapidly cropping up, many through PC user groups. Local electronic networks are low cost and they only take the time of the system operator (sysop) whose computer hosts the network. On these networks, HBEs and the vendors who have established themselves as insiders discuss common issues, exchange information about products, and download computer files with business tips.

Electronic networking is not putting face-to-face networking out of business, only supplementing it. Many HBEs participate in networking opportunities available through local Chambers of Commerce (cited on page 197). In addition, leads exchange groups have sprung up all over the country. In these groups, members meet regularly, often over breakfast, and share information that will help the other members of the group.

They also review information, such as business relocations, that can benefit all the members. Leads exchange groups are another low-cost but highly effective resource that many home business owners are using to succeed. Look for HBE networks, electronic or otherwise, to increasingly be a major source of new product and service information throughout the 1990s.

Electronically Linked Cottagers

The Association of Electronic Cottages (AEC) is one of a new breed of organizations serving the electronic cottage market. Registration is free once one has subscribed to the Compuserve Information Service. Meetings are held electronically on CompuServe's Working From Home Forum, which provides a live conference for members to network as well as bulletin boards that cover topics of concern to home business owners.

CompuServe subscriptions can be bought at any computer store for a nominal fee, and are often included as an introductory offer when one purchases a modem. Write to: Association of Electronic Cottagers, 677 Canyon Crest Drive, Sierra Madre, CA 91024.

Another effective way to target HBEs is through state
and local PC users groups, whose memberships often number in the thousands, and many of whom are HBEs or future HBEs. There are powerful groups throughout the
United States, particularly in California, Oregon, and
Washington, and along the Eastern Corridor.

As part of its continuing effort to foster PC user group
activities, *PC World* Magazine publishes an annual roster
of organizations throughout the U.S.

NATIONWIDE GUIDE TO PC USER GROUPS

ALABAMA
Birmingham IBM PC
User Group
c/o Fred Hilbers
P.O. Box 19248
Birmingham, AL
35219-9248
205/871-1939
$20/yr., NL, 15 SIGs,
TS, TE, SL

Huntsville IBM PC User
Group
c/o Bill Born
P.O. Box 16013
Huntsville, AL 35802
205/539-5940
$15/yr., NL, 3 SIGs,
TE, BBS

Montgomery PC Users
Group
c/o James Morrow
3505 McGehee Rd.
Montgomery, AL 36111
205/288-4434
$25/yr., NL, 3 SIGs,
TS, TE, BBS

ALASKA
Polar PC User Group
c/o Glen Wilcox
P.O. Box 72934
Fairbanks, AK 99707
907/452-2500
$10/yr., NL, TS, TE

ABBREVIATIONS KEY:

NL: newsletter SIG: special interest group TS: technical support TE: training
and education BBS: bulletin board service SL: software library (User groups are
listed alphabetically by state and city, not by user group name.)

ARIZONA
Phoenix IBM PC Users
Group
P.O. Box 44150
Phoenix, AZ 85064
602/943–7907
$40/yr., NL, SIGs, TE,
BBS, SL

Tucson IBM PC Users
Group
c/o Don Williams
P.O. Box 1489
Tucson, AZ 85702
602/577–3261
$24/yr., NL, 15 SIGs,
TS, TE, BBS, SL

ARKANSAS
Central Arkansas PC
Users Association
c/o Gary Davis
P.O. Box 2095
Little Rock, AR 72203
501/224–2568
$24/yr., NL, TE, BBS

NW Arkansas IBM PC
Users Group
c/o Bill Shook
Rt. 4, Box 376
Springdale, AZ 72764
501/361–2963
$15/yr., NL, TS, TE

CALIFORNIA
Gold Country PC
Users Group
1260 Taylor Ln.
Auburn, CA 95603
916/885–8022
$25/yr., NL, 1 SIG, TS,
TE, BBS

Kern Independent PC
User Group
c/o Jim Harrer
P.O. Box 2780
Bakersfield, CA 93303
805/395–0223 (days)
$20/yr., NL, 4 SIGs,
TS, TE, BBS

Berkeley PC/
Compatibles User
Group
c/o Mel Mann
1145 Walnut St.
Berkeley, CA 94707
415/526–4033
No fee, NL, TS, TE,
BBS

South County IBM PC
User Group
c/o Bob McCloud
17982 Walnut Rd.
Castro Valley, CA
94546
415/537–9899
$30/yr., NL, TS, TE

ABBREVIATIONS KEY:

NL: newsletter SIG: special interest group TS: technical support TE: training and education BBS: bulletin board service SL: software library (User groups are listed alphabetically by state and city, not by user group name.)

FOG International
Computer Users
Group
P.O. Box 3474
Daly City, CA 94015
415/755–2000 (days)
$30/yr., NL, 4 SIGs,
TS, TE, BBS

UCLA PC Users Group
c/o Richard Katz
P.O. Box 661189
Los Angeles, CA
90066
213/473–6668
$20/yr., NL, 18 SIGs,
TS, TE, BBS, SL

SLO Bytes PC Users
Group
c/o Bob Ward
2100 Andre Ave.
Los Osos, CA 93402
805/528–0121
$18/yr., NL, 4 SIGs,
TS, TE

Monterey Bay Users
Group IBM PC
c/o Fred Brownell
177 Webster St.
#A–354
Monterey, CA 93940
408/373–6245
$20/yr., NL, 3 SIGs,
TS, TE

North Orange County
Computer Club
P.O. Box 3616
Orange, CA 92665
714/998–8080,
714/730–6743 (BBS)
$25/yr., NL, 25 SIGs,
TS, TE, BBS

Pasadena IBM Users
Group
c/o Steven Bass
711 E. Walnut St.
#306
Pasadena, CA 91101
818/795–2300 (days)
$36/yr., NL, TS, TE,
BBS

Riverside IBM
Computer Club
c/o James Heidecke
7860 Live Oak Dr.
Riverside, CA
92509–5339
714/685–5407
$25/yr., NL, TS, TE,
BBS

ABBREVIATIONS KEY:

NL: newsletter SIG: special interest group TS: technical support TE: training
and education BBS: bulletin board service SL: software library (User groups are
listed alphabetically by state and city, not by user group name.)

Sacramento IBM PC
Users Group
c/o Milt Hull
P.O. Box 162227
Sacramento, CA
95816-2227
916/386-9865,
916/395-3153 (BBS)
$25/yr., NL, 20 SIGs,
TS, TE, BBS, SL

San Diego Computer
Society
c/o Hank Blake
P.O. Box 87770
San Diego, CA 92138
619/284-7802
$22/yr., NL, 20 SIGs,
TS, TE

PC Clone User Group
P.O. Box 15000-324
San Francisco, CA
94115
415/861-9321
$25/yr., NL, BBS

San Francisco Business
Computers
c/o Jordan Rosenberg
455 Vallejo St.
San Francisco, CA
94133
415/788-5338
No fee, TS, BBS

San Francisco
Computer Society
c/o Ralph Gallagher
P.O. Box 783
San Francisco, CA
94101
415/929-0252
$30/yr., TS, TE

San Francisco PC
Users Group
3145 Geary Blvd. #155
San Francisco, CA
94118-3316
415/221-9166
$30/yr., NL, 17 SIGs,
TS, TE, BBS

UCSF IBM PC User
Group
c/o Mark Slichter
Computer Center
Room U-76
U.C. San Francisco
San Francisco, CA
94143
No fee, NL

Lab PC Users Group
c/o Glenn Ouchi
5989 Vista Loop
San Jose, CA 95124
408/723-0947
$48/yr. (foreign $68/
yr.), NL, TS, TE, SL

ABBREVIATIONS KEY:

NL: newsletter SIG: special interest group TS: technical support TE: training
and education BBS: bulletin board service SL: software library (User groups are
listed alphabetically by state and city, not by user group name.)

Silicon Valley
Computer Society
c/o Kent Safford
1330 S. Bascom Ave.,
Ste. D
San Jose, CA
95128–4502
408/286–1271
$30/yr., NL, 20 SIGs,
TS, TE, BBS

Santa Barbara IBM PC
Users Group
c/o Eric Pedersen
281 Oak Rd.
Santa Barbara, CA
93108
805/969–9961
$15/yr., NL, 5 SIGs,
TS, TE, BBS

Stanford/Palo Alto
User Group
P.O. Box 3738
Stanford, CA 94305
415/322–3850
$25/yr. (student $10/
yr.), NL, SIGs, TS, BBS

Stockton PC Users
Group
P.O. Box 99052
Stockton, CA 95209
209/478–9697
$25/yr., NL, 4 SIGs,
TS, TE, BBS

COLORADO
PC Users Group of
Colorado
c/o Henry Lopez
P.O. Box 944
Boulder, CO 80306
303/447–2813
$22/yr., NL, TE, BBS

Chaffee County
Computer Club
c/o Mark Emmer
P.O. Box 1123
Salida, CO 81201
719/539–3884
$24/yr., NL, TS, TE

CONNECTICUT
Connecticut IBM PC
User Group
c/o John McGinley
P.O. Box 291
New Canaan, CT
06840
203/762–0229
$20/yr., NL, 6 SIGs,
BBS

Southeast Connecticut
PC Users Group
c/o Catherine Winslow
P.O. Box 909
Norwich, CT 06360
203/442–3844 (BBS)
$12/yr., NL, 3 SIGs,
TS, BBS

ABBREVIATIONS KEY:

NL: newsletter SIG: special interest group TS: technical support TE: training
and education BBS: bulletin board service SL: software library (User groups are
listed alphabetically by state and city, not by user group name.)

DELAWARE

PC Professional Users Group
c/o Glenn Bleakney
P.O. Box 2350
Wilmington, DE 19899
302/656–8200
$30/yr., TS, TE

DISTRICT OF COLUMBIA

Capital PC User Group
51 Monroe St.,
Plaza E #2
Rockville, MD 20850
301/762–6775
$35/yr., NM, 30 SIGs,
TS, TE, BBS

FLORIDA

Manatee PC Users Group
c/o Dan Crumpler
4411 100th St. W
Bradenton, FL 34210
813/792–3437
$15/yr., NL,4 SIGs,
TS, TE

Pinellas IBM PC Users Group
3118 Gulf to Bay Blvd.
#319
Clearwater, FL

34619–4509
813/797–7002
$25/yr., NL, 35 SIGs,
TS, TE, BBS

South Polk County PC Users Group
c/o Bill Goddard
815 N. Lake Reedy Blvd.
Frostproof, FL 33843
813/635–3381
No fee, TE

The Hog Town Hackers
c/o Bruce Ruiz
4623 N.W. 13th Ave.
Gainesville, FL 32605
904/392–3151 (days),
904/378–9700
(nights)
$15/yr., TS, TE, BBS

IBM PC Medical Users Group
c/o Bruce Ruiz
Department of Anesthesiology
P.O. Box J254
Gainesville, FL 32610
904/392–3151
No fee, NL, TS, TE,
BBS

ABBREVIATIONS KEY:

NL: newsletter SIG: special interest group TS: technical support TE: training and education BBS: bulletin board service SL: software library (User groups are listed alphabetically by state and city, not by user group name.)

IBM PC Users Group
of Jacksonville
c/o Rich French
P.O. Box 47197
Jacksonville, FL 32247
904/725-9075
$20/yr., NL, 8 SIGs,
TS, TE, BBS

Charlotte County PC
Users Group
c/o Gene Davis
P.O. Box 3530
Port Charlotte, FL
33949
813/625-6574
$15/yr., NL, 3 SIGs,
TS, TE, BBS

University of South
Florida PC/Users
Group
University of South
Florida
SVC 409
c/o U.C.S. Infocenter
Tampa, FL
33620-7250
813/974-3190
No fee, NL, 4 SIGs,
TE, BBS

GEORGIA
Atlanta IBM PC User's
Group
c/o Jack Bolton
P.O. Box 28788
Atlanta, GA 30358
404/662-0803
$30/yr., NL, 5 SIGs,
TS, TE, BBS

CSRA Computer
Society, Inc.
c/o Bob Kiernan
P.O. Box 284
Augusta, GA 30903
404/790-5241,
404/798-3864
$12/yr., TS, TE, BBS, SL

IDAHO
Idaho PC Users Group
c/o Richard Chambers
P.O. Box 9136
Boise, ID 83707
208/939-9120
$20/yr., NL, 5 SIGs,
TS, TE, BBS

ABBREVIATIONS KEY:

NL: newsletter SIG: special interest group TS: technical support TE: training
and education BBS: bulletin board service SL: software library (User groups are
listed alphabetically by state and city, not by user group name.)

ILLINOIS
The Chicago
Computer Society
P.O. Box 8681
Chicago, IL
60680–8681
312/794–7737
$40/yr., 11 SIGs, TS,
TE, BBS

LAWMUG (for lawyers)
Electronic Bar Assoc.
P.O. Box 11191
Chicago, IL
60611–0191
312/951–8264
$250/yr., NL, TS, TE,
BBS

Central Illinois PC
Users' Group
c/o Jack Beebe
307 W. Jackson
Petersburg, IL 62675
217/632–7284
$20/yr., NL, TS, TE

INDIANA
The Northeastern
Indiana PC Club
c/o Gordon Samra
4422 Bridgetown Run
Fort Wayne, IN 46804

219/436–7827
$20/yr., NL, 6 SIGs,
TS, TE, BBS

IBM PC Users Group,
Inc.
c/o Ken Fuffichen
P.O. Box 2532
Indianapolis, IN
46206
317/897–5166
$25/yr., NL, 8 SIGs,
TS, TE, BBS

IOWA
Hawkeye PC Users
Group
c/o Ben Blackstock
P.O. Box 2966
Cedar Rapids, IA
52406
319/393–5416,
319/363–3314 (BBS)
$15/yr., NL, 2 SIGs,
TS, TE, BBS

Northeast Iowa PC
User Group
c/o Barbara Blow
320 Oak Park Circle
Waterloo, IA 50701
319/234–0654
$15/yr., NL, 2 SIGs, TE

ABBREVIATIONS KEY:

NL: newsletter SIG: special interest group TS: technical support TE: training
and education BBS: bulletin board service SL: software library (User groups are
listed alphabetically by state and city, not by user group name.)

Des Moines Area IBM
PC Users Group
c/o Jim Nixon
1804 Hillside St.
West Des Moines, IA
50265
515/223–0328 (BBS)
$20/yr., NL, 1 SIG, TS,
TE, BBS

KANSAS
Topeka PC Users Club
c/o Bob Bowser
P.O. Box 1279
Topeka, KS 66601
913/272–7832
$10/yr., NL, 5 SIGs,
TS, TE

Wichita IBM PC Users
Group
P.O. Box 781200
Wichita, KS
67278–1200
$20/yr., NL, 6 SIGs, TS

KENTUCKY
Kentucky-Indiana PC
Users Group
c/o Elliot McGuire
P.O. Box 3564
Louisville, KY 40201
502/897–6668
$25/yr., NL, 15 SIGs,
TS, TE, BBS

Bluegrass IBM PC
Users Group
c/o Randall Goodwin
1894 Rio Vista Dr.
Paris, KY 40361–1235
606/269–6902
$12/yr., NL, TS, BBS

Powell County PC
Users Group
c/o Compserve
Limited
P.O. Box 399
Stanton, KY
40380–0399
606/663–2472
$10/yr., NL, 2 SIGs,
TS, TE

LOUISIANA
IBM Serious Users of
Baton Rouge
c/o Jay Brohn
Computer Electronics
1955 Dallas Dr.
Baton Rouge, LA
70806–1430
504/924–8066,
504/273–3116 (BBS)
No fee, NL, TS, TE,
BBS

ABBREVIATIONS KEY:

NL: newsletter SIG: special interest group TS: technical support TE: training
and education BBS: bulletin board service SL: software library (User groups are
listed alphabetically by state and city, not by user group name.)

Northwest Louisiana
IBM PC User Group
c/o H.G. Friedman
945 Dudley Dr.
Shreveport, LA 71104
318/868–5950
$25/yr. (student $10/
yr.), NL, TE

MAINE
Portland Maine IBM
User Group
c/o Louis De Angelis
26 Cascade Rd.
Old Orchard Beach,
ME 04064
207/934–5521
No fee, TS, TE

MARYLAND
Chesapeake PC Users
Group
c/o Steve Smith
2315B Forest Dr. #31
Annapolis, MD 21401
301/647–7139
$24/yr., NL, 4 SIGs,
TS, TE, BBS

Columbia-Baltimore
PC Users Group
c/o Ed Kidera
P.O. Box 125

Columbia, MD 21045
301/997–9333
$20/yr., NL, 2 SIGs,
TS, TE, BBS

MASSACHUSETTS
The Boston Computer
Society
One Center Plaza
Boston, MA 02108
617/367–8080 (days)
$35/yr., NL,45 SIGs,
TS, TE, BBS

Environmental
Protection Agency PC
Users Group
c/o Greg Charest
JFK Federal Bldg.
Boston, MA 02203
617/565–3357
No fee, NL, TS, TE

Pioneer Valley PC User
Group
c/o Donald Lesser
P.O. Box H
North Amherst, MA
01059
413/549–4856 (days),
413/549–6747
(nights)
$5/yr., NL, 7 SIGs, TS,
TE, BBS

ABBREVIATIONS KEY:

NL: newsletter SIG: special interest group TS: technical support TE: training
and education BBS: bulletin board service SL: software library (User groups are
listed alphabetically by state and city, not by user group name.)

MICHIGAN
Librarians Using
Computers
c/o Blaine Morrow
10 Kercheval
Grosse Pointe, MI
48236
313/343–2340
$5/yr., NL, TS, TE, BBS

The Cursors IBM PC
Users Group
Gogebic Community
College
E. 4946 Jackson Rd.
Ironwood, MI 49938
906/932–4231
$12/yr., NL, TS, TE

Southwestern Michigan
IBM PC Users Group
c/o R. K. Schmitt
2320 Crosswind Dr.
Kalamazoo, MI 49008
616/349–5381
$20/yr., NL, 2 SIGs, TS

MINNESOTA
Twin Cities PC User
Group
c/o Scott Young
P.O. Box 10360
Minneapolis, MN
55458–3360
612/888–0557
$24/yr., NL,10 SIGs,
TS, TE, BBS

MISSISSIPPI
Mississippi State
Microcomputer Users
Group
c/o Dr. Gene Boggess
MSU Computing
Center
P.O. Drawer CC
Mississippi State, MS
39762
601/325–2079
No fee, 3 SIGs, TS,
BBS

NEVADA
Las Vegas PC Users
Group
c/o Vic Sipin
4820 Alpine Pl.
#G202
Las Vegas, NV 89107
702/363–4032
(nights)
$25/yr., NL, 9 SIGs,
TS, TE

NEW JERSEY
Morris PC Users
Group
c/o Bill Traywick
P.O. Box 245
Cedar Knolls, NJ
07927
201/635–5393
$10/yr., NL, 1 SIG, BBS

ABBREVIATIONS KEY:

NL: newsletter SIG: special interest group TS: technical support TE: training
and education BBS: bulletin board service SL: software library (User groups are
listed alphabetically by state and city, not by user group name.)

Philadelphia Area IBM
PC Club
c/o Steve Longo
2041 Harbour Dr.
Palmyra, NJ 08065
215/951–1255
$30/yr., NL, 60 SIGs,
TS, TE, BBS

New Jersey PC Users'
Group
c/o Neil Stewart
P.O. Box 14
Paramus, NJ
07643–0014
201/664–3311
$25/yr., 2 SIGs, BBS

Amateur Computer
Group of New Jersey
c/o David Wrobel
P.O. Box 135
Scotch Plains, NJ
07076
201/264–8242
$15/yr., NL, 9 SIGs,
TS, TE, BBS

Computer Connection
c/o Ted Hare
P.O. Box 382
Voorhees, NJ 08043
609/783–7444
$15/yr., TS, BBS

NEW YORK
Buffalo IBM PC User
Group
c/o Peter Calendo
P.O. Box 1487
Buffalo, NY
14231–1487
716/832–1415
$20/yr., NL, 13 SIGs,
TS, TE, BBS

Long Island Computer
Assoc.
c/o Al Levy
P.O. Box 71
Hicksville, NY 11802
516/293–8368,
516/561–6590 (BBS)
$25/yr., NL, 22 SIGs,
TS, TE, BBS

New York IBM Users
Group
40 Wall St. #2124
New York, NY 10005
212/533–6972
$25/yr., NL, 24 SIGs,
TS, TE, BBS

ABBREVIATIONS KEY:

NL: newsletter SIG: special interest group TS: technical support TE: training and education BBS: bulletin board service SL: software library (User groups are listed alphabetically by state and city, not by user group name.)

Central New York PC
Users' Group
c/o Ted Williamson
P.O. Box 6411
Teall Station
Syracuse, NY
13217–6411
315/455–2833,
315/458–6812 (BBS)
$15/yr., NL, TS, TE,
BBS

Westchester PC User's
Group
P.O. Box 349
White Plains, NY
10602–0349
914/762–5248
$25/yr., NL, 3 SIGs,
TS, TE, BBS

NORTH CAROLINA
IBM PC Users Club of
Asheville
c/o Bruce Rogers
P.O. Box 2942
Asheville, NC 28802
$15/yr., 3 SIGs

PC Club of Charlotte
c/o John Callahan
1813 Kenwood Ave.
Charlotte, NC 28205
704/377–0400
$15/yr., NL, TS, TE,
BBS

NORTH DAKOTA
Fargo IBM PC Users'
Group
c/o J. Grettum
P.O. Box 9121
Fargo, ND 58109
701/232–3332
$12/yr., TE, BBS

OHIO
IBM PC Users Group
c/o Edward Baum
Ohio University
Athens, OH 45701
614/593–1334
$15/yr., NL, 2 SIGs,
TS, TE, BBS

Cincinnati Personal
Computer Users
Group
c/o Darrel Booth
P.O. Box 3097
Cincinnati, OH 45201
513/745–9356
$20/yr., NL, 6 SIGs,
TS, TE, BBS

Columbus Computer
Society
c/o George Rowcliffe
P.O. Box 1556
Columbus, OH 45216
614/878–8925
$25/yr., NL, 16 SIGs,
TS, TE, BBS

ABBREVIATIONS KEY:

NL: newsletter SIG: special interest group TS: technical support TE: training
and education BBS: bulletin board service SL: software library (User groups are
listed alphabetically by state and city, not by user group name.)

Lake Ashtabula IBM
PC Users Group
c/o John Dakos
5920 Shore Dr.
Madison, OH 44057
216/428–4512
$12/yr., NL, 3 SIGs,
TS, TE

Southwest General
Hospital PC Users
Group
c/o Bob Dykas
18679 E. Bagley Rd.
Middleburg Heights,
OH 44130
216/826–8077
$10/yr., NL, TS, TE

Toledo PC Users
Group
c/o Jim Yoder
P.O. Box 13085
Toledo, OH 43613
419/471–9444
$20/yr., NL, 2 SIGs,
TE, TS, BBS

Western Reserve IBM
PC Assoc.
c/o Gerald Kolar
P.O. Box 8828
Warren, OH 44484
216/373–2745
$15/yr., NL, TS, TE

Greater Cleveland PC
Users Group
c/o Roy McCartney
30704 Royalview Dr.
Willowick, OH 44094
216/944–5173
$20/yr., NL, TS, BBS

OREGON
Eugene PC Users
Group
c/o Jim Cox
P.O. Box 11436
Eugene, OR 97440
503/726–2221
$25/yr., NL, 3 SIGs,
TS, TE

PENNSYLVANIA
Harrisburg PC Users
Group
c/o Jack Stahl
1195 Fairmont Dr.
Harrisburg, PA 17112
717/652–9097,
717/944–6877
$10/yr., NL, 2 SIGs,
TS, BBS

ABBREVIATIONS KEY:

NL: newsletter SIG: special interest group TS: technical support TE: training
and education BBS: bulletin board service SL: software library (User groups are
listed alphabetically by state and city, not by user group name.)

Philadelphia Area
Computer Society
c/o Steve Longo
LaSalle University
P.O. Box 312
Philadelphia, PA 19141
215/951–1255
$20/yr., NL, 72 SIGs,
TS, TE, BBS

Pittsburgh Area
Computer Club
c/o Phil Cutrara
P.O. Box 6440
Pittsburgh, PA 15212
412-321–3181
$20-yr., NL, 6 SIGs,
TS, TE, BBS

RHODE ISLAND
Greater Rhode Island
IBM Satellite Group
c/o Hilde Gesch
University of Rhode
Island
Academic Computer
Center, Tyler Hall
#048
Kingston, RI 02881
401/792–2301 (days)
$35/yr., NL, 20 SIGs,
TS, TE, BBS

SOUTH CAROLINA
The Charleston
Computer Club

c/o Michael Finefrock
P.O. Box 520
Charleston, SC
29402–0520
803/722–7445,
803/792–5806 (BBS)
$19/yr., NL, 2 SIGs,
TS, TE, BBS

Palmetto PC Users
Group of South
Carolina
c/o H.D. "Skip" Mann
120 Parkshore Dr. W
Columbia, SC 29223
$20/yr., 8 SIGs, SL,
BBS

TENNESSEE
E. Tennessee PC Users
Group
11123 Concord Woods Dr.
Knoxville, TN 37922
$10/yr., NL, TE

Memphis PC Users
Group, Inc.
c/o John Slavick
P.O. Box 241756
Memphis, TN
38124–1756
901/767–3493
$25/yr., NL, TS, TE,
BBS

ABBREVIATIONS KEY:

NL: newsletter SIG: special interest group TS: technical support TE: training
and education BBS: bulletin board service SL: software library (User groups are
listed alphabetically by state and city, not by user group name.)

Music City IBM PC
Users Group
c/o Alan Ashendorf
488 Saddle Dr.
Nashville, TN 37221
615/662–0322
$25/yr. ($35/yr. family, $200/yr.
corporation), NL, TE,
BBS

IBM PC Users Group
c/o Ross Burrus
Scientific Applications,
Inc.
Plaza Tower #801
Oak Ridge, TN 37830
615/482–6649
$25/yr., NL, TE

TEXAS
Golden Triangle PC
Club
c/o Judy Allen
Rt. 3, Box 502
Beaumont, TX 77630
409/898–2191
$10/yr., NL, TS, TE,
BBS

North Texas PC Users
Group, Inc.
c/o Zach Porterfield
P.O. Box 780066
Dallas, TX
75378–0066

214/746–4699
$24/yr., NL, 22 SIGs,
TS, TE, BBS

Southwest IBM PC
Users Group
P.O. Box 870236
Dallas, TX
75287–0236
214/790–8960 (BBS)
$30/yr., NL, 3 SIGs,
TS, TE, BBS

Forth Worth IBM PC
Users Group
c/o Marie Schaefer
P.O. Box 1476
Fort Worth, TX
76101–1476
$24/yr., NL, 4 SIGs,
BBS

Bay Area PC
Organization
c/o Earl Rubenstein
P.O. Box 58098
Houston, TX 77058
713/483–0540
$15/yr., NL, 4 SIGs,
TS, TE, BBS

ABBREVIATIONS KEY:

NL: newsletter SIG: special interest group TS: technical support TE: training and education BBS: bulletin board service SL: software library (User groups are listed alphabetically by state and city, not by user group name.)

Houston Area League
PC Users, Inc.
P.O. Box 61266
Houston, TX
77208–1266
713/524–2572
$25/yr., NL, 45 SIGs,
TS, TE, BBS

Dallas-Fort Worth
Users Group
c/o Samuel Cook
309 Lincolnshire
Irving, TX 75061
214/986–9228
$30/yr., NL, TS, TE,
BBS

Longview Computer
Users Group
c/o W.C. McLendon
P.O. Box 9284
Longview, TX 75608
214/753–4626
$15/yr., NL, 1 SIG, TS,
TE, BBS

North Dallas PC Users
Group
c/o John Keohane
735 Scottsdale Dr.
Richardson, TX 75080
214/690–8092
No fee, TE

SPE Microcomputer
Applications Committee
Society of Petroleum
Engineers
c/o Pamela Kelly
P.O. Box 833836
Richardson, TX
75083–3836
214/669–3377
$10/yr., NL, BBS

Ft. Bend Computer
Users Group
c/o Cal Wainwright
P.O. Box 292
Richmond, TX 77469
713/341–0220
$25/yr., NL, 4 SIGs,
TS, TE

Tyler Computer Club
c/o Marionetta Smith
4928 Richmond Rd.
Tyler, TX 75703
214/561–6136
$20/yr., NL, 4 SIGs, TE

Baylor PC Users
Group
c/o Gary Fleming
1912 S. 5th #458
Waco, TX 76706
817/755–7603
$10/yr., NL

ABBREVIATIONS KEY:

NL: newsletter SIG: special interest group TS: technical support TE: training
and education BBS: bulletin board service SL: software library (User groups are
listed alphabetically by state and city, not by user group name.)

UTAH

The Computer
Pioneers
c/o Robert Posey
P.O. Box 338
Orem, UT 84057
$30/yr., NL, TS, TE

Utah Blue Chips
P.O. Box 510811
Salt Lake City, UT
84151
801/521-7830
$15/yr., NL, 5 SIGs,
TS, TE, BBS

Utah Corporate PC
Users Group
c/o Ross Nichol
First Security Corp.
P.O. Box 25247
Salt Lake City, UT
84125
801/350-6714
No fee, TE

VIRGINIA

Central Virginia IBM
PC Users Group
P.O. Box 34446
Richmond, VA 23234
$15/yr., NL, 4 SIGs, TE

WASHINGTON

Pacific Northwest IBM
PC Users Group
c/o Roland Cole
P.O. Box 3363
Bellevue, WA 98009
206/525-3452
$20/yr., NL, 15 SIGs,
TS, TE, BBS

Lower Columbia IBM
PC Users Group
c/o Fred Mattfield
P.O. Box 978
Long Beach, WA
98631
206/642-4786
$10/yr., NL, TS, TE

Tacoma Area PC Users
Group
c/o Lewis Chichester
2811 Bridgeport Way
#24
Tacoma, WA 98466
206/565-4917
$15/yr., 9 SIGs, TS, TE,
BBS

ABBREVIATIONS KEY:

NL: newsletter SIG: special interest group TS: technical support TE: training and education BBS: bulletin board service SL: software library (User groups are listed alphabetically by state and city, not by user group name.)

WEST VIRGINIA
Huntington PC Users
Group
c/o Jim Forbush
PC HUG
P.O. Box 2173
Huntington, WV
25722–2173
304/525–0404,
304/525–2031 (BBS)
$12/yr., NL, 4 SIGs,
TS, TE, BBS

WISCONSIN
Madison IBM PC
User's Group
c/o Denise Rall
P.O. Box 2598
Madison, WI
53701–2598
608/238–8119
$20/yr., NL, 4 SIGs,
BBS

Milwaukee Area IBM
PC Users Group
P.O. Box 2121
Milwaukee, WI 53201
414/679–9075
$12/yr., NL, 6 SIGs,
TS, TE, BBS

CANADA
North Alberta PC User
Group
c/o James Laviolette
8 Greenwood Pl.
Saint Albert, Alberta
T8N 2H5 Canada
403/458–9066
SL, BBS

IBM PC Users Group
of Winnipeg
c/o Membership
Secretary
P.O. Box 3149
Winnipeg, Manitoba
R3C 4E6 Canada
204/474-8319
$30/yr., NL, TS, BBS

Montreal IBM PC Users
Club (French language group)
c/o Carlos Verrando
P.O. Box 587
Station K
Montreal, Quebec
H1N 3R2 Canada
514/355–7070
$30/yr., NL, 8 SIGs,
TS, TE, BBS

ABBREVIATIONS KEY:

NL: newsletter SIG: special interest group TS: technical support TE: training and education BBS: bulletin board service SL: software library (User groups are listed alphabetically by state and city, not by user group name.)

Here is a closer look at the two largest Eastern Corridor PC Users Groups.

New Jersey PC User Group (NJPC)

NJPC is composed of individuals who want to learn more about personal computers, network with fellow members, and share the wealth of their collective knowledge. The first hour of their meeting is devoted to questions and answers: ideas, insights, problems, and solutions related to the PC are discussed. After a short break, they reconvene for the evening's scheduled presentation, usually an expert discussing a specific topic or a representative from a vendor such as IBM, WordPerfect, Hayes, or Lotus.

The NJPC meets monthly at Bergen Community College, Room 155 in East Hall, on the second Thursday of each month. Admission is free to members; nonmembers are welcome and asked to contribute a nominal fee for the evening. Most groups similar to NJPC choose similar meeting facilities.

A monthly newsletter is mailed to all members and other user groups. It contains notices on scheduled speakers, articles, and reviews written by NJPC members or reprinted from the newsletters of other user groups across the U.S., Canada, England, and Australia.

The NJPC User Group maintains a public domain software library with over 100 programs on diskette. These programs can be purchased for a nominal charge during monthly meetings. In addition, every member receives a free diskette listing NJPC User Group membership and current information.

NJPC's electronic Bulletin Board Service is operated on an AT Clone using PC Board, a Hayes 9600 V-series modem and contains over 100 megabytes of programs. It is available to the public 24 hours a day.

Membership is open to anyone with an interest in the personal computer, and dues are nominal. For more information write NJPC User Group, P.O. Box 14, Paramus, NJ 07653–0014.

New York PC User Group (NYPC)

NYPC is the New York metropolitan area's largest personal computer user group. Founded in 1982, NYPC originally fulfilled the critical need for exchange of information in the early days of PC computing. That's still their primary mission, but in the 1990s, the group has grown to embrace a wide range of users, from corporate managers, small business owners, and consultants to those just interested in PCs for the fun of it.

While most members still use DOS-based machines, the group's focus has expanded to include OS/2, Unix, and the Mac platforms. NYPC now has over 40 special interest groups (SIGs) meeting most of the year.

NYPC's highlight each month is the General Meeting, open to members and nonmembers alike. At least half of each meeting is devoted to random access and networking. Members can seek recommendations; report bugs and incompatibilities; solve others' problems; and make personal contact with each other. Every month a major presentation is given by a vendor or an industry leader. Speakers have included Bill Gates, Peter Norton, Esther Dyson, and Bill Machrone—all heavyweights in the PC industry. NYPC has also hosted product introductions from Microsoft, Lotus, and Borland among major PC vendors.

Monthly meeting information is available on the NYPC Hotline. NYPC membership is required for continued attendance at SIG meetings. Some of the SIGs have a small yearly membership fee of their own to cover expenses, demonstration equipment, and reproduction of program code and other materials.

NYPC publishes an 80-page magazine 10 times a year. It features reviews and columns by members, many of whom are recognized experts in their specialty areas. The magazine also features news about SIGs, classified ads (free to members), and special discounts and offers. A separate, four-page calendar is published each month detailing SIG meetings and other events.

NYPC has its own bulletin board system. There are several conferences on the BBS and a wide range of downloadable free software, utilities, and shareware is available. The BBS can be used by anyone, but current NYPC members are granted extended access time. NYPC also operates a 24-hour voice information system, accessed from any touch-tone phone. NYPC Hotline is easy to use, there are up-to-date announcements on our SIGs, the General Meeting and other activities.

NYPC conducts on-going classes and semi-annual seminars. From basic DOS, to some very advanced topics available nowhere else, NYPC devotes much of its resources to a continuing educational program.

NYPC offers the following types of membership:

- Regular individual members each receive the monthly NYPC Magazine and the monthly Calendar listing Special Interest Group activities and other meetings. Regular members can attend SIG meetings, participate in all other NYPC activities, receive discounts, and vote in elections.
- Student memberships, with the same benefits as regular memberships, are available to senior citizens, full-time students, or others with financial hardship.
- Corporate memberships are governed by special plans for corporations and organizations. Individuals joining under a corporate plan receive the same benefits as individual members, plus special discounts and other benefits. If your firm is not a corporate sponsor of NYPC, you can join by contacting the NYPC Vice President.

In a typical month the New York PC Users Group holds conferences, seminars, and workshops on such diverse topics as nonprofits, computing, using Lotus, project management, security, desktop publishing, investments, experts systems, voice technology, using consultants, census and public data, local area networks, CD-ROM, graphics, spreadsheets, computing for religious groups, new software, and computer design.

With such a diverse array of interest and topics, it is easy to see how, as a vendor, one may contact such groups, make presentations, offer a service, or advertise within their publications. The key in marketing to PC users groups, and a general key to marketing in the 90s is to become an insider. Know the niche well, know their needs, and appeal to them in language they are responsive to.

For more information write to: New York PC Membership, 40 Wall Street, Suite 2124, New York, NY 10005–1031.

SMALL BUSINESS SUPPORT GROUPS WITH SIGNIFICANT HBE MEMBERSHIP

Several small business association and advocacy support groups exist whose membership contains significant numbers of HBEs or traditional entrepreneurs who often work at home.

The Powerful Chamber

The Chamber of Commerce of the United States, with more than 260,000 members, is organized on three levels, including local, state, and national. On the national level, the Chamber of Commerce works with developing local and state Chambers and represents national business interests to the federal government.

State Chambers coordinate local Chamber programs and represent the state business community to the state government. Information on small business programs in the state is available through the state Chamber. Local Chambers serve the local business community with programs in economic development, community and human resources, and public affairs. Programs may include small business development, group and individual counseling on business problems, group seminars on management and start-up assistance, and lending and equity capital programs.

The Chamber's Small Business Programs Office serves as a central clearinghouse for information on getting started in business, expanding business overseas, and managing a business. The State and Local Chamber List provides a complete list of state and local Chambers that have small business and export assistance programs.

For more information write to: Chamber of Commerce of the United States, 1615 H St., NW, Washington, DC 20062.

The Largest Small Business Association in the World

The National Federation of Independent Business (NFIB) represents more than 570,000 business owners in the legislatures as well as with state and federal agencies. It is the largest organization representing small and independent merchant-oriented businesses, ranging from one person to more than 300 employees.

NFIB offers information on free enterprise, entrepreneurship and small business, and provides surveys on economic trends, lobbies for members on particular issues, and provides entrepreneurship educational materials. Of particular interest to marketers, NFIB launched *Independent Business* in 1989, a full-featured, high-quality monthly magazine with articles and information on the full gamut of entrepreneurship. For more information, write to: The National Federation of Independent Business, 150 West 20th Avenue, San Mateo, CA 94403. (415) 341–7441.

The National Small Business Association

The NSBA is a membership-based association of business owners representing all types of business. The NSBA presents small businesses's point of view to all levels of government and Congress and develops programs of national policy that are of concern to the small business community.

Key services include providing members with a monthly newsletter and other materials that keep them up-to-date on issues affecting their businesses and alerting members to Federal contracting opportunities through the Bidder's Early Alert Message system. Write to: National Small Business Association, 1604 K St., NW, Washington, DC 20006.

Manufacturers Large and Small

The National Association of Manufacturers (NAM) D. C., a group widely recognized by large corporations, consists of 15,000 manufacturing firms, with a majority classified as small business. Member firms account for 80 percent of the nation's industrial capacity. NAM is a strong voice in Washington, D. C. for the manufacturing community. It provides members with an opportunity to participate in the public policy process through membership on 14 policy committees. Major subject areas include:

- Resource and technology—energy, environment, innovation, and natural resources.
- International economic affairs—international investment, finance, and trade.
- Industrial relations—labor relations, human resources, employee benefits, loss prevention, and control.
- Government regulation, competition, and small manufacturing.
- Taxation and fiscal policy.

NAM services include a roster of 100 subject specialists, including legislative specialists, lawyers, communications advisors, and public affairs experts, who help members with questions and problems. The NAM Member Service Guide provides the names and telephone numbers of these specialists. Also, *Enterprise,* NAM's monthly magazine, focuses on emerging issues. Write to: NAM, 1776 F St., NW, Washington, D. C. 20006.

Women Business Owners Unite

The National Association of Women Business Owners consists of 40 local chapters and several thousand members nationwide. NAWBO helps female business owners to expand their operations and represents female business interests to federal and state governments.

NAWBO services include providing counseling and technical assistance at the local level, primarily through networking with local members, holding monthly programs at the local chapters, which address female business owner problems, and sponsoring an annual national conference which provides management and technical assistance training through workshops and seminars.

NAWBO is the only dues-based national organization representing the interests of all women entrepreneurs in all types of businesses. It is affiliated with the World Association of Women Entrepreneurs (Les Femmes Chefs d'Entreprises Mondiales) in 23 countries.

Membership in NAWBO offers opportunities for members to expand their business horizons to national and international levels. Among the member benefits are:

- National and international networking opportunities.
- Multi-state regional retreats, seminars, and training programs.
- National health insurance programs.
- A professional lobbying network in Washington, D.C.
- National membership directory.
- Bi-monthly newsletter and special member reports outlining national and international events, and business and legislative developments.
- Discounts on travel, car rentals, business equipment, credit cards, and business publications.

- International trade missions.
- A nationally syndicated radio program.
- Annual Public Affairs Day in Washington, D.C.
- National and international leadership and managerial opportunities.

For more information write to: NAWBO, 221 N. La Salle Street, Suite 2026, Chicago, IL 60601.

The largest chapter of NAWBO is the New Jersey Association of Women Business Owners (NJAWBO). Its primary objective is to support and encourage business ownership by women. Incorporated in 1978, today NJAWBO has approximately 1,000 members in 15 chapters throughout New Jersey.

Membership in NJAWBO offers one many opportunities to make new business contacts. Among the benefits are:

- Local, regional, and statewide networking opportunities.
- Monthly chapter meetings and semi-annual regional meetings with guest speakers, panel discussions, and participatory programs.
- Educational programs, workshops, seminars, and retreats.
- Legislative advocacy through lobbying on business issues.
- Life, health, and dental insurance.
- Speakers bureau.
- Membership directory listing members alphabetically, by business and by chapter.
- Monthly statewide newsletter.
- Annual conference with informative workshops, a formal dinner honoring women of achievement, networking opportunities, exhibit areas, and a business meeting that establishes policy and elects state officers.
- Affiliation with other business organizations.
- Interaction with state agencies.
- Leadership and managerial opportunities.

Like its sister organizations in other states, NJAWBO offers four categories of membership: Active, Associate, Student, and Sustaining. An Active Member is a woman who is a sole proprietor, or a partner (or corporate officer) owning at least 15 percent of the partnership (or corporate shares) or less than 15 percent if the partnership (or corporation) is 51 percent female-owned and holds policymaking roles in the partnership (or corporation). Or, a woman who financially maintains business facilities as her major source of employment and income (includes commissioned agents, brokers, independent contractors, and consultants).

An Associate Member acknowledges and follows the objectives of NJAWBO but does not qualify for Active membership. A Student Member is not a business owner but attends an educational institution on an undergraduate, full-time basis or as a postgraduate.

A Sustaining Member has retired from business, has previously been a NJAWBO member and is at least 62 years of age. When one joins NJAWBO as an Active or Associate member, NAWBO membership is included.

To contact NJAWBO write to: New Jersey Association of Women Business Owners, Inc. 120 Finderne Avenue, Bridgewater, NJ 08807.

UNITED WE STAND

Small Business United (SBU) is a network of regional small business organizations, representing these organizations and the concerns of small business before lawmakers. SBU works regularly with Congressional and Executive Branch officials in Washington and the field. SBU offers no direct services to small business in particular, rather it is a networking organization. Write to: SBU, 69 Hickory Drive, Waltham, MA 02154. (617) 890–9070.

Direct services are offered by SBU-member organizations. Member organizations often offer publications that provide key regional information. Below is a listing of these organizations.

Smaller Business Association of New England
69 Hickory Drive
Waltham, MA 02254
(617) 890–9070

Smaller Manufacturers' Council
339 Boulevard of the Allies
Pittsburgh, PA 15222
(412) 391–1622

> Serves western Pennsylvania, eastern Ohio, and northern West Virginia.

Independent Business Association of Wisconsin
3 S. Pinckney Street, Suite 26
Madison, WI 53703
(608) 251–5546

Council of Smaller Enterprise
690 Huntington Building
Cleveland, OH 44115
(216) 621–3300

> Serves the greater Cleveland and surrounding region.

Small Business Association of Michigan
P.O. Box 16158
Lansing, MI 48901
(517) 482–8788

Independent Business Association of Illinois
8565 W. Dempster,
Suite 200
Niles, IL 60648
(312) 692–7306

Ohio Small Business Council
Ohio Chamber of Commerce
35 E. Gay Street
Columbus, OH 43215
(614) 228–4201

Other small business support groups include:

American Woman's Economic Development Corp.
60 East 42nd Street, #405
New York, NY 10165
(212) 692–9100

Offers telephone counseling for fee and sponsors an annual Spring conference. This group has trained more than 100,000 women on how to launch a business. Publishes *Woman Entrepreneur,* a monthly newsletter.

Center for Entrepreneurial Management
180 Varick Street
New York, NY 10014
(212) 633–0600

Offers a variety of intensive courses on entrepreneurship. Also publishes several texts. A one-stop center for serious small business owners.

International Franchise Association
1350 New York Avenue, NW Suite 900
Washington, DC 20005
(202) 628–8000

Membership organization of more than 800 franchisors, member fee is based on franchise sales. Publishes a directory of franchisors and several guides to successful franchising.

National Small Business United
1155 15th Street, NW #710
Washington, DC 20005
(202) 293–8830

A lobbying group for 50,000 members, publishes a monthly magazine, sponsors special conferences, issues retreats, and seminars.

Other HBE and small business support groups can be found through several key directories, available in anylibrary. Also, cited here for their value in pinpointing HBE conventions and meetings, some of the leading directories include:

Directories in Print,
Julie E. Towell, editor. Gale Research: Detroit, MI. An annotated guide to more than 10,000 business and industrial

directories, professional and scientific rosters, directory data bases, and other lists and guides published in the United States that are national or regional in scope.

Encyclopedia of Business Information Sources,
James Woy, editor. Gale Research: Detroit, MI. Name, address, phone number, and citation on more than 9,000 different organizations, publishers, and institutions providing business information resources.

Gales Encyclopedia of Associations,
published by Gale Research: Detroit, MI. A four volume set describing more than 22,000 active associations, organizations, clubs, and other nonprofit membership groups in every field of human endeavor. Volumes arranged by national organizations of the United States, geographic and executive indexes, new associations and projects, and international organizations. Also provides two periodical issues of updated information for associations listed in volume one.

National Trade Associations of the United States,
John J. Russell, managing editor. Published by Columbia Books Inc., Washington, D.C. Provides 6,200 active national trade and professional associations and labor unions, including the year founded, the name of the executive director, number of members, staff size, annual budget, historical note, names of publications and date, place, and expected attendance of the annual meeting.

Hot Tips and Insights from Chapter 8
- One effective way to penetrate HBE's niches is by becoming an insider to the groups you've targeted.
- Your ability to sense, serve, and satisfy needs of targeted HBEs in ways in which they perceive the value will result in marketing success.
- Developing an insider's reputation in targeted HBE groups minimizes the amount of rejection you will experience when marketing to the niche, and helps to prompt new business inquiries from those who know and trust you. When members of the niche regard you as one of

them, you've built the trust and rapport that lead to marketing success.

- There are at least four strategies for developing an insider's reputation among HBEs groups, including becoming an active, accepted, visible, and working-serving member of the infrastructure; creating, maintaining, and enhancing a favorable awareness of themselves, their firm, and its services; stimulating inquiries from high-potential customers; and paving the way or gaining acceptance on the part of targets when making mailings and telephone contacts.
- The key to effectively penetrating a targeted niche and attaining insider status, however, is maintaining an image and reputation that you are different and/or better than the competition, and then living up to that reputation.
- Promotional activities and marketing opportunities emerge by being involved in "forums"—organizations, networks, groups, and publications made up of, and read by, your targets.
- The HBE support groups fall into three major categories, including HBE-Focused Groups, PC User Groups, and Small Business Groups.
- Many HBE entrepreneurs network through subscriber services such as CompuServe and join forums on home-based business.
- Local and regional electronic networks are rapidly springing up, many through PC users groups. These electronic networks are low-cost and they only take the time of the system operator (sysop) whose computer hosts the network.
- On these networks, HBEs and the vendors who have established themselves as insiders discuss common issues, exchange information about products, and download computer files with business tips.
- An effective way to target HBEs is through state and local PC users groups, whose memberships often number in the thousands, and many of whom are HBEs or future

HBEs. Every August *PC Magazine* publishes a roster of PC user groups.

- Several small business association and advocacy support groups exist whose membership contains significant numbers of HBEs or traditional entrepreneurs who do work at home on many occasions.
- Other HBE and small business support groups can be found through several key directories, available in any library, such as *Directories in Print, Gales Encyclopedia of Associations,* and *National Trade Associations of the United States.*

CHAPTER 9

USING TRADE SHOWS TO BOLSTER MARKETING EFFORTS

---

*All the world's a stage and all men
and women merely actors and
actresses playing their parts.*
William Shakespeare

Home-based entrepreneurs attend trade shows and conventions to learn about the latest equipment that can help increase their productivity. Trade shows are a real time-saver for them; they can spend a few hours picking up what would have taken them many more hours of reading and can easily visit the booths of many vendors. One way to gain maximum marketing leverage of your time and resources is by exhibiting at trade shows. Another more challenging approach is to sponsor your own.

Trade shows are sacred turf. If something can be shown to prospective buyers or clients—even if only in a picture—there is probably an annual or semi-annual trade show related to it. Trade shows are a major and fast growing method for demonstrating products and services and represent key positioning opportunities for savvy vendors. In the 1990s, trade shows for HBEs will grab hold and become exceedingly well-attended events.

Well over 1,700 exhibits and trade shows are held annually in the United States. More than 20,000 association-based conventions and exhibitions are held annually, with many listed in the book *Directory of Conventions*. See address on page 211.

Trade Shows Offer Many Opportunities

• Low cost per prospect
• A chance to create your own forum
• Obtain roster of participants and attendees
• Gain instant visibility
  Make on-the-spot sales
• Monitor competitors
• Test sales offerings
• Gain immediate feedback

A growing number of vendors to HBEs have found that using trade shows as a marketing vehicle can provide an effective cost-to-benefit ratio. In fact, the cost per new customer of exhibiting at trade shows can be lower than many of the other marketing vehicles.

CREATING YOUR OWN FORUM

The creation of a publicity event, such as a regional or national forum, is advanced strategy for those vendors who are ready to make a bold statement about their relationship to the HBE niche targeted. Hosting events makes a powerful declaration to the niche: "We own the niche," "We preempted it," and "We are the educational force."

There are many organizations that have achieved this type of positioning in their respective niches. If you don't have the resources or wherewithal to host your own event, as part of your ongoing task in developing an insider's understanding of your selected niche, you'll want to at least ascertain which groups, if any, are hosting such meetings.

Let's look at a prime example of an organization that serves HBEs, which made a decisive step to take a position of leadership within the industry.

The Home Office Computing Small Business Conference and Expo

From October 26 to 28, 1990, a historic occasion for the home-based business revolution occurred in the Harmon Meadow Convention Center in Secaucus, New Jersey. *Home Office Computing* magazine, published by Scholastic Press in New York, held its first home office/small business conference and exposition for thousands of HBEs. HOC, with more than 400,000 subscribers, was already a major force among HBEs, providing key information and information services to a fiercely loyal readership. By launching the expo, HOC carved out an undisputable lead position among HBE information services.

The Harmon Meadow exposition provided an opportunity for vendors to showcase products and to meet with customers face-to-face. Everything from laptop computers to supplies, office furniture, copiers, fax machines, printers, security, voice recognition technology, and books were on display. Other vendors presented insurance and credit card services, information on support groups, software to assist with negotiating, marketing, and totally integrating one's home-office management system, and financial services.

Among the big name vendors, products and services were on display from AT&T, American Express, Apple Computer, Avery Products, Borland International, Fuji, Hewlett-Packard, IBM, Intel, Lotus, NEC, Plantronics, Prodigy, SYBEX Computer Books, Tandy/Radio Shack, Toshiba, WordPerfect, WordStar, and XTree Company.

To attract such a large crowd, conference planners charged only a modest fee, and also provided several helpful workshops and hands on sessions on Saturday and Sunday, including "How to do Your Own Public Relations," "Shopping for Software," "Government Giveaways," "A Self Test for Entrepreneurs," "Walk-in Computer Clinic," "Desktop Publishing," "Getting Business to Come to You," "Getting Organized," "Hardware for the Office," and "Starting a Business."

"Press day," held on Friday before the official opening of the expo, drew more than a hundred members of the media, as well as product vendors, association executives, and other key players in the home office market. They assembled at 11:30 A.M. to hear the renowned Alvin Toffler, who has long-championed the home office, and author of *Power Shift, The Third Wave,* and *Future Shock.* Toffler was followed by Claudia Kohl, editor in chief of *Home Office Computing,* and by Paul Reiss, associate publisher of *Home Office Computing.*

Attendees were then treated to an in-depth marketing research presentation by Thomas Miller, vice president and director of LINK Resources, and another by Raymond L. Boggs, director of small business market strategy for BIS CAP International. Then, vendors from Microsoft, Lotus, Xerox, and Hewlett Packard gave detailed presentations on where they thought the home office market was going and how to best penetrate it. In all, the expo represented a bonanza for anyone seeking to enter the home office market or refine his skills in being successful in it. The free flow of information, instant accessibility to experts, and overall tone of friendliness and cooperation made this an event not to be missed.

Fortunately for you, the Home Office Expo will be held in seven additional cities this year, with more planned throughout the 1990s, and will be publicized in *Home Office Computing Magazine* and to attendees of previous conventions.

The beauty of conventions like this and others that will surely follow is the chance to not only meet and interact with key players within the industry but to gain valuable data and insight that might otherwise require extensive time or energy.

Directories Available

Beyond keeping up with the numerous HBE associations and support groups that often sponsor events, there are several resources available to keep tabs on who's meeting where, and when. Trade show directories are available for a small fee or through the local library. The *Directory of Conventions,* published annually by Bill Communications, provides listings of conventions by geographic location. A key word index by industry group or interest is included for reference. Contact:

Research Department—Directory of Conventions
Bill Communications
633 Third Avenue
New York, NY 10017
(212) 986–4800

The *Trade Shows and Professional Exhibits Directory,* edited by Robert J. Elster, gives detailed information for more than 2,200 scheduled exhibitions, trade shows, association conventions and other sales events. It focuses on the United States, but also includes many international shows. It is arranged by subject, gives type of audiences, anticipated attendance and display prices. Write to:

Gale Research Inc. Company
Book Tower
Detroit, MI 48226
(800) 877–GALE

National Trade and Professional Associations (NTPA) contains any annual meeting or convention dates and locations for each association of the 6,200 listed. The geographic, subject (key word), and budget indices permit cross referencing to appropriate associations for small business and HBEs. The same publisher also offers a companion directory entitled *State and Regional Professional Associations.* Contact:

National Trade and Professionals Associations
Columbia Books, Inc.
1212 New York Avenue, NW #330
Washington, DC 20005–3920
(202) 898–0662

One of the associations listed, the International Association of Convention and Visitors' Bureaus, Box 758, Champaign, Illinois 61820, is a good source for information since there is at least one convention bureau in every state. Another good source is the International Exhibitors' Association, 5103 Backlick Road, Annandale, VA 22003.

The *Tradeshow Week Data Book,* published annually by the Tradeshow Bureau, features marketing and statistical data on over 5,000 trade shows. This can be obtained by writing:

Tradeshow Week Data Book
12233 W. Olympic Blvd. #236
Los Angeles, CA 90064
(213) 826–5696

Key Periodicals
In addition to all of the directories cited above, here are a few key periodicals that offer important information on trade-show, expositions and major events. *Tradeshow Week* lists trade shows scheduled by week, for up to six months in advance. Each listing includes the location, contact name, address, phone number, projected square footage of exhibit space, number of booths, number of exhibiting companies, and professional attendance expected.

Tradeshow Week, Inc.
12233 W. Olympic Blvd. #236
Los Angeles, CA 90064
(213) 826–5696

The *Special Events Reports* is an international newsletter on events, festivals and promotions which is published biweekly.

Special Event Reports, Inc.
213 West Institute Place #303
Chicago, IL 60610
(312) 944–1727

The American Society of Association Executives produces a calendar of various programs of affiliated societies that may provide information on relevant trade shows and meetings.

American Society of Association Executives
1575 Eye Street, NW
Washington, DC 20005
(202) 626–2773

EXHIBITING AT TRADE SHOWS

Being part of a trade show is not at all inexpensive, but when you realize how many interested HBEs you will see face-to-face in a short time, especially compared to the time it would take to personally visit each of those, the cost becomes a bargain. To get good exposure by presenting your business at a trade show, don't skimp. You need trained staff on hand to demonstrate your wares, hand out brochures, and answer questions.

You'll have to pay for registration and space rental, and you need to either rent or ship a booth to set up in your space. You also need healthy amounts of written product or service information such as handouts, possibly demonstration models, or a film or video that visually depicts what you are selling.

In addition to these obvious costs, there are substantial costs in terms of your time and the time of other staff, not just during the trade show itself, but in the planning process and in the follow-up that occurs afterwards. The cost of exhibiting can range anywhere from $800–$1,400 for a local or a small scale show to $3,000 or more for a regional or a national show.

Objectives of Exhibiting

Setting very specific objectives for trade show participation allows you to accurately direct every effort you make for the show—from training personnel who will staff the booth to drafting written materials and determining which potential clients to take out to lunch or dinner.

Consider the approach used by many financial services companies when they exhibit at shows. They know most HBEs come to see products, and they also know that they don't have a product to "show." So, they try to get a booth in a central location and decorate it with colorful signs and banners and possibly, some well-produced, lively videos.

They staff it with plenty of trained personnel who are ready to smile and offer, "I'd like to tell you about our outstanding services," to HBEs who just slow down as they are walking by. More importantly, they are ready to sign up clients on the spot. They have stacks of forms to be completed by an HBE. They are ready to offer a membership card or other symbolic token to signify a completed transaction. This is a more active and successful approach than "Here's my card and brochure; give me a call."

Good Prospecting Opportunity

To come away from the show with a list of blue chip prospects for follow-up—HBEs who might not actually buy or sign up for anything on the spot, but who are worth your time in terms of follow-up contacts—can be ensured by securing the roster and addresses of attendees.

If you have not exhibited before, you'll have plenty of homework to do before attempting such a venture. It's easy to make a bad showing if you have no idea of the level of preparation and professionalism required to be successful.

The companies that are most thorough in this regard assemble everybody involved in their exhibit, including company employees, the day before the opening. At that time, they clarify objectives, train local temporary personnel, and prepare a schedule for "working" the booth. Everyone gets the same message about how to handle interested show attendees and how to best represent the company.

Joe Jeff Goldblatt, author of *Special Events: The Art and Science of Celebration,* and former President of the Wonder Company, a Nashville, Tennessee-based special events production company, suggests the following 16 tips to boost booth sales:

1. Send potential attendees (HBEs) a printed piece containing an offer.
2. Make the offer strong enough to motivate them to come buy! Strong offers include free items, major discounts good only the day of the show, and free information and consulting.
3. Design the booth to allow optimum room to demonstrate the product and to negotiate the sale.
4. Make certain the product is illuminated well and is the central focus of the booth design.
5. Ask for business cards for a drawing that will be held after the show.
6. Display the "prize" next to the entry vessel so the prospect can easily see what he might win.
7. Prepare a short, five-question survey that includes space to write down the HBE's name, prior knowledge or use of your product, annual needs for your services, current satisfaction with the product they are now using, and ability to make a decision to try your product.
8. When appropriate, ask the salespeople to try to close sales in the booth. Use the advertised offer as the entry to closing. "Did you receive our special offer in the mail?"
9. Always keep the conversation focused on the product.
10. Be concise, direct, and engaging. The average booth visit is less than one minute! You are producing a live commercial.
11. Keep something like candy in the booth to sweeten up your clients! (If acceptable to show management).
12. Visit all other booths fifteen minutes before opening and tell salespeople of your location and special offer.

13. Consider using a free, instant photo giveaway with an imprinted photo mount for your clients.
14. Make certain that each HBE prospect leaves as a potential client. Give them printed material with your name and phone number so they can follow-up.
15. Rest the day before the trade show. Treat the trade show as a chance to appear in the olympics of your industry. Train!
16. Training includes rehearsing and role playing with your salespeople. Rehearse a script so that it becomes a natural and honest conversation with the potential client.

Once you are back in your office, be sure to follow up on whatever contacts or information you've developed. The contacts you've met also met 200 other people at the show, so your follows up must be swift, informative, and professional.

Here's a quick summary of the benefits you can derive through trade shows:

- Demonstrate new products.
- Find new customers.
- Take orders.
- Develop mailing list.
- Promote the company image.
- Determine what competitors are doing.

If you haven't considered them before, don't overlook the significant opportunities trade shows can offer for reaching HBEs. It's an investment that can pay off in a big way. HBEs are flocking to tradeshows—perhaps you should be there, too.

Hot Tips and Insights from Chapter 9
- Home-based entrepreneurs go to trade shows and conventions to learn about the latest equipment that can help increase their productivity.
- Trade shows are a real time-saver for them; they can spend a few hours picking up what would have taken

them many more hours of reading, and can easily visit the booths of many vendors.

- One way to gain maximum marketing leverage of your time and resources is by exhibiting at trade shows; another more challenging approach is to sponsor your own.
- The creation of a publicity event, such as a regional or national forum, is advanced strategy for vendors ready to make a bold statement about their relationship to the HBE niche targeted.
- *Home Office Computing* magazine in New York held its first home office/small business conference and exposition for thousands of HBEs. With more than 400,000 subscribers, it's already a major force among HBEs, providing key information and information services to a fiercely loyal readership. By launching the expo, HOC carved out an undisputable lead position among HBE information services.
- There are several resources available to keep tabs on who's meeting where, and when, such as the *Directory of Conventions, Trade Shows and Professional Exhibits Directory,* and *National Trade and Professional Associations.*
- Set very specific objectives for trade show participation. This allows you to accurately direct every effort you make for the show—from training personnel who will staff the booth, to drafting written materials, and determining which potential clients to take out to lunch or dinner.
- To come away from the show with a list of blue chip prospects for follow-up—HBEs who might not actually buy or sign up for anything on the spot, but who are worth your time in terms of follow-up contacts—can be ensured by securing the roster and addresses of attendees.

CHAPTER 10

PENETRATING THROUGH PUBLICATIONS

To be able to associate with journalists as
friends, and know what is a good piece of
news, means more than all the well-planned
P.R. activities combined.

Sture Lindmark,
Swedish Association of Wholesalers

HBEs are getting a boost from the proliferation of organizations and associations that publish how-to guidebooks, monthly magazines, newsletters, and special reports all geared to help run home-based businesses profitably. The availability of publications for selected HBE niches makes it easier for you to:

- Collect data and key information on selected groups.
- Use key publications for their mailing lists.
- Write articles to impact selected groups.
- Run low-cost advertisements.
- Gain notice of meetings and events.
- Maintain an insider's understanding.

ORGANIZING YOUR APPROACH TO HBE PUBLICATIONS

The birth of magazines such as *Inc.* in the 1970s marked a new maturity in the small-business market, and the home-based business market is now served its own magazines as well. The publishers of *Entrepreneur* have launched *New Business*

Opportunities, a quarterly magazine devoted solely to business start-ups, with significant coverage of home-based ventures.

In Business is geared to environmental entrepreneurs (the environment already is one of the hottest growth areas for small and home-based business). *Home Office Computing* provides coverage of HBEs who use a computer in some way, and is regarded as the bible of the HBE. Other computer magazines, such as *Personal Computing* and *PC Week,* now provide essential information for the home-based business using a computer. More of these magazines are likely to crop up in the 1990s.

Fortunately, today, identifying the publication read by niche members is relatively easy. The directories listed below collectively list more than 12,000 publications in every topic area. You will be able to identify 90 percent or more of all publications serving your target niche. Each of these directories can be found in your public library:

Bacon's Publicity Checker is published by Bacon Publishing Company in Chicago, IL. It's a two-volume media guide to magazines and newspapers in the United States and Canada containing listings of more than 7,600 business, trade, industrial consumer, and farm publications, and more than 9,000 daily newspapers, weekly newspapers, multiple publishers, news services, and syndicates.

Bacon's provides information as to which publications include new product news, trade literature, general news, personnel news, coming events, byline articles, staff articles, letters to the editor, questions and answers, book reviews, announcement of contract awards, and other information.

Gebbie Press All-In-One Directory is published by Gebbie Press in New Paltz, NY. It provides name, address and phone number, name of editor, number of subscribers, and description of readership in 10 major fields, including daily newspapers, weekly newspapers, AM and FM radio stations, television stations, consumer magazines, business papers, trade press, minority press and radio, farm publications, and news syndicates.

National Directory of Addresses and Telephone Numbers is published by General Information Inc. in Bothell, Washington. It contains 66,000 alphabetical listings of the biggest and most influential organizations in the U.S., including publishers. It also contains 35,000 fax numbers and 9,400 toll-free numbers— 210,000 listings in all.

National Directory of Magazines is published by Oxbridge Communications in New York. It lists all large and small U.S. magazines including description of publication, staff, advertising rates, circulation, and competitive analysis.

Oxbridge Directory of Newsletters is also published by Oxbridge Communications and lists more than 15,000 newsletters including title, publisher, address, telephone number, editor, description of editorial context, year established, frequency, circulation, average number of pages and, of particular importance to home-base marketers, list rental cost.

In addition, *Writers Market, Working Press of the Nation* and *Hudson's Newsletter Directory* are all helpful directories of publications.

INSIDE THE PUBLICATIONS

There are many ways to use niche publications to quickly gain an insider's understanding and to effectively penetrate the niche. Let's examine the wealth of information that is available from these publications that can be used to support your HBE marketing efforts.

Readership Demographics

Nearly all publications maintain information on their readership, including average age, income, sex, job title, and other valuable data. The key to obtaining such information is to write to the advertising department and ask for a copy of the advertising-rate card and readership demographics. The advertising-rate card will explain the various costs and procedures for placing a single or continuous ad within the publication. You can also use *Standard Rate and Data,* which contains information on all major U.S. publications and a directory of advertising-rate cards.

A World of Information Through Publications

- Readership demographics
- Editorial guidelines
- Special issues
- Subscriber mailing lists
- Contents that reveal trends
- Classified advertisements that reveal need
- Opportunity to advertise

Editorial Guidelines

Those who regularly write for magazines know that most editors of larger publications maintain a published set of editorial or author's guidelines. These are available to any-one who asks. These guidelines define the nature and scope of the material the editor is seeking to serve the interest of the readers.

Special Issues

Many publications periodically offer a special issue that highlights developments and trends in the industry. For example, *Home Office Computing* has special issues listing resources. Other publications, such as *Inc.,* are noted for their special directory and industry-focused issues. The editorial calendar will pinpoint when a special issue will be published and outlines the topics and issues for the following year.

Subscriber Mailing Lists

Most publications have subscriber mailing lists for sale. A good mailing list is essential to any direct mail campaign or promotional mailing. Although some publications sell their entire list of subscribers (representing overkill if you only want subscribers in a particular locality), others offer a more targeted list.

In addition, many publications sell their subscriber lists to the direct-mail catalog houses that sometimes offer them to you at a lower cost than the publisher because of high-volume sales. Some established mailing-list houses are presented below. Others can be found in the yellow pages of any phone book.

Alvin B. Zeller, Inc.
475 Park Avenue South
New York, New York 10016
(212) 689–4900
(800) 223–0814 out of state

> Offers lists by state, county, city, metro area, ZIP code and/or SIC on label, magnetic tape, floppy disk, or 3 × 5.

American Business List, Inc.
P.O. Box 27347
Omaha, Nebraska 68127
(402) 331–7169

> Compiles and frequently updates large scale prospect lists from the Yellow Pages.

Hugo-Dunhill Mailing List, Inc.
630 Third Avenue
New York, New York 10017
(212) 682–8030
(800) 223–6454 out of state
Also:
(404) 885–1490 - Atlanta
(312) 726–2177 - Chicago
(213) 469–8231 - Los Angeles
(202) 783–5988 - Washington, D.C.

Offers comprehensive mailing lists and related services and multiple formats.

Professional Mailing List
450 Seventh Avenue
New York, New York 10001
(212) 563–9100
(800) 221–3156 out of state

Presents lists categorized by industry, profession, SIC number, and special markets.

Inside the Magazine Itself

In reviewing any particular publication read by your targeted niche, pay close attention to the following items.

The Masthead. Who publishes, edits, advertises, and circulates the publication? How often is it distributed? Who owns the publication? Is it published in affiliation with some association or other organization? The masthead provides this information.

Table of Contents. In addition to the normal feature articles look for the following:

- Book reports.
- Washington watch.
- Trend watch.
- Columnist.
- Reader surveys.
- Letters to the editor.
- "My say" or opinion pieces.
- HBE profiles.
- New products and services.
- Advertising index.

Classified Ads. This section, particularly if there is a "wanted to buy" section is a give away as to the needs of the readership. Still, many marketers rarely read these sections in their own industry publications.

Other things you will find inside of publications are fairly obvious. Who writes the articles and what kind of bylines are offered? Are articles accompanied by pictures, charts or art work? The publications read by your targets are among the least expensive and the most effective ways to gain inside information, and all while you're seated at your desk.

ADVERTISING THROUGH PUBLICATIONS

Any successful advertising program within HBE publications must be of an ongoing nature. Just one or two ads are not likely to generate the kind of impact necessary to keep the inquiry pipeline open. If you choose to place advertisements, carefully examine several issues of the publication, noting who advertises, what they offer, and the image they convey.

Next, write to the advertising department of the publication and ask for the rate card. Normally, you can achieve substantial discounts by running an ad several times. To determine whether to place an ad, check the cost-per-thousand, the cost of reaching 1,000 members of your targeted niche.

Roster of HBE Publications

The following list, like any list today, is quickly subject to change. Within a twelve-month period, 20 percent of the information provided is likely to be obsolete due to changes of address and phone number, reorganization, merger and acquisition, bankruptcy or cessation of publication, and a host of other reasons.

Advertising, Marketing, Public Relations

Communication Arts
Coyne & Blanchard
P.O. Box 10300
Palo Alto, CA 94303

> Published eight times per year for 55,000 graphic designers, art directors, illustrators in advertising, display, photography, and the arts.

Public Relations Journal
PRSA Publications
33 Irving Place
New York, NY 10003

> Monthly magazine sent to 17,000 members of the Public Relations Society of America; nonmember PR practitioners, students, and executives.

Arts, Graphics

Artist's Magazine
F&W Publications
1507 Dana Avenue
Cincinnati, OH 45207

> Monthly magazine sent to 210,000 serious amateur artists interested in today's artists, their working methods, tools, and material information.

Graphic Studio News
Graphic New York
210 E 38 Street
New York, NY 10016

> Bimonthly tabloid sent to 30,000 decision makers at small ad agencies, graphic design studios, in-house advertising, and graphic departments.

How
RC Publications
104 Fifth Avenue
New York, NY 10011

Bimonthly magazine sent to 43,000 graphic designers, illustrators, commercial photographers, computer graphic designers, and type directors.

Business, Commercial, Stores

Bottom Line-Personal
Boardroom Reports
330 W 42 Street
New York, NY 10036

Bimonthly magazine sent to 600,000 readers (general public) interested in money management; investments; income, gift, and estate taxes; and securities.

Business Age
Business Trend, Inc.
135 W Wells
Milwaukee, WI 53203

Bimonthly magazine sent to 126,000 owners or managers of businesses with staffs of 1 to 50 interested in comprehensive business information.

Business to Business
17222 Armstrong Avenue
Irvine, CA 92714

Monthly magazine sent to 30,000 management personnel of small and medium size business interested in how-to operating information.

Entrepreneur's Magazine
Entrepreneur Group Inc.
2392 Morse Avenue
Irvine, CA 92714

Monthly magazine sent to 208,000 readers (general public) interested in investing in or starting a small business. Subscribers include career agencies, and high schools.

In Business
J.G. Press Inc.
P.O. Box 351
Emmaus, PA 18049

Bimonthly magazine sent to 63,500 individuals interested in starting or managing a new or growing ecology-related businesses; office equipment manufacturers and sellers.

INC. Magazine
38 Commercial Wharf
Boston, MA 02110

Monthly magazine sent to 630,000 managers and owners of expanding companies concerned with all phases of administration.

Journal of Accountancy
AICPA
1211 Avenue of Americas
New York, NY 10036

Monthly magazine sent to 305,000 members of American Institute of Certified Public Accountants; financial, accounting corporation officials.

National Public Accountant
NSPA
1010 N. Fairfax Street
Alexandria, VA 22314

Monthly magazine sent to 23,500 members of National Society of Public Accountants; office managers; bankers; lawyers; and EDP personnel.

Nation's Business
U.S. Chamber of Commerce
1615 H Street, NW
Washington, DC 20062

Monthly magazine sent to 917,000 leaders in business, industry, and national affairs; city, state, federal officials; and general business leaders.

New Business Opportunities
2392 Morse Avenue
Irvine, CA 92714

Quarterly, full-feature magazine offering anecdotes and information on starting a small business. Heavy on entrepreneur profiles.

NSBU Newsletter
1155 15th Street, NW #710
Washington, DC 20005

Monthly newsletter sent to 50,000 NSBU members on lobbying and legislation; contains some how-to advice, and other issues affecting small business.

Personal Sales Power
P.O. Box 5467
Fredericksburg, VA 22403

Monthly magazine sent to 10,000 sales representatives, sales managers, meeting planners, trainers, and consultants.

Practical Accountant
Warren, Gorham, Lamont
One Penn Plaza
New York, NY 10019

Monthly magazine sent to 51,000 accountants in both public and private practice, tax personnel, and estate planners.

Small Business America
National Association for the Self-Employed
P.O. Box 612067
Dallas/Ft. Worth, TX 76118

Published monthly, this tabloid newsletter is for 10,000 self-employed and independent business people.

Small Business Report
Business Research/Communications
203 Calle del Oaks
Monterey, CA 93940

Monthly magazine sent to 52,000 presidents and top management in small businesses interested in banking, legal, tax, insurance, and benefits news.

Training
Lakewood Publications
50 S 9 Street
Minneapolis, MN 55402

Monthly magazine sent to 51,000 specialists in training programs for business, industry, government, universities, colleges, and trade schools.

Woman Entrepreneur
AWED
60 East 42nd Street
New York, NY 10165

>   Monthly newsletter featuring advice for the female entrepreneur, from start-up to veteran.

Building, Management, Real Estate

Apartment Owner/Builder
3220 East Willow St.
Long Beach, CA 90806

>   Monthly magazine sent to 60,000 established and prospective apartment owner/builders interested in legislative, tax, maintenance, and construction news.

Real Estate Today
National Association of Realtors
430 N. Michigan Avenue
Chicago, IL 60611

>   Nine issues per year sent to 770,000 real estate brokers, sales personnel, land developers, and others in related industries nationwide.

Cottage Industry

Alliance
National Alliance of Home-Based Businesswomen
P.O. Box 306
Midland Park, NJ 07432

>   Bimonthly newsletter about home-based business issues especially for women with children.

Family in Business
Center for Family Business
Box 24268
Cleveland, OH 44124

>   A monthly publication that covers all aspects of managing growth and continuity in a successful family business.

Home Business Advocate
Home Business Network
195 Markville Road
Unionville, Ontario L3R4V8
(416) 470–7930

Monthly newsletter targeting regional HBEs featuring advice, information, and tips. Also publishes the *Home Business Directory.*

Home Businessline
397 Post Road
Darien, CT 06820

Monthly newsletter with tips on taxes, marketing, and promotion, as well as information on issues specific to home-business entrepreneurs.

Home Office Computing
Scholastic, Inc.
730 Broadway
New York, NY 10003

Sent to 430,000 monthly. A magazine on home/small business computing covers family business, desktop publishing, and business basics for new and prospective users of home computers interested in integrating computers into everyday life.

Home Run Business Newsletter
Front Office Systems, Inc.
19751 Frederick Road, Suite 326
Germantown, MD 20874

Bimonthly geared toward people who are operating a business from their home with articles on management, law, accounting, and computers.

Home Venture
Home Venture Enterprises
10 Michel Court
Thornhill, ON L4J 3A9 Canada

Monthly newsletter highlighting people who started home based businesses, also includes general tips.

Home Work Digest
EJP Publishing Company
Box 420126
Houston, TX 77242

> Monthly publication offering articles and tips on working from home.

Homebased Business Directory News
Mountain View Systems
930 S. Washington Ave.,
Suite 111
Scranton, PA 18505

> Offers tips and techniques for one-person businesses.

Mind Your Own Business at Home
P.O. Box 14460
Chicago, IL 60614

> Bimonthly newsletter for home-business entrepreneurs.

Mothers' Home Business Network
P.O. Box 423
East Meadow, NY 11554

> Monthly networking newsletter for mothers who work at home. Chapter news, forthcoming seminars and events, how-to information, and encouraging articles.

National Home Business Report
Brabec Productions
Box 2137
Naperville, IL 60565

> Published quarterly, it offers news, information, and guidance with a personal touch for home-based business owners.

Small Business America
National Association for the Self-Employed
2328 Gravel Road
Fort Worth, TX 76118

> Bimonthly tabloid on all aspects of self-employment, entrepreneurship, employee hiring and supervision, and administrative aspects of running a business.

Sideline Business Newsletter
Box 323
18 South 7th Street
Emmaus, PA 18049

Worksteader News
2396 Coolidge Way
Rancho Cordova, CA 95670
Geared towards anyone who works at home.

HBE DIRECTORIES

Some of the publishers listed above, particularly those affiliated with HBE association or support groups, offer membership directories. With both publishers and the organizations listed in the previous chapter, it's always worthwhile knowing if a directory is available and in what form—mailing label, software disk, hardcopy, annual issue, etc.

The *Homebased Business Directory of North America,* for example, published by Mountain View Systems, lists about 2,500 HBEs. The publisher bills it as the "first comprehensive directory to include all types of products and services offered by home-based business owners from every state, province, and territory in North America."

Entries are listed by location, product/service, business name, and owner for easy access. For more information write to: Russ Buchanan, MLS, Mountain View Systems, 930 S. Washington Avenue, Suite 111, Scranton, PA 18505.

EDP, Computers, Publishing

Compute!
Compute Publications
825 7 Avenue
New York, NY 10019

Monthly magazine sent to 270,000 readers (general public) interested in application of personal computers at home, education, and consumer settings.

Computerland Magazine
Computerland Corp.
2901 Peralta Oaks
Oakland, CA 94605

Bimonthly magazine sent to 365,000 ComputerLand customers interested in high-tech information systems used by the general public and manufacturers.

Computerpeople Monthly
Logic Publications
700 N. Green Street
Chicago, IL 60622

Monthly tabloid sent to 45,500 business computer users interested in how technology affects businesses, especially small business operations.

Consumer Electronics Monthly
International Thomson Press
345 Park Avenue, South
New York, NY 10010

Monthly that contains an "office at home" column that discusses what can be done in a home-office.

COSMEP
International Association of Independent Publishers
P.O. Box 703
San Francisco, CA 94101
(415) 922–9490

Home Office
Scholastic, Inc.
730 Broadway
New York, NY 10003

Monthly magazine sent to 455,000 new, prospective, or casual users of home computers interested in integrating computer use into family life.

Lotus
Lotus Publishing Co.
P.O. Box 9123
Cambridge, MA 02139

> Monthly magazine sent to 360,000 management and other personnel using computers; Lotus and other software users interested in in-depth information.

Mac User
Frederic Davis
950 Tower Lane
Foster City, CA 94404

> Monthly magazine.

Macweek
Dan Ruby
525 Brannan
San Francisco, CA 94107

> Weekly magazine.

Macworld
Jerry Borrell
501 Second
San Francisco, CA 94107

> Monthly magazine.

Microtimes
Bam Publications
5951 Canning Street
Oakland, VA 94609

> Monthly magazine sent to 135,000 personal computer owners in California interested in how-to articles, product information and evaluation.

PC Computing
Ziff-Davis Publishing
80 Blanchard Road
Burlington, MA 01801

> Monthly magazine sent to 150,000 highly active PC users interested in information advancing their professional and personal PC applications.

PC Magazine
Ziff-Davis Publishing
One Park Avenue
New York, NY 10016

> Biweekly magazine sent to 550,000 users of IBM/MS DOS PCs software, peripherals, and accessories; also retailers and manufacturers.

PC World
501 Second
San Francisco, CA 94107

> Monthly magazine sent to 475,000 users or potential users of personal computers. Readers are interested in all information including hardware and software.

Personal Computing
Hayden/VNU Business Publications
10 Mullholland Drive
Hasbrouck Heights, NJ 07604

> Monthly magazine sent to 540,000 users interested in the benefits of personal computers, equipment, manufacturers, and retailers.

Publish!
PCW Communications
501 Second Street
San Francisco, CA 94107

> Monthly magazine sent to 100,000 desktop, publishers interested in integrating text graphics and laser printing.

Rainbow
Falsoft, Inc.
P.O. Box 385
Prospect, KY 40059

> Monthly magazine sent to 62,000 current and prospective users of TRS–80 Color, TDF–100, and Dragon–32 interested in programs and general information.

Run
IDG Communications
80 Elm Street
Peterborough, NH 03458

Monthly magazine sent to 180,000 owners of Commodore 64, VIC–20 computers interested in expanding possibilities, applications, and programs.

Engineering, Construction

Carpenter
UBCJA Publishing
101 Constitution Avenue, NW
Washington, DC 20001

Monthly magazine sent to 586,000 members of United Brotherhood of Carpenters and Joiners of America, state, and federal officials.

Construction Times
Webco Publishing
110 S Greeley
Stillwater, MN 55082

Monthly magazine sent to 17,000 architects and builders in the residential construction and remodeling industry interested in industry-related news.

Engineering Times
National Society Professional Engineers
1420 King Street
Alexandria, VA 22314

Monthly tabloid sent to 75,000 engineers in various fields interested in legislative, ethical, competency, and employment practices.

Farm Publications

Cooperative Farmer
Southern States Co-op
Box 26234
Richmond, VA 23260

Nine issues sent to 177,000 members of Southern State Cooperative, agricultural colleges personnel, farm owners and operators.

Farm & Ranch Living
Bob Ottum
Box 643
Milwaukee, WI 53201

> Bimonthly magazine sent to 330,000 full-time farmers and their families interested in a broad range of life-enrichment topics for home and farm.

Farmer
Webb Publishing Company
1999 Sheppard Road
St. Paul, MN 55116

> Twenty-one issues per year sent to 117,500 crop and livestock farmers in Minnesota and North and South Dakota, farm owners, and county agents.

Progressive Farmer
Progressive Farmer, Inc.
P.O. Box 2581
Birmingham, AL 35202

> Monthly magazine sent to 475,000 farm owners, managers, and foremen in the south and southwest; equipment and feed, manufacturers; and suppliers.

Successful Farming
Meredith Corporation
1716 Locust Street
Des Moines, IA 50336

> Fourteen issues per year sent to 575,000 farmers, owners, managers, operators, business managers, bankers, and farm equipment dealers.

Hobbies, Crafts

Antiqueweek
Mayhill Publication
P.O. Box 9
Knightstown, IN 46148

> Weekly tabloid sent to 64,000 interested in antiques, collectibles, historic preservation, auctions, and antique shops.

Craftrends
Archibald Press
6405 Atlantic Blvd.
Norcross, GA 30017

> Monthly magazine sent to 27,000 retailers and wholesalers of craft needlework, home sewing needs, accessories; manufacturers and distributors.

Homesewing Trade News
P.O. Box 286
300 Sunrise Highway
Rockville Centre, NY 11571

Threads
Taunton Press, Inc.
Box 355
Newtown, CT 06470

> Bimonthly magazine sent to 128,000 readers interested in techniques, materials, and design for knitting, sewing, and weaving; manufacturers and retailers.

Quilting
National Quilting Association
P.O. Box 393-AQ
Ellicott City, MD 21043-0393

> Monthly published by a small profit organization serving quilting entrepreneurs and enthusiasts.

Mobile Office

Car Audio & Electronics
CurtCo Publishing
21600 Oxnard Street, # 675
Woodland Hills, CA 91367

> Monthly magazine offering the latest on technology for the car.

Mobile Office
CurtCo Publishing
21600 Oxnard Street, # 675
Woodland Hills, CA 91367

Monthly magazine that offers tips on maintaining high productivity while on the road and integrating car and travel routines with one's office.

Purchasing, Selling, Franchises

Agency Sales Magazine
Manufacturers Agents National Association
Box 3467
Laguna Hills, CA 92653

Monthly magazine sent to 18,000 members of Manufacturers' Agents National Association; business owners, agents, and manufacturers.

Income Opportunities
Davis Publications
380 Lexington Avenue
New York, NY 10017

Monthly magazine sent to 325,000 readers interested in owning their own business, profitable sidelines, direct selling, and franchises.

Making Profit
Communication Channels
6255 Barfield Road
Atlanta, GA 30328

Circulation of 150,000 individuals and distributor sales firms engaged in multi-line franchised sales.

Money Making Opportunities
11071 Ventura Blvd.
Studio City, CA 91604

Eight issues per year sent to 220,000 independent sales personnel, route operators, managers, franchise holders, and small business owners.

Opportunity Magazine
Opportunity Press
6 N. Michigan Avenue
Chicago, IL 60602

Monthly magazine sent to 187,000 jobbers, independent salesmen and saleswomen, party plan operators, agents, and franchise operators.

Spare Time
Kipen Publishing
5810 W. Oklahoma Avenue
Milwaukee, WI 53219

Nine issues sent to 313,000 men and women in full- or part-time sales, route operators and owners, and franchise holders.

Success
Success Magazine, Inc.
342 Madison Avenue
New York, NY 10173

Monthly magazine sent to 425,000 readers interested in motivational and inspirational information relating to greater self-reliance.

Travel

Country Inns Bed & Breakfast
Country Inns
Box 182
S. Orange, NJ 07079

Bimonthly magazine sent to 150,000 readers interested in bed & breakfast travel in the United States and Canada, innkeepers, hotels and motels.

Tour & Travel News
Prescott Visitor
600 Community Drive
Manhasset, NY 11030

Forty-eight issues in tabloid format sent to 50,000 leisure travel agents, tour operators, wholesalers, incentive houses, and leisure travel professionals.

WRITING FOR TARGETED PUBLICATIONS

The publications listed above represent excellent sources to which you may send an article. Given all of the information you have assembled about serving HBEs, it would not be difficult to determine several interesting topics. Your article need not be more than 750 to 1,000 words (three or four double-spaced typed pages). As long as you simply address a hot issue or recurring need of readers, the chance of your article being accepted and published will be high.

Each time you write an article make about 15 copies of it. On the average, every 15 times you mail out a well-written manuscript targeted to appropriate publishers, you will ultimately achieve at least one acceptance. Most editors do not mind receiving simultaneous submissions. In other words, you are also mailing the same article to other editors. You can also mail two or three different articles to one editor at the same time. Mass-mailing increases your chances of getting in print.

Each year between 800,000 and 1 million people in the United States alone have their first article published. Take advantage of the pyramiding process when trying to get published. It is far easier to get a small column published in an HBE newsletter than in a major, nationwide magazine such as *Entrepreneur.*

Once you get published, even in a newsletter, make an attractive reprint, write the words "previous publication" in the corner and include that reprint when sending out other manuscripts to editors of larger publications.

Successful marketers, those who have well-developed systems for penetrating markets, often have mastered techniques for getting into print. Review the most prominent magazines in the niche, and you undoubtedly will find published articles authored by those who have something to sell to HBEs.

Unfounded Fears

Perhaps the greatest obstacle to breaking into print is the concern that what you have to say is not important or how you say it is unacceptable. Both of these fears are unfounded. If you have done your homework, you will know what topics are of concern to the niche.

Continually be on the lookout for reports and written materials you have already developed from which articles can be extracted. Often, with a little work, product or service announcements or press releases you've already written can be converted into articles.

Once you have actually written your article and had it published, many more leveraging opportunities become available. The article reprint can be used to influence editors and accelerate the process of getting published in the future. Beyond that, the article reprint can be used as a promotional tool when contacting prospective clients.

PREPARING ARTICLES TO APPEAL TO HBEs

An advanced strategy in preparing articles to develop an insider's reputation is to include you, your company, and its products and services as the subject of your article. Done skillfully, the article in print, and its reprint, are effective means of establishing a reputation and gaining high visibility. If done as a major feature story, it should be loaded with illustrative applications of how HBEs you have served are better off since being served by you. A variation on this theme is to prepare the same type of article but much shorter, focusing on a particular problem or portion of the problem-solving process.

To produce the major feature story we have been discussing, hook the reader into the case history by quantifying the benefits that you helped the HBE achieve. In other words, at the outset of the article provide a basic summary of what was accomplished and a foreshadowing of what is to follow. Then put the story in perspective by describing the customer and his need. This could include improving sales, reducing costs, or some other objective. Somewhere after the article's midpoint, elaborate on how the product service you provided continues to be used to master the problem. Bring the reader up to the present. Offer an extended explanation of what the HBE is presently doing.

Look through your own files and examine the articles that you have saved. What was it that attracted you to them? The chances are it was the company that had developed a good understanding of your needs and had an ongoing program for developing an insider's reputation.

AN ALTERNATIVE TO ARTICLES

Another way to influence HBE targets through their memberships or publications is through educational flyers. Writing articles may not be your cup of tea. Educational flyers are a useful tool to generate publicity and demonstrate concern for the marketplace. Many marketers to HBEs produce such items. They have titles such as: *Eight Things to Look for in Selecting Database Software, Five Services Your Accountant Should be Providing,* and *How a Fax Board can Streamline Your Business.*

Notice that these are not titles that highlight the specific benefits of your product or service. Rather, they provide general education about the item or service, with the implication being that since your company is aware of such criteria, they also meet them. The educational flyer can readily be converted into an article with minimum effort.

Quill's Booklet Series

Quill Corporation is one of America's largest independent distributors of office products. The company takes a proactive stance in marketing to HBEs nationally as well as marketing to commercial accounts. Quill has found booklets to be particularly effective promotional vehicles.

Quill recently produced a 64-page booklet, for example, entitled *How to Win through Great Customer Service* which emphasized the importance of handling customers with care in an increasingly competitive marketplace. This booklet, the fifth in a series of booklets published by the company, reveals how to hire, train, and supervise service-oriented employees; develop a company-wide commitment to customer service; build and maintain customer loyalty; and monitor customer service operation.

Quill announces the publication of each free booklet through press releases to the organizations and publications serving Quill's market. When a member or reader writes for the free booklet, Quill also encloses their latest office products catalog, complete with bargains, a toll-free number and other ordering conveniences. The recipient of the catalog and booklet is far more likely to remember Quill than if the company had simply mailed a catalog, however captivating its design. The kind of information in Quill's booklets is routinely available in books and magazines on customer service and management. Yet, Quill, and other vendors to HBEs like them, gain many advantages using them.

First, the booklets are a handy size. Many people are inundated by too much information today. Second, it's a product that many recipients will retain, or at least retain for a longer time, than an advertisement or catalog. Third, and perhaps most important, it portrays the company in a highly favorable light. Booklets such as this tend to position the distributors as a caring, committed organization interested in not only selling to its customers, but ensuring that its customers achieve success.

The customer service booklet goes on to describe step-by-step ways to handle customer problems, regain the confidence of disappointed customers, maintain present customers, and win new customers through improved service programs. It also illustrates how losing just one customer each day, each of whom spend only $5.00 per week, can add up to a yearly loss of $9,400.

Quill president Jack Miller says, "providing good service means that a company sets high standards in service and keeps its customers. Customers shouldn't have to choose between low prices and good service." A customer service policy must begin with a commitment by top management. Miller says, "It isn't a question of what customer service costs, failure to meet customers' expectations can be disastrous."

To receive a copy of the booklet as a model for producing one in your own business, or to simply benefit through the suggestions offered, write to Quill Corporation, 100 South Schelter Road, P.O. Box 464, Lincolnshire, IL 60069. The company requests $2.25 for postage and handling.

Hot Tips and Insights from Chapter 10
- HBEs are getting a boost from the proliferation of organizations and associations that publish how-to guidebooks, monthly magazines, newsletters, and special reports all geared to help run home-based businesses profitably.
- The availability of publications for selected HBE niches makes it easier for you to collect data and key information on selected groups; use key publications for their mailing lists; write articles to impact selected groups; run low-cost advertisements; gain notice of meetings and events; and maintain an insider's understanding.
- Identifying the publication read by niche members is relatively easy. The following directories, found in any library, collectively list more than 12,000 publications in every topic area: *Bacon's Publicity Checker, Gebbie Press All-In-One*

Directory, National Directory of Addresses and Telephone Numbers, National Directory of Magazines, Oxbridge Directory of Newsletters, as well as *Writers Market, Working Press of the Nation,* and *Hudson's Newsletter Directory.*

- Nearly all publications maintain information on their readership, including average age, income, sex, job title, and other valuable data. The key to obtaining such information is to write to the advertising department and ask for a copy of the advertising-rate card and readership demographics.
- Those who regularly write for magazines know that most editors of larger publications maintain a published set of editorial or author's guidelines. These are available to anyone who asks. These guidelines define the nature and scope of the material the editor is seeking to serve the interest of the readers.
- Most publications have subscriber mailing lists for sale. Although some publications sell their entire list of subscribers (representing overkill if you only want subscribers in a particular locality), others offer a more targeted list.
- The publications read by your targets are among the least expensive and the most effective ways to gain inside information, and all while you're seated at your desk.
- Some of the publishers listed above, particularly those affiliated with HBE association or support groups, offer membership directories. It's always worthwhile knowing if a directory is available, and in what form—mailing label, software disk, hard copy, annual issue, etc.
- Once you get published, even in a newsletter, make an attractive reprint, write the words "previous publication" in the corner, and include that reprint when sending out other manuscripts to editors of larger publications.
- Successful marketers, those who have well-developed systems for penetrating markets, often have mastered techniques for getting into print. Review the most prominent magazines in the niche and you undoubtedly will find published articles written by those who have something to sell to HBEs.

CHAPTER 11

CASE HISTORIES: MARKETING TO HBES

Better to master one
mountain than a thousand
foothills.
William Arthur Ward

HBES MARKETING TO EACH OTHER

With a minimum of 34.4 million home-based workers just within the United States, marketing from home-based business to home-based business is a channel already in strong formation. HBEs understand and readily respond to one another. They communicate faster, more freely, and with less formality than traditional business-to-business or traditional business to home-based business.

If you are an HBE, consider that a large and growing number of home-based entrepreneurs already exists within three to four blocks of your home and within your community, and await your service or product, if they only knew that you exist.

Depending on your selected targets, a full-scale advertising campaign may not be necessary. An effective promotional program is. You may need a brochure or flyer, perhaps a capability statement, business cards, mailers, and specifications or boiler plate sheets, depending on the nature of your product or service.

You may or may not want to be listed in the yellow pages; directories of HBEs groups and associations are likely to give you a better return for your dollar. You'll want to join at least one HBE group and at least one professional society or local civic group such as the Chamber of Commerce, the Rotary Club, or Kiwanis.

Maintaining contact with customers and prospects keeps your firm's name in front of them. You can do this by mailing greeting cards, newsletters, or announcements of new products and services in the form of a press release.

Quick Tips for Identifying Other HBEs

Given the market potential of calling on HBEs within your local area, how can you quickly and easily identify appropriate targets?

- In the white pages in many metropolitan telephone books, the latter half of the book is devoted to business and professional entities. Often, these listings contain smaller, entrepreneurial enterprises including a bevy of home-based entrepreneurs. Many of those listed within these white pages do not maintain listings in the yellow pages.
- Home-based businesses that do advertise in the traditional yellow pages often can be detected from their listing. For example, is the street address one that you know to be residential as opposed to commercial? Many single line entries, as opposed to a quarter- and half-page advertisements, tend to be the home-business variety.
- Mini yellow pages serve the suburban areas of many major metropolitan areas. For example, in the Philadelphia suburbs, a half-inch thick mini yellow pages directory serves Jenkintown, while another serves Bala Cynwyd, and others serve other communities. Each of these mini-directories contain but a fraction of a number of businesses listed in the Philadelphia

yellow pages. Using the "minis" will enable you to more quickly spot other home-based businesses.

- The Chamber of Commerce in your town may maintain a roster of businesses or members and, once again, from the addresses you can detect who is operating from a residential address.
- The business card bulletin boards at local printers and office supply stores are worth checking. Many HBEs display their business cards on such bulletin boards.

In this chapter, we'll take a look at a variety of techniques, all in the form of brief case histories, that smaller vendors to the HBE market have employed to market their products or services.

TOTAL SUPPORT FOR HOME-OFFICE DESIGN

Lawrence La Porta, president of At Home Office Works, Inc., designs workspaces to meet a home-based professional's needs. "We offer our customers a total package of quality and support, and that's what makes us different from a lot of companies," says La Porta.

"For example, there are lots of people selling software to home businesses, but they don't offer their customers ongoing support. Customers may hire someone to design a system for them and after it has been installed, lose contact with the vendor and find there's nobody who can answer their questions.

"We know that this is a problem, so we make sure that we are always there to help our customers understand and use the software and equipment we sell to them."

At Home Office Works was founded in February 1989, when La Porta recognized what he had to offer the home-based professional community. He was working at an electronics firm, where he serviced computer hardware. His brother Dennis, a home-based pharmaceutical sales representative, teamed up with him as a business partner. The addition of two full-time consultants completed the vision of La Porta's plan.

At Home Office Works helps its customers make informed and practical choices for their workspaces. The company specializes in home office equipment and furniture. High tech advice may also be gained through At Home Office Works consultants.

The company works with local distributors to offer a wide selection of office furniture, computers, software, fax machines, and even training tapes—anything and everything needed to create an efficient, professional home workspace. La Porta recently opened a showroom to demonstrate the possibilities to prospects.

La Porta's clients include home-based professionals in law, sales, finance, and design who trust him to help them create a workspace that works. Many come to him through referrals from satisfied customers. Others discover At Home Office Works through trade shows and association contracts. La Porta's personalized approach is catching on among HBEs. To get in touch write to P.O. Box 88752, Carol Stream, IL 60188–0752.

IS A TYPICAL DAY IN YOUR HOME OFFICE LIKE MINE USED TO BE?

If it is, it probably involves a lot of stress, trying to do
several things at once:

- Answering the phone, looking up the information
  your client called for, and trying to remember
  what/why/where and how many!

- Keeping up with your appointment schedule and your
  to-do list.

- Writing a letter, checking the spelling and
  wondering about the correct usage of a certain word.

- Stopping everything to print a document and running to the
  local postal service to use the FAX machine.

- Tracking expenses and keeping your eye on the bottom
  line.

And in the middle of all this chaos, you've <u>still</u> got to try to
get your work done.

SOUND FAMILIAR?

Guess what? You're not alone! That's exactly the same situation I
faced when I moved my office to my home. I found I was spending
more time doing things my support staff used to do than getting <u>my</u>
work done. The only things I missed about the "old office" was
that there was always someone to answer the phone, send my FAXes,
and take care of those time consuming details I didn't have time to
worry about.

I thought the solution would be simple. Given my many years in the
computer business and today's powerful desktop computers, I really
believed I could build a support system to take the place of the
one I had in my "formal" office. After two frustrating years spent
searching for a workable home office system (and a sizable
investment in hardware and software), I found myself drowning in a
sea of details and accomplishing less and less each day. I gave up
and decided to create my own.

The result is a system called **FYI: Work Smarter**. And it's worth a
few minutes of your time to find out more about it.

The problem with all the, so-called, "home office software" on the
market today is that it's not designed to work as a complete
system. The products all work well on their own, but just try and
get them to work together!

That's where **Work Smarter** is different. It's been conceived,
designed and developed as a complete support system. Every detail
of day-to-day office operation has been thought out and is covered
by a **Work Smarter** function -- and they all work together! This
means that your work flows uninterrupted from one operation to
another -- make a call, set an appointment, add a to-do task, write
and FAX a letter -- all without leaving the comfortable, intuitive
and productive **Work Smarter** environment.

WORK SMARTER IS NOT ONLY <u>SOFTWARE</u>, IT'S <u>HARDWARE</u>, TOO!

Included with Work Smarter is <u>The Complete Communicator</u>, an add-in board which provides high speed send/receive facsimile (FAX) at 9600-bps, sophisticated Voice Mail messaging, a 2400-bps Modem and a scanner port for an optional Complete PC Scanner. Just plug in this easy-to-install board and give your PC these capabilities without any additional equipment.

BUT **WORK SMARTER** IS MUCH MORE THAN THAT.

We call **Work Smarter** a <u>total</u> support system, which includes ongoing support from us. You see, we want to do more than just sell you a solution. We want to establish a long-term working relationship between your company and ours, because we know that for home office professionals, it's the one-on-one relationships that really count.

Our commitment starts with free customer support over the phone. And, it goes a step further....

Because support is so important to us, we've built a special function into **Work Smarter** for problem solving. If you have a question or problem -- day or night -- you can FAX us a report so we can quickly pinpoint the trouble and respond with a solution. If an internal problem occurs within the software, the system FAXes us a report <u>automatically</u> and we'll call you back just as soon as the problem is resolved.

When you buy **Work Smarter**, you're making an investment in your personal life. I guarantee your investment will pay off handsomely, in terms of your time and your productivity.

PROVE IT FOR YOURSELF.

Please take time to read over the materials we've enclosed. Watch our demonstration Slide Show and see how **Work Smarter** can help <u>you</u> Work Smarter in your home office.

Then, call our Home Office Products Group and let us know what you think. Thank you for your interest in our products.

Sincerely,

John J. Shea
President

JJS/ws
Enc.

P.S. As you look through these materials, keep in mind that we used **Work Smarter** to print this <u>letter</u>, the enclosed <u>coupon</u> and the <u>mailing label</u> - all as a result of entering your name and address information into Contact Management. We'll then use the same information to track and report our leads and sales!

HOW FYI SYSTEMS POSITIONED ITSELF
THROUGH WORK SMARTER

FYI Systems, based in San Diego, developed a product
called WORK SMARTER, designed to provide an office support system for home and single worker offices. The company bills it as "The Complete Office Support System You
Can Bring Home," and employs the following advertising
copy: "WORK SMARTER helps transform a PC into a
personal communications center by incorporating send/re-
ceive high-speed FAX (9,600-bps), voice mail messaging
and Modem (2,400-bps) hardware technologies on a single
board with a logical, intuitive, task-oriented software in-
terface."

In developing this product Jeff West, Vice President of
Sales for FYI Systems, observed that WORK SMARTER
solves the problem of having to buy separate office equipment and software programs, then trying to make them
all work together. The WORK SMARTER environment is
divided into management tasks which makes it easy to
switch from one operation or task to another, the way people normally work. Another company ad reads: "WORK
SMARTER is more than just software and hardware. It's a
fully-integrated electronic support system providing users
with an effective solution to managing their day-to-day activities while greatly increasing their productivity."

The preceding pages are a self-explanatory illustration of
how FYI Systems appeals directly to the HBE market.

HQ BUSINESS CENTERS

The phone is ringing, the baby is crying, and you need to
get your shipment out today. Isn't there any way a home-
based business can operate more like a Fortune 500
company without losing its home base? Thanks to HQ
Headquarters Companies, there is a way.

HQ, based in San Francisco, is an executive business center that has branches in 92 cities throughout the United States, as well as Brussels, and Windsor, England. They offer their clients an office and conference room as well as a number of services not available to the home-based worker.

Cynthia Bronte, Vice President of Sales and Marketing, says "there is no average client." Bronte estimates that approximately half of all clients are single office users, while the other half are branch offices of larger companies. While many clients are in sales, others have diverse backgrounds, and include lawyers, entrepreneurs, and real estate agents.

One program offered by HQ is their Business Identity Plan. With this plan, the client can use the HQ business center as their mailing address; HQ will forward your mail on to you. By doing this, the client will have a mailing address as well as a suite number, and have their company name listed on the building directory. The receptionist will answer your phone, and, says Bronte, "our people don't act as an answering service, we will act as a personal secretary as much as possible."

With this program, clients also have access to fax and copy machines. Other benefits of the program include car and hotel discounts and group insurance rates. Bronte estimates that the average cost is between $200 and $225 per month. Short-term leases are available to those who are undecided about the program.

For more information about this service concept write to HQ Headquarters Companies, 120 Montgomery Street, Suite 1040, San Francisco, CA 94104.

THE COTTAGE SEMINAR

One effective technique that HBEs who market to other HBEs can employ has been dubbed the "cottage seminar." Here is how it works. Suppose you offer seminars or training to corporate clients but are continually asked by attendees where else you will be giving seminars. It is not feasible for you to continue to rent expensive space in hotels or meeting rooms, yet you know a significant number of noncorporate types would show up if you advertise your seminar.

Pamela Rhody, an Atlanta-based family financial planner who schedules a weekly cottage seminar in her home, says that the cottage approach "is a good way to attract couples, not just individuals." Those offering counseling or financial business or professional service are well positioned to appeal to both household buyers at the same time.

More and more HBEs who market to other HBEs are turning to establishing cottage seminars. With this marketing strategy, the host is able to schedule the time and date. Other HBEs have no problem attending a seminar in someone's home, because they, too, work out of their own homes.

Regardless of how much space you have, almost any living quarters can accommodate 8 to 10 people. While this size seminar may seem small, it can be far more friendlier, personal, and effective than seminars in traditional corporate settings.

Not to be mistaken, cottage seminars are not freebies designed to attract people in hopes of urging them to buy more. Each attendee pays a set price for the seminar. After, an attendee may wish to do more business but he or she gets his or her money's worth that night. If they wish to attend future seminars on different topics, they pay again.

Thus far, cottage seminars have appealed largely to women. Men still associate gatherings in one's home with kitchen ware parties and baby showers. Also, some men are unable to overcome what they see as the stigma of being an HBE.

More men, particularly younger ones, are becoming amenable to attending or sponsoring such seminars. Rhody says that regardless of who conducts a particular seminar, most attendees are still primarily women. For nongender

related types of products and services, heavy female attendance poses no hardship to those presenting seminars, since
the number of female entrepreneurs has increased markedly every year since 1975.

GETTING IT RIGHT THE THIRD TIME

Ron Wagner is an HBE, inventor and enthusiastic marketer to HBEs. For a change of pace, here is Ron's own
account of the trials of marketing to HBE targets.

"There is no such thing as a product that will sell itself.
Regardless of any product's inherent or obvious superiority
over its competition, it will merely be a source of personal
pride for its creator unless it is marketed properly. I maintained the belief that if I could make my invention *even
better*, they would catch and reap a bonanza.

"There is more to a product than merely creating it.
Many products and services are perfectly sound, useful, and
desirable, and, save the entrepreneur's lack of marketing
capability, would be selling now. Any product will remain
merely a source of personal pride for its creator unless the
market has been properly defined and targeted.

"My first product for the HBE was a software program.
The tax laws years ago required HBEs to document the
percentage of time that a personal computer was used for
business, with only that portion being deductible. When I
discovered that there was no software package on the market to accomplish that automatically, I decided to write one
myself. Thus was born the program entitled "PC-Log,"
which instantly logged and categorized personal computer
usage, producing a year-end report for tax records.

"Targeting the home-based business market was a good
idea because it was growing rapidly. I was not prepared for
this growth to be my undoing. Knowing I had a program
that was useful and easy to learn, I blitzed the home-based

computer news world with copies of the program and a press release. PC-Log was well received by the magazines, and I got several good review articles out of the promotional mailing. This put me in a position to implement the next phase of my marketing plan: taking the program to the computer store chains.

"My approach paid off when PC-Log appeared in one of the nation's largest retail chains. I remember the first time I saw my program in a shopping mall in another city when I was travelling. Seeing a national distribution channel in place for my program was highly encouraging, but there was to be an unforeseen twist.

"PC-Log was developed at a time when the personal computer software market was small compared to today. Also, much of the software itself was less sophisticated. One day, when I called the buyer at the headquarters of the chain which was carrying my program, he told me that he could no longer place orders directly with software companies. The chain's policy had changed and he could now only order from the catalogs of national software distributors. He assured me he would continue to order PC-Log as soon as it was available through one of the distributors, and kindly provided addresses, phone numbers, and contact names.

"My call to the first distributor went well because the program's current status in major stores quickly established my credibility. They requested evaluation copies and mailed me forms asking detailed information about my company. That call would be the last time anything went smoothly for PC-Log.

"The marketing lesson that I learned was you must research the distribution system behind a product you wish to sell. If it targets a rapidly changing market, find out if the rules may suddenly change. The distributor's job—what they do for the "middleman's" cut—is to screen companies for the major buyers. My small company did not meet the criteria established by the distributors. Although it was already selling in a major chain store, no distributor would add a small company to its vendor list. The chain never reordered PC-Log."

Getting Back on the Horse

"I had learned several lessons the hard way, remembering them well as I developed my next product. My next venture was into the computer keyboard template market. Templates were just beginning to appear in stores. I got involved early through a local company that later became one of the most successful in the business. Their templates can still be bought today in nearly every shopping mall.

"My idea was to have this company produce a template expressly for me. It was for a program that they did not plan to support, but I had arranged a deal with the software company to include a brochure for the template, an order form, and my business reply envelope with each copy of the program.

"The demand for my template certainly existed; everyone who opens a new software package would want the template. The publicity would be the most direct possible; every user of the program would get a copy of my brochure and an order form. The pricing target was easy to hit because it was well established by templates for other programs. Finally, my long-term contract with the software developer protected me from a major change in the distribution system.

"My template marketing plan had a bonus for me. The program it supported would be used mainly by home-based businesses. This gave me another vehicle to distribute my unsold copies of PC-Log.

"The template orders were soon pouring in, increasing every week. Although I did not have a huge mark-up margin on the template, each order produced a guaranteed profit, so I was pleased.

"Then I got a call from the executive vice president of the software company who excitedly told me of their plans for a major upgrade to their program. They wanted another template for the new version, however my template business was doomed. The unrecouped costs on the remaining stock prohibited me from funding the new version.

"I've since concluded that a product must either address a static need or easily be updated to accommodate the new demands as rapidly as they evolve. The demand for the old version of the program lingered long enough for me to turn a small profit. Nevertheless, I've got thousands of templates left. Here are a few lessons from that venture.

- Check out the pricing structure of the market to ensure your product fits a pricing niche with which your potential customers will be familiar.
- Research the distribution system. Don't risk being caught with unsold products because some force outside your control changes the rules on you. If the system seems to be changing rapidly, look for nontraditional market avenues which will allow you some consistency.
- Offer a product that meets a demand with static requirements. Or, make sure your product can quickly and easily be adapted—on short notice and with little cost—to keep up with the changing demands."

The Perfect Ruler

"My newest product is "The Perfect Ruler," which is a layout ruler designed specifically for WordPerfect. My training experience as a WordPerfect Certified Instructor demonstrated that nearly every WordPerfect user could benefit from a ruler designed expressly for WordPerfect. The Perfect Ruler has a see-through layout scale, which is calibrated in tenths of an inch, exactly the units displayed on the WordPerfect screen. With this ruler in hand, the layout and planning of complicated documents becomes a cinch.

"The Perfect Ruler answers another demand, one brought out by today's ubiquitous laser printers. The Perfect

Ruler has a "Font Point Size" window that eliminates the guesswork from font size selection. With these two exclusive features, The Perfect Ruler satisfies my first rule— meeting a demand that I could easily identify. I felt that users would not want to live without a Perfect Ruler once they knew of the product's existence.

"Armed with prototypes and good documentation, I was able to secure an order large enough to assure profitability before the first ruler was manufactured. The pricing structure was not a big factor because the ruler is priced so low that its purchase is not a major decision.

"Because the initial order made the entire venture profitable, I proceeded with production without considering whether distributors would carry it. Finally, my rule concerning static and dynamic demands was satisfied because the ruler meets a static need. Well, okay, the United States will adopt the metric system in a few years and I may be stuck with a bunch of "inches" rulers, but that's a risk I willingly took.

"The Perfect Ruler marked the first time I had a project apply to each of the marketing lessons I had learned. It produced an instant profit. Further, it could remain viable for many more years, giving it a long marketing life."

For more information write to: The Perfect Ruler, Heartwood Creations, P.O. Box 2293, Springfield, VA 22152 (703) 455−4195.

DIVING IN WITHOUT LOOKING

Fred Arons (name disguised) has been working feverishly so that his copy machine sales and service center will open on schedule. The store is located in the Middleton Plaza shopping area, a medium-sized, convenience goods, open-air mall. The plaza has four customer entryways. Fred's shop is located just to the left of the second most prominent, visible entryway.

There are two anchor stores within the plaza including a large Trak Auto store, and a national chain drugstore. Far in advance of the site selection, Fred was able to obtain pedestrian and vehicular traffic counts. He felt reasonably sure that the chosen location could support his new venture.

Seeking to appeal to a small business and HBE clientele, Fred called the advertising representative of a stylish, county-focused monthly magazine. Fred was dazzled by the promotional package that the magazine sent him. The demographics of their readership were just the kind of people Fred wanted to reach. The ad representative with whom he spoke was encouraging.

Fred was interested in placing a large advertisement during the opening month and, depending on the costs, a second ad the following month. After reviewing the prices for a half-page ad, Fred was stunned. "It couldn't be that expensive." Nevertheless, Fred went ahead and committed several thousand dollars to run an attractive half-page ad for two consecutive months.

Though the cost of these ads nearly consumed Fred's marketing and promotion budget, Fred knew that he had to take some calculated risks. He further reasoned that these ads would reach the widest number of potential customers and would cause the most immediate impact. Had he instead used the money for handbills, flyers, smaller community shopper ads, and the like, Fred believed he would get no better response, with a lot more work.

During the grand opening week, sales were encouraging, but not exactly what Fred had expected. The owners and employees of the other stores in the plaza all made a visit and several came back to run off copies of various announcements. Regular customers of the nearby stores looked in the windows and some even came in, but copier sales were negligible. In a matter of weeks there was a noticeable decline in the number of store visitors. Only the quick-copy service was bringing in revenue, but not much.

Fred was diligent in asking customers how they heard about the store and if any saw his ad in the magazine. Virtually everybody who came by did so only as a result of their habit of coming to the plaza. Only three people vaguely recall "seeing something about the store" in some magazine.

The second ad, already paid for, ran in the next issue. Fred was sure that running ads for two consecutive months would pull in some customers. There was little change however. Fred now realizes that he had spent a "chunk of change" without doing enough investigative groundwork. Moreover, he couldn't change his product mix—he lacked the cash to display an inventory of more expensive high-speed copiers for large offices.

Later, in conversation with other business owners, Fred learned he could have attracted far more small business and HBEs through flyers, handbills, and ads in the community shopper—the strategy Fred had first contemplated, but abandoned, and through specialized newsletters such as those of the local PC users group and the Middleton Association of Entrepreneurs.

It's easy enough for any entrepreneur to misallocate crucial marketing funds. Many rely on some percentage from a chart or book indicating how much to spend and expect that that will do the job. The major error in this approach is that it does not reflect the prevailing environment and any unique circumstances.

For example, the size of Fred's trade radius, the number of people who could reasonably be expected to patronize his copy center, would be equal to the size of the Middleton Plaza trade radius, and not any where near the readership of the county magazine. The number of people residing in the Middleton Plaza trade radius is largely an established figure. From that figure the HBEs could be reasonably estimated. Both the plaza Trak Auto and the drugstore had already compiled this data.

Suppose that the trade radius extends for a half mile to the south, one and one-half miles east, one mile north and, because of the river, only three blocks to the west.

The number of households and businesses in this trade radius represents less than 1 percent of the number of households reached by the county magazine. In essence, 99 percent of the cost of Fred's ads were dissipated among readers who could not be expected to respond, even if they: (1) saw the ad, (2) read it, (3) were interested in what was being offered, and (4) actually drove in that direction.

Fred's business failed not merely because he placed ads in the wrong medium, but because prior to opening his store he failed to take crucial steps that could have bolstered his cash flow during the early critical months when money would be extremely tight. Fred was product and service focused, but never took the time to gain an insider's understanding of the niche.

Selling to HBEs—All the Wrong Moves

- Not doing initial research on the target market
- Inadequate revenue forecasting
- Less than adequate location
- Underdeveloped strategies
- Inappropriate advertising vehicles
- Lack of marketing flexibility

Hot Tips and Insights from Chapter 11

- With 34.4 million home-based workers just within the United States, marketing from home-based business to home-based business is a channel already in strong formation.

- HBEs understand and readily respond to one another. They communicate faster, more freely, and with less formality than traditional business-to-business or traditional business-to-home-based business.
- Depending on your selected targets, a full-scale advertising campaign may not be necessary. An effective promotional program is.
- Given the market potential of calling on HBEs within your local area, you can quickly and easily identify appropriate targets.
- The cottage seminar is an effective technique that HBEs who market to other HBEs can employ.
- When devising your own unique product, check the pricing structure of the market to ensure your product fits a pricing niche that your potential customers are familiar with.
- Research the distribution system. Don't risk being caught with unsold products because some force outside your control changes the rules on you. If the system seems to be changing rapidly, look for nontraditional market avenues which will allow you some consistency.
- Offer a product that meets a demand with static requirements. Or, make sure your product can quickly and easily be adapted—on short notice and with little cost—to keep up with the changing demands.

CHAPTER 12

PROSPECTS FOR THE FUTURE

Empires of the future will be
empires of the mind.
Winston Churchill

The pace of change and ease of mobility is accelerating. Young adults today, for example, are apt to travel more in the first 21 years of their lives than their grandparents did in a lifetime. Only since the 1980s have the majority of American women begun working outside the home, which has impacted the family unit and childbirth and divorce rates.

Acceptance of VCRs, cable television, and personal computers as standard home equipment and services required less than 10 years each. It took less than five years to generate the first million cellular customers, as compared to the twenty years to sell the first 1 million television sets.

Many aspects of the future are not subject to reliable forecast. Who could predict the outbreak of aids and the long-term battle to find its cure? Other aspects of the future can be predicted with varying degrees of reliability. For example:

- Renewable energy is on the rise. According to a study by the Union of Concerned Scientists in Washington, D.C., our country could draw up to 50 percent of its energy supply from renewable sources by the year 2020. In the next 10 years alone, the use of renewable energy could double to 15 percent.

- Residential water purification products are now a $1.7 billion industry. Retail sales of bottled water and water appliances for conservation and purification will double over the next five years, according to FIND/SVP, a market research firm.
- Investments in computers and robots are expected to double to more than 19 percent of all business investments.
- By the year 2000, as much as 85 percent of all field sales operations will be automated, with the laptop computer becoming as common as the attache case or the cellular phone.
- A shorter work week among traditional office workers will increase the demand for leisure-related goods and services.
- Year-round schooling is inevitable.
- The number of self-employed individuals will grow more rapidly in the next 15 years than it has during the last 15 years. The U.S. Small Business Administration estimates that by the year 2000, small firms will produce about 40 percent of the U.S. output.

INEVITABLE DEVELOPMENTS IN MARKETING AND DISTRIBUTION

Micro-Targeting

Competition in the 90s is going to be savage, from all predictions, with both small and large companies falling to the wayside if they don't think globally and arm themselves for the fray with marketing tools and strategies. Companies are segmenting their markets with finer and finer precision, and going after the tiniest of the tiny—the HBE. Both the marketer and the HBE can thrive under this microscopic attention.

Can't Miss Marketing Trends

- Micro-targeting
- Global competition
- Decline in mass marketing
- National account management
- Upgraded advertising appeals
- Overnight delivery and satisfaction as norms
- Records and inventory control kept by the vendor

More companies are looking to pull apart markets into many different parts and from these many parts seek the small but profitable areas that were hidden. Once they have identified the small segments, they then develop products and services that key into the specific needs of each one of those segments.

Global Competition

International competition is heating up in the 90s, growing at unprecedented rates, and coming from all parts of the globe. In Asia, industrial centers are maturing fast, and in Europe, the former communist bloc nations are gearing for growth from market-based economies. If current trends are an indicator, world trade will be at the top of every country's agenda, leading the way to worldwide global capitalism.

As individual corporations scramble to find the tools and techniques to adapt to a new way of marketing, so must the marketer to HBEs. Sales must be automated, and communication and data systems tailored to the individual needs of the HBE. Quality and service must become more than just words or symbols, but resources to be managed wisely.

A Eulogy for Mass Marketing

Mass marketing is in rapid decline as characterized by automobile manufacturing. General Motors is now wooing the single buyer, rather than a collection of buyers. The new trend is direct contact on a massive scale. United States Fortune 100 companies have led the way in the now firmly-tested strategy that companies must establish strong give-and-take relationships with their customers.

Critical in these relationships is the company's ability to deliver a product or service on time, sometimes just in time, and create an atmosphere of trust and friendship with the client. Companies with vision have already sought closer customer relationships to be competitive in the changing global economy of the 1990s.

The Large Customer or "Chain" Sales Strategy of the Future

National account management is the sales strategy of the future. It caters standard quality and delivery of products and services to large customers with facilities in many locations, while responding to the individual needs of different segments.

Automation, such as electronic messaging, electronic data interchange, and computer-to-computer communication, will help tighten up the efficiency of national account management while allowing the marketer to spend more time selling—and answering the needs of individual customers.

Advertising and Marketing in the 1990s Will Go Beyond Focusing on the Five Ps

Marketing will go from price, product, placement, positioning, and promotion to a new arena—focusing on the ability of marketers to form a responsive relationship with prospects and customers. In the context of marketing to HBEs, by building the responsive relationship, marketers will close their customers off from the competition outside their tight circle of involvement.

Have Item, Will Guarantee Overnight
Delivery and Satisfaction

Technology will accelerate the entire marketing process, clear through delivery of the product to the end-user. Delivery of nearly all goods is bound to become an overnight affair. The express delivery services are expanding globally and exponentially. Catalog mail order deliveries can now be accomplished overnight. The speed of direct marketing in the near future will make the present seem like slow motion.

You Keep Their Records of Your Products
And Their Inventories

McKinsey & Company management consultants interviewed 18 marketers in large grocery and personal care companies. They found that in order to lower the costs of selling, manufacturers are cutting their daily calls and upgrading the skill levels of key account representatives. Computers are being used to decipher data about customers, both large and small, and deliver that information almost simultaneously to field representatives. Salespeople are becoming more involved in developing strategies and plans, and allocating budgets. Marketers are relying more and more on the valuable information gathered from their clients. Maintaining clients records of one's own deliveries and inventories is not far off.

THE RE-EMERGENCE OF THE
PROSUMER

One of the most grand-sweeping predictions that appears evermore certain is the re-emergence of the prosumer.

Alvin Toffler sees the post-industrial age moving toward a synthesis of First and Second Wave societies. According to Toffler, the First Wave was characterized by a majority of the world's population engaged in agriculture and what he calls prosumers, people who produce goods and services for their own consumption. The Second Wave was marked by industrialized and exchange networks created to trade goods and services.

In the Third Wave, the two previous waves will be synthesized. For many reasons, most people, particularly HBEs, will once again become prosumers, engaging in various forms of production and consumption within their home and offices. People will be elated when they can produce better quality products than they can buy.

In fact, Toffler predicts that a growing number of people will actually seek self-expression through the production of their own goods and services. Combined with the rising cost of skilled labor, untold masses of people will begin to do their own plumbing, carpentry, and electrical work.

Toffler sees most markets becoming more segmented and personalized, with emphasis on individual rather than mass consumption. People will want more physical activity as their main job involve sitting at a workstation terminal.

The challenge—and frustration—of marketing to prosumers, a group that will contain substantial numbers of HBEs, will be that these new type of targets have less interest in brand names, and less interest in mass-produced goods and services. The trick is to pinpoint what goods and services prosumers are most likely to produce for themselves.

Current Prosumption

Grocery stores now offer bulk food items, like cereal and dog food, carrying no brand name. Shoppers bag it for themselves, selecting their own quantities. Other grocery stores offer cheaper prices if people bag all the groceries themselves using their own bags and boxes.

Warehouse clubs, such as the Price Club, sell HBEs office supplies, groceries, and even home furnishings at very low prices by offering a large inventory and selection. The brand name is not nearly as important as the size and the savings of the product, from toilet paper packaged in 30-roll packs to copying paper at a substantial cost reduction for 10 reams.

One of the growth markets spurred by the trend toward prosumption and working from home is the market for instruction. More HBEs want to obtain skills on their own, through classes, how-to books, magazine subscriptions geared to home businesses, audio and video instruction tapes, as well as computer-aided instruction disks.

Telemarketing to HBEs

The way to reach the HBE office of the future increasingly will be through telemarketing as companies continue to expand their operations while reducing the cost of selling the HBEs, and these marketers will rely heavily on automation. The trend toward telemarketing will drastically reduce the number of sales representatives on the road across the nation.

Your message will need to perform a double duty: build a positive image and bring in a response by starting a dialogue with the customer. Also, value-added propositions will help make the sale, whether it is a toll-free number for software support, or an offer of purchase loss insurance on a credit card.

THE "HOFFICE"—PRODUCE DOWNSTAIRS, CONSUME UPSTAIRS

A very small but growing number of HBEs are buying homes with complete offices already in them. "Hoffice" is a term coined at Creekside Commons, a development in Stuart, Florida. A hoffice has a professional office on the ground floor with the residence on the floors above. New as it is, it has already spawned a new genre of mixed-use development—professional, residential, and retail—around the country.

The spread of hoffices is really representative of a deeper change which the work-at-home movement is producing. Americans are growing tired of commuting hours to work. They are weary of city troubles and the declining quality of life in urban centers, but they are also dissatisfied with the isolation and sameness of the suburbs. They want to live in communities where they know their neighbors, and can walk, not drive, to stores and activities.

Professional Builder magazine, commenting on the "New Neighborhoods for the Nineties," said, "In many ways, the new American neighborhoods of the 1990s will look like the 1890s, with architecture reflecting resurgent traditional values and the joys of unfettered wandering. Look closely at the suburbs of today, and you'll see deep disillusionment with suburban sprawl and the problems growth spawned."

Creekside Commons was developed in this new spirit. It is the brainchild of developer James Smith. The town of Stuart is north of Palm Beach. It's a small village whose main street went downhill fast after the interstate and business passed it by. The town has renovated the old downtown, and Creekside Commons' architecture blends in with the old-Florida style called for in Stuart's master plan—screened verandas, cupolas, tin roofs, and French doors. Boat dockage is also provided.

Smith is building 20 three-story townhouses. Zoning laws restrict office use to the first floor. The upper two floors contain two bedrooms and two-and-one-half baths, for the residence. The hoffice concept is applicable to development in large or mid-sized cities as well.

The first wave of HBEs inhabiting hoffices gain many advantages:

- The IRS has given its blessing to the hoffice concept, in part because the office part is separately metered.

- Mortgages for hoffices are generally residential loans with lower interest rates than commercial loans.
- The hoffice owner can obtain an occupancy permit, put up a business sign, and accept large deliveries. Most home businesses experience difficulties in these areas.

THE PORTABLE OFFICE ENTREPRENEUR

From the smog-choked freeways leading into Los Angeles to the backed-up beltway around the waistline of Washington, D.C., HBEs are beginning to equip their cars for high productivity.

An HBE on the road buying and selling real estate in California had a mobile office custom-built into a stretch limo. The office seats up to nine in the back—perfect for having a meeting, giving a presentation, or entertaining his clients. The equipment includes a central console containing two video monitors, a VCR, two laptop computers, and a fax machine.

Communications equipment in the front includes a separate audio system, three handsets for a cellular phone, intercom and amateur radio, and a two-way radio handset for a CB radio. Eight antennas are mounted on the back exterior of the limousine.

Communications equipment in the passenger compartment includes a cellular phone with hands-free speaker and microphone for conference calls, an amateur radio with a 200-mile range, and a standard CB radio with a public address system.

All this keeps the hard-working HBE in business on the road, while the high-tech, well-to-do impression it gives his clients and business associates is public relations gold. It better be worth something since the monthly cost equals that of a stationary office in a prestigious location.

While most HBEs cannot afford a custom-built stretch limo, each day more of them are looking for ways to get the business mileage out of their vehicles. Mark Eppley, founder and chief executive officer of Traveling Software, one of the fastest growing privately held companies in the country, developed the Battery Watch. The Battery Watch tells how much remains on a computer's battery charge while on the road. Eppley's idea came from many years of working as a traveling consultant and the frustrations he experienced trying to be productive without high-tech help.

Eppley's own mobile office equipment includes a laptop computer, a fax modem, a phone modem, and a customized tool kit with telephone jacks for 14 countries. His latest interest is in developing an electronic organizer—a wireless communications, handwriting recognition, and voice-mail capability built into a pocket-sized, eight-ounce, battery operated product much like the Dick Tracy watch of the comics.

The Global HBE Is Also Emerging

Marketing to global HBEs will be a multi-pronged approach, starting with the basic equipment and ranging to high-tech enhancements that make business faster and easier. Sophisticated sales and marketing software, for example, will make it possible for HBEs to do their own research and segmentation in a cost-effective way. The HBE who has already automated specific functions, such as direct mail advertising and call reporting, for example, can be sold on linking those functions for greater efficiency.

IN CONCLUSION

Marketing to HBEs successfully, as with all marketing, will be rooted in your ability to help these customers fulfill needs. HBEs, because they have broken away from traditional companies and whatever security was gained by working for someone else, have proven that they want to be active participants in deciding their own futures. The wise marketer will help them meet their goals.

Hot Tips and Insights from Chapter 12
- The number of self-employed individuals will grow more rapidly in the next 15 years than during the last 15 years.
- By the year 2000, small firms will produce about 40 percent of the U.S. output.
- Competition in the 90s is going to be savage, from all predictions, with both small and large companies falling to the wayside if they don't think globally and arm themselves for the fray with marketing tools and strategies.
- Companies are segmenting their markets with finer and finer precision, and going after the tiniest of the tiny—the HBE. Both the marketer and the HBE can thrive under this microscopic attention.
- Express delivery services are expanding globally and exponentially. Catalog mail order deliveries can now be accomplished overnight. The speed of direct marketing in the near future will make the present seem like slow motion.
- Many HBEs will once again become prosumers, engaging in various forms of production and consumption within their homes and offices. People will be elated when they can produce better quality products than they can buy.
- A growing number of people will seek self-expression through the production of their own goods and services. Combined with the rising cost of skilled labor, untold masses of people will begin to do their own plumbing, carpentry, and electrical work.
- One of the growth markets spurred by the trend toward "prosumption" and working from home is the market for instruction. More HBEs want to obtain skills on their own, through classes, how-to books, magazine subscriptions geared to home businesses, and audio and video instruction tapes, as well as computer-aided instruction disks.
- A small number of HBEs are buying homes with complete offices already in them. A hoffice has a professional office

on the ground floor with the residence on the floors above.
New as it is, it has already spawned a new genre of mixed-
use development—professional, residential, and retail—
around the country.
- HBEs are beginning to equip their cars for high productivity. The global HBE is also emerging.
- Marketing to HBEs successfully is rooted in one's ability
to help these customers fulfill needs. The wise marketer
will help them meet their goals.

BIBLIOGRAPHY

Auerbach, Stewart. "Slower Growth Predicted for U.S. Industries". *The Washington Post,* December 29, 1989, Section F-1.

Bertrand, Kate. "Get Ready for Global Capitalism". *Business Marketing,* January 1990, pp. 42–44, 49–54.

Bigham, Barbara J. "Prospecting in the Home". *Nation's Business,* November 1987, pp. 55–56.

Castro, Janice. "Staying Home is Paying Off". *Time Magazine,* October 26, 1987, pp. 112–113.

Churbuck, David. "Attention, PC Shoppers!". *Forbes,* March 5, 1990, pp. 42–43.

Cotler, Phillip. "Prosumers". *The Futurist,* September/October 1986, pp. 24–30.

Dykeman, John. "How Corporate America Takes Its Work Home, Part II". *Modern Office Technology,* August 1989, pp. 45–50.

Farhi, Paul. Marketers Angling for Ways to Hit Tough-to-Target Consumers". *The Washington Post,* December 29, 1989 Section C, p. 1.

Furger, Roberta. "Nationwide Guide to User Groups". *PC World,* August 1990, pp. 125–131.

Goldstein, Jerome. "Proving Grounds for Entrepreneurs". *In Business,* March/April 1990, pp. 32–33.

Goldstein, Jerome. "Trends". *In Business,* March/April 1990, p. 62.

Golembo, Eri. "A Channel Too Big Too Ignore". *Marketing Computers,* February 1990, p. 31.

Hollander, Barbara S. "Hot Points for Married Partners, Family Business". *In Business,* March/April 1990, p. 60.

Kane, Karen and Williams, Steve. "Trend for the 1990s, The Home Office Hits Puberty". *Home Office Computing,* September 1989, p. 12.

Kelley, Bill. "Is There Anything That Can't be Sold by Phone?". *Sales and Marketing Management,* April 1989, pp. 60–64.

Kelly, Marsha M. "The Work at Home Revolution". *The Futurist,* November/December 1988, pp. 28–32.

Koblenz, Jay. "Mobile Offices". *Mobile Office,* June 1990, pp. 53–56.

Lazzareschi, Carla. "Discounters Plug Into PC Market". *Los Angeles Times,* Business Section B, August 22, 1990, pp. 1, 5.

Makey, Betty Barr. "Longwood Cottage Publishing". *Worksteader News,* 1990, p. 4.

Miety, Melanie. "HQ-Business Centers". *Cottage Connection,* May/June 1990, p. 1.

Miller, Steven. "Mine The Direct Marketing Riches in Your Data Base". *The Journal of Business Strategy,* November/December 1989, pp. 33–37.

Morrill Tazelaar, Jane. "Working at Home with Computers". *Byte,* March 1986, pp. 155–158.

Rapp, Stan. "Taking a Look Ahead to the 1990s". *Direct Marketing,* January 1990, pp. 80–81.

Reiman, John. "Profiles in Mobility, Mark Eppley". *Mobile Office,* June 1990, pp. 43–46.

Romei, Lura K. "The Home Office: Alive and Well". *Modern Office Technology,* August 1990, pp. 23–26.

Schwartz, John. "Three Views of Working at Home". *Personal Computing,* February 1987, pp. 87–90.

Sniff, Roger. "Creating a 21st Century". *The Futurist,* November-/December 1986, pp. 21–23.

Taylor, Thayer C. "How the Game Will Change in the 1990s: Sales Management, An Interview with Andrew Parsons of McKinsey and Company". *Sales and Marketing Management,* June 1989, pp. 52–59.

Veilleux, C. Thomas. "Soft Warehouse Expands Lines, Stores". *HFD,* October 1, 1990, p. 3.

Ward, Bernie. "At Home at the Office". *Sky Magazine,* July 1990, pp. 20–25.

Wolpin, Stewart. "In Search of the Home Office Market". *Marketing Communications,* January 1989, pp. 46–54.

"1990 Annual Readers' Survey Results." *Home Office Computing,* June 1990 Survey.

"Computerized Category Killer". *Discount Merchandiser,* April 1990, p. 2.

"The Frustrated Superbrowser: A Golden Opportunity Going Begging". Compiled by Merrin Information Services. *The Channelmarker Letter,* July 1989, pp. 1, 3–5.

"Reaching for New Heights, Small Business Growth Opportunities in the 1990s". An Advertising Supplement. *Fortune,* September 21, 1990.

"Working at Home Adds Up to Big Bucks". Short Takes-Emerging Markets. *Sales and Marketing Management,* February 1990, p. 31.

SPECIAL REPORTS

"Highlights of the 5th Annual 1990 National Work at Home Survey". Thomas E. Miller, Director of Research. New York: ESU Telework Group of Link Resources, 1990.

"Lotus Backgrounder—Selecting Software for the Home". Lotus Development Corporation, 1990.

"Small Business and Home Offices to Drive PC Market Through 1995". From presentations made by Raymond Boggs. Norwood, MA, BIS CAP International, 1990.

"Specialty Retailing in the 1990s: A Superstore Homerun". McNulty, Robert J. An economic study conducted by A.B. Lafer, V. A. Canto and Associates, LaJolla, CA, April 19, 1990.

"Work at Home: New Findings from the Current Population Survey". Division of Data Development and User Services, Office of Employment and Unemployment Statistics, Bureau of Labor Statistics, U.S. Department of Labor.

BOOKS

Davidson, Jeffrey P. *Breathing Space: Living and Working at a Comfortable Pace in a Sped-Up Society.* New York: Master Media, 1991.

Cetron, Marvin. *American Renaissance.* New York: Simon and Schuster, 1989.

Contrucci, Peg. *The Home Office, How to Set It Up, Operate it, and Make it Pay Off!.* Englewood Cliffs, NJ: Prentice Hall Inc., 1988.

Flemming, Lis. *The Electronic College Handbook II, Making Money With Your Home Computer.* Davis, CA: Flemming, Ltd., 1988.

HELPFUL DIRECTORIES

AT&T Toll-Free 800 Directory, published by AT&T: Bridgewater, NJ. Two sections including the 800 consumer white pages which contains alphabetical listings by name or business, organization and government agencies providing toll-free numbers to the public. The consumer Yellow Pages index lists the various products and service categories by category.

Facsimile User's Directory, published by Monitoring Publishing Company: New York, New York. A 100 percent verified fax number phone book listing fax numbers for corporate headquarters of business, financial institutions, law and accounting firms, media and publishing companies, advertising and public relations firms, federal and state agencies, nonprofit organizations, professional and trade associations and leading foreign companies.

ADDITIONAL READING

Boone, Louis E. and Kurtz, David L. *Contemporary Marketing.* 6th ed., Takoma Park, MD: Dryden Press, 1988.

Davidson, Jeffrey P. *Marketing for the Home-Based Business.* Holbrook, MA: Bob Adams, Inc., 1990.

Davidson, Jeffrey P. *Marketing on a Shoestring.* New York: Wiley, 1988.

Debelak, Don. *Total Marketing: Capturing Customers with Marketing Plans that Work.* Homewood, IL: BusinessOne Irwin, 1989.

Greenblatt, Joe Jeff. *Special Events: The Art and Science of Celebration.* New York: Van Nostrand Reinhold, 1990.

Ries, Al and Trout, Jack. *Bottom-Up Marketing.* New York, NY: McGraw Hill, 1989.

Yoho, Dave and Davidson, Jeffrey P. *How to Have a Good Year Every Year.* New York: Berkley, 1990.

INDEX

A

Accessory boards, 79

Accounting, and accounting software, 25, 80, 81, 82

Additional reading, 282

Advantage Line, 165

Advertising, 222, 224–25
of future, 270–71
and publications, 225–33

AEC. *See* Association of Electronic Cottages (AEC)

After-marketing, 109, 111

Age, 36, 133

AHBI. *See* American Home Business Institute (AHBI)

Aisles, 98

Alvin B. Zeller, Inc., 223

American Baby, 164

American Business Lists, Inc., 223

American Express, 209

American Home-Based Business Association, 5, 17

American Home Business Association, 14, 34

American Home Business Institute (AHBI), 22–23, 162–63

American Society of Association Executives, 213

American Telephone and Telegraph (AT&T), 53, 209

American Woman's Economic Development Corporation, 203

Annual Guide to Telemarketing, 116

Answering service, 82, 84

Apple Computer, 209

Armstrong, Colleen, 145, 146

Armstrong Computer Products, 145

Articles, preparation and altervatives to, 243–46

Arts, publications, 226–27

Association convention information, 213

Association of Electronic Cottages (AEC), 23, 173–74

AT&T. *See* American Telephone and Telegraph (AT&T)

At Home Office Works, Inc., 249–50

Attic office, 122–23

Austin, Jo-Ann, 143, 145, 146, 149, 150, 151, 154

Austin Tayshus Communications, 143

Avery Products, 209

Avis Rent-A-Car, 163

Integrated package software, 80
Intel, 209
Internal Revenue Service. *See*
  United States Internal
  Revenue Service (IRS)
International Association for
  Business Organizations, 161
International Association of
  Convention and Visitors'
  Bureaus, 212
International Business Machines
  (IBM), 14, 78, 104, 149, 150,
  193, 209
International Exhibitor's
  Association, 212
International Franchise
  Association, 203
Inventory adjustment, 99
IRS. *See* United States Internal
  Revenue Service (IRS)

J

Jacobs-Gardner, 91
Jellek, Tom, 39
JS & A Products, 115

K

Kelley, Marcia M., 24, 27
Kern, Walter M. D., 25
*Kids & Careers: New Ideas and
  Options for Mothers*, 165
Kiwanis, 255
K-Mart, 152, 156
Kohl, Claudia, 210
Kuhn, Susan, 16

L

Lacroix, Rod, 155
Landon, Charles, 147
Langdon, Dave, 149, 155

La Porta, Lawrence, 249–50
Laptop computers, 78
Laventhol & Horwath, 147–48
Laws, zoning, 30
Learning curve, 49
Leave, maternity, 43–44
Les Femmes Chefs d'Entreprises
  Mondiales, 199
Lewis, Eliana, 73–74
Lindmark, Sture, 219
LINK Resources, Inc., 8, 9, 13,
  24–25, 34–35, 36, 38, 42, 53,
  210
Lists, mailing. *See* Mailing
  lists
Location-independent, 15
Loita, Barbara, 29
Loss leaders, 97
Lotus, 193, 194, 209, 210

M

MacArthur, Douglas, 33
McCabe, Brian, 156
Machrone, Bill, 194
Macintosh, 78
McKinsey & Company, 271–72
Mail
  electronic mail (E-Mail), 82, 83
  and mailing lists, 222, 223–24
Mainstream, becoming, 25–28
Management, publications, 230
Manufacturers, and markets,
  154–56
Marken, G. A. "Andy," 130, 133
Marken Communications, 130
Marketing
  and after-marketing, 109, 111
  areas, 136–40
  and Canada, 143–58
  case histories, 249–66
  and catalogs, 112–16
  consulting, 82, 84

For more information or for inclusion in the next edition of *Marketing to Home-Based Businesses,* send Jeff Davidson a self-addressed stamped envelope with your organization's literature:

HBEs
Jeff Davidson MBA, CMC
3713 S. George Mason Drive #705W
Falls Church, VA 22041

Or call 1 (703) 931-1984, 1 (800) 735-1994, or FAX: 1 (703) 931-4082.

PLAYING IN TRAFFIC ON MADISON AVENUE
Tales of Advertising's Glory Years
David J. Herzbrun

After a 40-year award-winning career in the ad business, David Herzbrun chronicles his adventures and paints a picture of the many characters with whom he worked closely, and who shaped the "Creative Revolution": Bill Bernbach, David Ogilvy, Lou Dorfsman, Bob Levenson, Helmut Krone, George Lois, and others. Herzbrun shows how they rebelled against the commonplace, the boring, and the mediocre to create truly memorable advertising.
$24.95

ADVERTISING AGENCY MANAGEMENT
Jay McNamara, former president McCann-Erickson Worldwide

"Jay McNamara has concisely and comprehensively compiled in one volume what every aspiring agency manager should be learning on the way up and what no advertising manager should ever forget after he or she gets there."
Allen Rosenshine, Chairman and CEO
BBDO Worldwide, Inc.
$29.95

Prices Subject to Change without Notice
Available in fine bookstores and libraries everywhere.